Praise for *The Bonnot Ga*

The first book on the subject in English, and one based on original research in the various libraries and collections in Paris, Amsterdam, and London. . . . Although the book is written as a history, the style is journalistic rather than stuffily academic, and paced so that the narrative gets progressively more exciting. All in all, this is that rare book indeed. It is a good read and action-packed; but also meticulously researched with an impressive attention to detail.
    —*New Anarchist Review*

Although Parry does not try to romanticize the protagonists, the conclusion of the book does try to interpret their story as a political event arising out of the class struggle. . . . It will be widely read; it ought to be widely discussed.
    —Nicholas Walter, *Freedom*

The book is original, almost naively frank, and instantly likeable. It requires no prior knowledge and although it describes itself as a history, it often reads more like a novel. All told this is a great introduction to the subject and well worth the read.
    —Katy Armstrong-Myers, *Socialist Lawyer*

Parry neither idealizes nor condemns the Bonnot Gang. Instead, he is trying to situate its activities in an ideological tradition and, at least as importantly, in the unforgiving class contradictions characterizing French society at the time.
    —Ulf Gyllenhak, *Dagens Nyheter*

André Soudy, as he appeared at Chantilly,
aiming his Winchester rifle.

The Bonnot Gang

The Story of the French Illegalists

Second Edition

Richard Parry

PMPRESS

2016

The Bonnot Gang: The Story of the French Illegalists
Richard Parry
Second Edition, PM Press, 2016
© Richard Parry 2016

ISBN: 978-1-62963-143-1
Library of Congress Control Number: 2016931126

Cover by John Yates/Stealworks.com
Interior by Jonathan Rowland

10 9 8 7 6 5 4 3 2 1

PM Press
PO Box 23912
Oakland, CA 94623
www.pmpress.org

Printed in the USA by the Employee Owners of Thomson-Shore in Dexter, Michigan.
www.thomsonshore.com

Contents

Preface to the Second Edition

THIS NEW EDITION appears after the hundredth anniversary of the death of Bonnot following the spectacular shoot-out at Choisy-Le-Roi in 1912. When he wrote "I am a famous man, my name has been trumpeted to the four corners of the globe" he could little suspect how much would be written about him in the future and how far he would penetrate into the French psyche as the image of furious and violent resistance to the existing order. And not just an antihero in the traditional mould, but an anarchist. An illegalist.

Since the book was published some thirty years ago, interest in the story of the Bonnot Gang has not waned. In fact, since the turn of the millenium, a new book has appeared almost every year, and older works have been republished. In 1988, the year following publication of the first edition, there was reprint of Rirette Maîtrejean's reminiscences of the Bonnot Gang, first published in 1913 after her trial and acquittal. The following year the Librairie Monnier in Paris printed the early writings of Victor Serge that had appeared in the pages of *l'anarchie* as well as the more obscure *Le Communiste* and *Le Révolté*. More recently, in 2007, Dieudonné's experiences of life in the penal colony of French Guiana, *La Vie des Forçats* (first published in 1930) was republished. As one of the few to escape, he may be considered as the real Papillon—but one who made it and lived to tell the tale. What Dieudonné did not do, however, was to tell the tale of his involvement or otherwise in the Bonnot Gang. Following a long and ultimately successful campaign over his supposed innocence, resulting in a presidential commutation of his sentence in 1927, he probably thought it wise to keep quiet.

And this is why authors have continued to be inspired by the story—because, while we have the bare bones of the historical facts, there is still enough mystery to be able to invent some fabulous fiction. Several new novels have appeared in the last few years, some taking as a central theme the supposed employment of Bonnot as chauffeur to Sir Arthur Conan Doyle in London in 1910. Although it is almost certainly untrue, the legendary status of Bonnot has lent credence to this mythical encounter.

In France, interest in the story of the Bonnot Gang has never died—it is their 'Bonnie and Clyde' and 'Dillinger' all rolled into one, but with some major differences. While these American antiheros were simple bank robbers without pretensions to be any more, the illegalists were consciously political, both on a personal level and in their view of the structure of the state and society. They are far more fascinating as individuals with their vegetarianism, teetotalism and belief in anarchy and free love, as well as for their daring exploits.

In my book I tried to adopt a both sympathetic and critical stance. It may be that I have been over-sympathetic, but this is the historian falling in love with his subject, and I admit that it was exciting both to research and to write. I have not, however, repeated matters of pure speculation; even where I describe intimate details of the gang's relationships this is, as far as possible, based on primary sources—from the memoirs of the actual participants, from contemporary police reports or the columns of the anarchist press. In this new edition I have tried to clear up some earlier inaccuracies in regard to the survivors, some of whom later returned to live back in Paris and Brussels for many years, although, as with Dieudonné, they appear not to have left any later memoirs of their younger anarchist days.

With the reappearance of the revolutionary movement in France in 1968, the story of the Bonnot Gang resurfaced. It was recalled by the Situationist International who admired their 'devil-may-care' attack on society, which they no doubt wished to emulate. They obviously caught the popular mood as in 1968 the film *La Bande à Bonnot* hit the screens, starring the singer Jacques Brel as Raymond-La-Science. With the decline of the revolutionary movement in the 1970s there was a reversal of perspective—now the story was told from the police point of view in the popular "Tiger Brigades" series, in which Bonnot featured in several episodes. A more recent film has repeated this adaptation.

With the contemporary crisis of capitalism it may be that the popular mood will turn again and Bonnot will feature once more on the silver screen, but with the story told from his perspective. Whatever may be, one thing is sure, the legend of the Bonnot Gang will remain.

Richard Parry
London, 2016

Preface to the First Edition

ON THE EVE of World War One a number of young anarchists came together in Paris determined to settle scores with bourgeois society. Their exploits were to become legendary.

The French press dubbed them 'The Bonnot Gang' after the oldest 'member', Jules Bonnot, a thirty-one year-old mechanic and professional crook who had recently arrived from Lyon. The other main characters, Octave Garnier, Raymond Callemin, René Valet, Élie Monier and André Soudy were all in their very early twenties. A host of other comrades (i.e. those of an anarchist persuasion) played roles that were relevant to the main story, and I apologize in advance for the plethora of names with which the narrative abounds.

The so-called 'gang', however, had neither a name nor leaders, although it seems that Bonnot and Garnier played the principal motivating roles. They were not a close-knit criminal band in the classical style, but rather a union of egoists associated for a common purpose. Amongst comrades they were known as 'illegalists', which signified more than the simple fact that they carried out illegal acts.

Illegal activity has always been part of the anarchist tradition, especially in France, and so the story begins with a brief sketch of the theory and practice of illegality within the movement before the turn of the century. The illegalists in this study, however, differed from the activists of previous years in that they had a quite different conception of the purpose of illegal activity.

As anarchist individualists, they came from a milieu whose most important theoretical inspiration was undoubtedly Max Stirner—whose work *The Ego and Its Own* remains the most powerful negation of the State, and affirmation of the individual, to date. Young anarchists took up Stirner's ideas with relish, and the hybrid 'anarchist-individualism' was born as a new and vigorous current within the anarchist movement.

In Paris, this milieu was centred on the weekly paper *l'anarchie* and the *Causeries Populaires* (regular discussion groups meeting in several different locations in and around the capital each week), both of which were founded by Albert Libertad and his associates. It was here that 'illegalism' found fertile soil and took root, such that the subsequent history of the illegalists is closely bound up with the history of *l'anarchie*.

One of the editors of this weekly was Victor Kibalchich, later to be better known as Victor Serge, the pro-Bolshevik writer and opponent of Stalinism. At the time of this story, however, he was not just a close associate of several 'illegalists' but was also one of the most outspoken of the anarchist-individualists, and editor of *l'anarchie* to boot. As such, his early career as a revolutionary is a central thread in the story of the Bonnot Gang, although this period of his life was glossed over by Serge himself and has been subsequently ignored by contemporary political writers who wish to keep him as 'their own'. It therefore seems more fitting for the purposes of this narrative to use his *nom de plume*, Le Rétif, or his real name, Kibalchich, rather than 'Serge', a pseudonym he did not adopt until five years after he found himself fighting for his life as a defendant in the mass trial of 1913.

Despite their sanguinary exploits, the 'Bonnot Gang' remain as much a chapter in the history of anarchism as the activities of Ravachol in France or the Durruti Column in Spain. To push their story to one side, or to treat it as a 'dark side' of anarchism to be glossed over or ignored, is to be unfaithful to the history of anarchism as a whole. On the other hand, however, those who would glamorize or make heroes of the illegalists are failing to see that they were not at all extraordinary people or anarchist supermen. What is remarkable about them is that although as young sons of toil their lives could easily have led to the slavery of the factory or the trenches, they chose not to resign themselves to such a fate.

This book is not a novel; the novelist's approach certainly adds dramatic tension and vigour, but I would not like to be guilty of spurious characterizations. In any case, I certainly could not have done better than Malcolm Menzies' book *En Exil Chez Les Hommes* (unfortunately only available in French) and so have written what I hope will pass as a 'history'.

Here, the question of 'historical truth' rears its ugly head: some of the story remains very obscure for several reasons. To begin with, none of the surviving participants admitted their guilt, at least until after the end of the subsequent mass trial. It was part of the anarchist code never to admit to anything or give information to the authorities. Equally, it was almost a duty to help other comrades in need, and if this meant perjury to save them from bourgeois justice, then so be it. Hence the difficulty in knowing who was telling 'the truth'. Those who afterwards wrote short 'memoirs' often glamorized or ridiculed persons or events, partly to satisfy their own egos and partly at the behest of gutter-press sub-editors.

In the trial itself there were over two hundred witnesses, mainly anarchists for the defence, and presumably law-abiding citizens for the prosecution. Much evidence from the latter was contradictory. While most were probably telling the truth as far as they could remember, others had told an inaccurate version so many times that either they believed it themselves, or, under police pressure, they found it too late and too embarrassing to withdraw it. A few were certainly motivated either by private, or a sense of social, revenge. Then of course there was the evidence of the police who, it was revealed during the course of the trial, had pressurized witnesses and fabricated evidence in order to make the case appear neat and tidy and secure easy convictions. Some policemen in their reports either lied to conceal their blunders, or exaggerated the importance of their role in order to promote their careers.

Lastly, there was the press, that guardian of bourgeois morality, though not averse to sniping at the police, depending on which administration was in power. Some newspapers gave space to the *auto-bandits* almost daily for six months, yet they were usually forced to rely on police reports which often withheld news or supplied deliberate misinformation. This, coupled with that normal journalistic practice of creating stories out of nothing, meant that many articles which appeared were confused, exaggerated or fictitious.

In other words, I have had to select my material and make a judicious *mélange* from conflicting sources. In the good old tradition of liberal historiography the story that follows is very much my own.

Richard Parry
London, 1986

List of Illustrations

Principal Characters

David Belonie (1885–?)

Born in Gignac to a single mother, who died when he was just twelve, he came to Paris in 1900 and worked as a chemist. He avoided conscription in 1905 by going to Switzerland, where he met Bonnot. He later travelled to London, where Bonnot visited him. In Lyon he introduced Bonnot to the art of counterfeiting. He tried to assist the gang by supplying hair dye and possibly cyanide and in retrieving the bonds stolen in the rue Ordener from Amsterdam. He was arrested as he went to pick up the bonds from the Gare du Nord. He claimed Dieudonné was innocent. He was sentenced to four years in prison.

Jules Bonnot (1876–1912)

Born in the Jura mountains in eastern France, his mother died when he was just ten. He began work at thirteen. By sixteen he had already been convicted of assaulting police and was marked down for his anarchist opinions. After his military service he married, he had a son and began work as a car mechanic. He was repeatedly sacked for his conduct and opinions, his wife left him, and he turned to crime—at which he was a success, priding himself on his professionalism. With the police in Lyon on his trail, and wanted for the murder of his friend Platano, he went to Paris and offered his services to some young illegalists. And so, at the end of 1911, the Bonnot Gang was born. He was the driver with the necessary *sang-froid*, and without whom this story could never have happened. He killed the Deputy Chief of the Paris Sûreté and for six months was France's Enemy Number One. He was killed at the end of the famous siege of Choisy-Le-Roi in April 1912.

Raymond Callemin (1890–1913)

Born in Belgium, he was the childhood friend of Victor Kibalchich and Jean De Boe, and together they formed the Brussels Revolutionary Group and published *Le Révolté*. Meeting up with Victor again in

Romainville, he threw in his lot with Garnier and the others. His belief in the progressive qualities of scientific advance led to his nickname 'La Science'. He opened fire first at Chantilly, killing a teenage bank clerk. Arrested, he admitted nothing but was condemned to death at the mass trial and executed by guillotine in April 1913.

Édouard Carouy (1883–1913)

Born in Belgium, he lost his mother at the age of three and began work at the age of twelve in a sugar refinery. He then worked as a metal worker and became an anarchist, meeting up with Kibalchich, Callemin, and De Boe in Brussels, and collaborating on *Le Révolté*, of which he later became nominal editor. In France, he went to live in Romainville in 1911. Although a friend of Garnier, he did not join in with the gang, preferring nocturnal burglary with his associate Metge, which however ended with them both convicted of a double murder in Thiais. Having been sentenced to forced labour for life in Cayenne, he committed suicide in prison. His lover, Barbe Le Clech, was implicated in the burglary but acquitted at trial.

Jean De Boe (1889–1974)

Born in Anderlecht in Belgium, he was an orphan raised by his grandmother and later became a typographer. A close associate of Kibalchich and Callemin, he founded the Brussels Revolutionary Group with them. In France, he was peripherally involved in the Bonnot Gang, assisting with safe houses and in trying to move the bonds stolen from the rue Ordener hold-up. Arrested early on and charged with conspiracy, he was sentenced to ten years' forced labour in Cayenne.

Eugène Dieudonné (1884–1944)

Born in Nancy, he was brought up in an orphanage and became a carpenter at seventeen. Unusually for the illegalists, he did his two years military service and went back to his profession as a carpenter. Married to Louise Kayser, they had one child. In Nancy he met with four brothers, all anarchist carpenters who converted him to anarchism. He arrived in Paris with Louise in 1909, meeting up with Lorulot, who promptly seduced his wife. He knew many of the illegalists but there was little evidence of his involvement until he was denounced by Rodriguez and wrongly identified by the victim of the rue Ordener robbery as the man who shot him. At trial he was sentenced to death, but the President commuted this to forced labour for life in Cayenne.

Anna Dondon (1884–1979)

Born in the Nièvre, she was in Paris at the age of twenty-one and made contact with comrades of *l'anarchie*. In 1906 she was sentenced to five years in prison for counterfeiting and sent to Rennes. She was released on licence in 1909 and met René Valet, who became her lover, and they later moved to Romainville with the other comrades. Despite being with Valet in the flat in rue Ordener even after the Chantilly raid in March 1912, she was fortunate to be in Paris at the time of the siege of Nogent. There was insufficient evidence to charge her with any crime.

Jean Dubois (1870–1912)

Born in Golta, Russia, into an old French Huguenot family, he joined the French Foreign Legion and settled in France. He was a comrade from the *l'anarchie* group and a defence witness at the affray trial of 1910. Separated from his wife and four children, he lived with his Alsatian dog over a workshop in Choisy funded by Alfred Fromentin, the 'anarchist millionaire'. He was the mechanic who gave sanctuary to Bonnot, a decision that was to cost his life. He was shot and killed by police during the siege in April 1912.

Octave Garnier (1889–1912)

Born in Fontainebleau, he began work at thirteen in a bakery but later worked as a navvy. Avoiding military service, he fled to Belgium where he met Carouy, De Boe and Callemin from the Brussels Revolutionary Group. Back in France with his lover Marie, he went to live in Romainville with other comrades of *l'anarchie*. The meeting with Bonnot was a turning point; the gang was formed. Garnier was responsible for shooting the bank clerk in their first attack in rue Ordener, gunning down a policeman at place du Havre, shooting an informer and killing a bank clerk in the attack at Chantilly. He died in the siege at Nogent in May 1912.

Antoine Gauzy (1879–1963)

Born in Nîmes, he had a shop in Ivry on the outskirts of Paris that had been funded by Fromentin. His association with Monier led to him allowing Bonnot to stay when he was on the run, with tragic consequences. The killing by Bonnot of the Deputy Chief of the Sûreté, Jouin, meant that he was charged with harbouring and was sentenced to eighteen months' imprisonment at the end of the trial.

Victor Kibalchich (1890–1947)

Born in Brussels to exiled Russian revolutionaries, his parents separated and his brother died young. Close friends with Callemin and De Boe, their first experience of anarchism was in a libertarian commune in the forest of Stockel. Taught typography by De Boe, he became a regular contributor, under the pseudonym *Le Rétif*, to both *Le Révolté* (until he was expelled from Belgium in 1909) and *l'anarchie*, becoming editor of the latter, aged twenty-one, when it moved to Romainville in 1911. His stance on illegalism sometimes appeared as outright support and encouragement, at other times he was more guarded. Indicted for conspiracy with the rest of the Bonnot Gang following the discovery of two Browning 9mm pistols at his home, he was sentenced to five years in prison.

Rirette Maîtrejean (1887–1968)

Born in Corrèze, as Anna Estorges, she married an anarchist and moved to Paris in 1904, aged seventeen, and had two daughters. Her husband Louis was imprisoned for counterfeiting in 1909 and she began a relationship with Mauricius, then editor of *l'anarchie*. Meeting Kibalchich in 1909 she soon began a passionate relationship with him, and they jointly became editors of *l'anarchie* while it was at Romainville and subsequently at rue Fessart, until they were both arrested and indicted for conspiracy. She was acquitted at trial and soon after published her memoirs of illegalism in the popular press.

Marius Metge (1890–1933)

Born in the Ardèche he was brought up by his grandmother, and began work as a chef. Dodging military service, he went to Belgium where he met Carouy and Garnier. Back in France he lived with the others in Romainville, conducting burglaries in suburban villages with Carouy. Convicted by fingerprint evidence at the trial of the Bonnot Gang, he was condemned to forced labour for life in Cayenne.

Élie Monier (1889–1913)

Born in the eastern Pyrénées, his parents were wine growers. He began work aged twelve as a gardener. Avoiding conscription, he went to Paris then Belgium. He began to associate with the anarchists, in particular Lorulot and others around *l'anarchie*. He was recruited by the gang to find a place to rob in the south of France, but this job did not work out. He joined in the attack on Chantilly, shooting and injuring a bank clerk. His connection to Gauzy led to the latter offering Bonnot a refuge, where Jouin was killed. Arrested and convicted of conspiracy and involvement in the Chantilly raid, he was executed in April 1913, his head being the last to tumble into the basket.

Giuseppe Platano (1883–1911)

Born in 1883 in Italy, he began work as a baker and moved to Toulon at first and then to Lyon in 1907. There he met Bonnot and they went into partnership together, successfully burgling houses, post offices, even a cathedral, in the Rhône valley, as far as Switzerland. Although parting company for a while, they met up again in Paris in October 1911, and it was Platano who initially introduced Bonnot to Garnier. Returning from a mission to Lyon together in November, Platano accidentally shot himself while examining Bonnot's Browning pistol, and Bonnot, seeing him mortally wounded, decided to put him out of his misery. Wanted for Platano's murder, Bonnot now had nothing to lose.

Louis Rimbault (1877–1949)

Born in Tours into a poor family of eight children, he was a locksmith and a strong advocate of vegetarianism. He tried to revive the libertarian community in Bascon in 1911 and invented the salad *La Basconnaise*. It was Rimbault's lorry that helped move Carouy's belongings to Dettweiler's garage where the Bonnot Gang's first stolen car was later hidden. Arrested in possession of firearms, his links to the illegalists were nevertheless tenuous, it being suggested he provided weapons to the gang. He feigned madness to escape trial and was eventually released.

Alphonse Rodriguez (1878–1969)

Born in Paris, he was an anarchist convicted in both France and England for counterfeiting currency. He knew Belonie, an associate of Bonnot, and with him went to Amsterdam to retrieve the bonds stolen from rue Ordener, and then re-negotiate them with a fence in Paris. Arrested, his extensive criminal record left him at the mercy of the police and he denounced Dieudonné for involvement in the rue Ordener hold-up. His cooperation doubtless helped in his acquittal at the trial of the Bonnot Gang in February 1913.

André Soudy (1892–1913)

Born in Beaugency, he began work at the age of eleven as a grocer's boy. At sixteen he moved to Paris, but within two years had contracted tuberculosis. A friend of Kibalchich and Rirette, he came into contact with the illegalists around *l'anarchie,* and was recruited to their cause for the robbery at Chantilly in 1912, where he gained notoriety as 'the man with the rifle' who kept the public at bay. Arrested and put on trial with the others, he was executed by guillotine at the tender age of twenty-one, the youngest member of the gang.

Judith Thollon (188?–1916)
Married to the keeper of the cemetery of La Guilltière in Lyon, she became Bonnot's lover in 1910 and they made plans to start a new life perhaps in Germany or England. Her husband appears to have condoned the affair, and their house became Bonnot's secret hiding place for his money and tools of the trade. Raided by the police, Judith was arrested along with her husband, leading to Bonnot's flight to Paris, with all the consequences that entailed. Refusing to denounce him, she stood trial in Lyon in 1912 for receiving stolen goods and was given a heavy four-year sentence.

René Valet (1890–1912)
Born in Verdun, he was said to come from a 'good family' and became a locksmith in Paris, to where his family had moved. Avoiding military service he obtained false papers. He became close friends with Kibalchich and Rirette, and became a convinced anarchist, with a passion for poetry and justice. He moved to Romainville with his lover Anna Dondon, but also threw in his lot with the illegalists and joined in the attack at Chantilly, where he shot a teenage bank clerk. He died with Garnier in the siege at Nogent in May 1912.

Marie Vuillemin (1889–1963)
Born in Mons, she went to Paris, was married, then separated, and returned to Belgium. In 1910 she met, and fell in love with Garnier. They went to live together in Romainville in 1911 until leaving for Paris. Arrested twice, she refused to talk and was released. Spirited away by Garnier from under the noses of the police, she went to live with him at Nogent for their final few days together. During a lull in the siege she was able to escape. She was acquitted of conspiracy at the trial.

Chronology

1900 First French edition of Max Stirner's *The Ego and Its Own* published as *L'Unique et sa propriété*.

1900 Bonnot finishes his military service with the 133rd Line Regiment.

August 1901 Bonnot marries Sophie.

10 April 1902 general strike in Belgium over reform of the electoral system lasts ten days. Twelve workers killed. Reform refused.

October 1902 Libertad and Paraf-Javal found the *Causeries Populaires* in Montmartre.

1903 Libertad and Paraf-Javal and others form the Antimilitarist League.

June 1904 International Antimilitarist Association congress in Amsterdam fails to support draft-dodging and desertion as primary tactics; Libertad and Paraf-Javal leave.

January 1905 Revolution breaks out in Russia. First Soviets formed. Uprisings and insurrections spread. Thousands of political prisoners are freed.

January 1905 Funeral of Louise Michel in Paris.

March 1905 Marius Jacob on trial in Amiens; sentenced to forced labour for life in Cayenne.

13 April 1905 First issue of *l'anarchie* appears, founded by Libertad, Paraf-Javal and the Mahé sisters. Armand, Lorulot and Mauricius are main contributors.

1905 Kibalchich and Callemin join the Socialist Young Guards in Brussels, meet De Boe.

December 1905 general strike in Russia; insurrection in Moscow crushed. Beginning of the repression.

1 May 1906 general strike in France calling for an eight-hour day. State of emergency declared, CGT leaders arrested on orders of Radical Party Minister of Interior, Clemenceau.

20 May 1906 'Radical' government elected in France, Socialist Party gain 10 per cent of the vote.

Summer 1906 Kibalchich, Callemin and De Boe join anarchist colony *L'Expérience* in Stockel, later moved to Boitsfort, south of Brussels. Kibalchich writes first articles for their paper, the *Communiste*.

October 1906 CGT Charter of Amiens proclaims the independence of unions from political parties.

1907 Bonnot gets his first driving licence. Works at Berliet in Lyon. Deserted by his wife and child.

June 1907 During the strike of the vineyard workers in the Midi the 17th Line Regiment revolts.

1908 Bonnot in Lyon takes out a subscription to *l'anarchie*, meets Belonie, Rodriguez, Platano.

1 May 1908 De Boe, Callemin and Kibalchich put out a Brussels Revolutionary Group manifesto.

May–July 1908 Strike of the quarry workers. Shot by police at Draveil and charged by dragoons at Villeneuve-St Georges.

September 1908 First edition of *Le Révolté* printed in Brussels by the Brussels Revolutionary Group.

12 November 1908 Death of Libertad aged thirty-three. Amandine Mahé and Jean Morand take over *l'anarchie*.

January 1909 Two anarchists from Latvian anarchist group Leesma killed in London after a wages snatch—the so-called Tottenham Outrage.

11 March 1909 Mauricius and Rirette Maîtrejean take over *l'anarchie*.

Spring 1909 Eugène and Louise Dieudonné arrive in Paris from Nancy.

12 August 1909 Lorulot takes over at *l'anarchie*. He and Louise Dieudonné now lovers.

August 1909 Victor Kibalchich arrives in Paris.

13 October 1909 Execution of Ferrer in Barcelona; riots outside Spanish Embassy in Paris.

February 1910 Carouy now editor of *Le Révolté* in Brussels. Kibalchich meets with Rirette and Valet in Paris.

May 1910 Fight between supporters of Paraf-Javal and *l'anarchie*—one dead, five arrested including Lorulot.

30 June 1910 Lorulot transfers *l'anarchie* to Romainville.

2 July 1910 Execution of Liabeuf. Riots outside the prison of La Santé.

July 1910 Bonnot and Platano burgle lawyer's house in Vienne. Bonnot starts liaison with a married woman, Judith Thollon.

October 1910 National strike of railway workers. Government mobilize strikers and enforce martial law. Two hundred leaders arrested. Strike collapses.

October 1910 Garnier crosses into Belgium to avoid military service, begins liaison with Marie, and meets Carouy, Callemin, De Boe, Rodriguez.

January 1911 Siege of Sidney Street in London. Two Latvian anarchists from Leesma killed.

February 1911 Callemin arrives at Romainville.

April 1911 Carouy, Garnier and Marie arrive at Romainville. Carouy meets Jeanne. Valet and Anna arrive from Paris around this time.

13 July 1911 Kibalchich and Rirette take over editorship of *l'anarchie*. Lorulot and Louise depart for Paris to start a new journal, *L'Idée Libre*.

July 1911 Bonnot stays with Dubois in Choisy-Le-Roi.

August 1911 At the end of the month Garnier, Marie, Carouy, Jeanne, Callemin, Valet and Anna all leave Romainville for Paris.

10 October 1911 *l'anarchie* transferred to rue Fessart in Paris.

October 1911 Police raid Bonnot's garage in Lyon; he flees to Paris.

26 November 1911 Platano dies of gunshot wounds to the head. Bonnot blamed, wanted for murder.

2 December 1911 Police seize Bonnot's twenty-five thousand francs in Lyon; Judith and her husband arrested.

13 December 1911 Bonnot, Garnier and Callemin steal a Delaunay-Belleville luxury car, take it to Dettweiler's.

21 December 1911 Attack outside the Société Générale bank, rue Ordener: Garnier shoots Caby, Bonnot drives the getaway car.

24 December 1911 Burglary of gun shop in rue Lafayette. Garnier and Callemin visit Kibalchich and Rirette.

2 January 1912 Murder of couple during course of burglary in Thiais; Metge and Carouy suspected.

4 January 1912 Kibalchich article in *l'anarchie*, "The Bandits".

9 January 1912 Burglary of Smith and Wesson armoury.

12 January 1912 Guichard takes over as head of the Sûreté Nationale.

31 January 1912 Kibalchich arrested.

15 February 1912 Theft of Peugeot limousine in Béziers.

26 February 1912 Theft of Delaunay-Belleville in St Mandé, Paris.

27 February 1912 Garnier shoots his police namesake at place du Havre.

28 February 1912 Arrests of De Boe, Dieudonné. Rirette arrested and released.

18 March 1912 Rodriguez arrested confirms Dieudonné was present at rue Ordener. Rirette re-arrested.

19 March 1912 Garnier's challenge to Guichard in *Le Matin*. Bonnot's in *Le Petit Parisien*.

25 March 1912 Bonnot, Garnier, Callemin, Monier, Soudy and Valet all participate in the hijacking of a car at Montgeron and subsequent attack on the Société Générale bank in Chantilly. Three people are killed and two wounded.

3 April 1912 Carouy arrested. Soudy arrested. Callemin arrested. Monier arrested.

4 April 1912 Émile Armand takes over *l'anarchie*.

24 April 1912 Bonnot kills Jouin, Deputy Chief of the Paris Sûreté, and injures Inspector Colmar.

28 April 1912 Siege of Choisy-Le-Roi and death of Bonnot and Dubois.

14 May 1912 Siege of Nogent-sur-Marne and death of Garnier and Valet. Marie unharmed.

3 February 1913 Trial of the 'Bonnot Gang' at the Palais de Justice. Rirette, Marie and Rodriguez acquitted. Carouy commits suicide in his cell.

3 April 1913 All appeals rejected.

22 April 1913 Execution by guillotine of Callemin, Soudy and Monier. Dieudonné reprieved by President Poincaré, sentence commuted to forced labour for life in Cayenne.

1. From Illegality to Illegalism

Property is theft. Property is liberty.
—Pierre-Joseph Proudhon (1809–65)

Making a Virtue of Necessity

ALMOST ALL THE illegalists who were associated with the Bonnot Gang were born in the late 1880s or early '90s, into a society completely torn by class division. Above all, it was the suppression of the Paris Commune in 1871 that had consolidated the climate of mutual hatred between the workers and the bourgeoisie. The Commune, a minimal attempt at social-democracy by workers and impoverished *petit-bourgeois*, was drowned in the blood of thirty thousand people by an army acting on the instructions of a ruling class infuriated at this challenge to their monopoly of power. The bloody repression of the Commune marked the birth of the Third Republic and served as a constant reminder to workers that they could expect nothing from this 'New Order' except the most brutal repression.

The memory of these tragic events of 1871 left a rich legacy in class-hatred, one with which French anarchists identified and which they hoped to exploit. With revolutionary organizations outlawed, and all forms of working class political activity banned, anarchists and trade-unionists were forced to operate in ways that were clandestine or outrightly illegal. As such modes of behaviour became the accepted norm, anarchists acquired a taste for illegality which lingered on into the 1900s when the Bonnot Gang came of age.

The 1870s were lean years for revolutionaries, and it was not until the 1880s that French anarchism really took off. The amnesty granted to deported Communards in 1880 signaled the return of thousands of hardened revolutionaries from exile in New Caledonia. A strong and fresh impetus was given to the revolutionary movement and "Paris quivered with excitement", according to one police observer. Within a couple of years there were an estimated forty anarchist groups in France with two thousand five hundred active members, including perhaps five hundred in Paris and in Bonnot's town of Lyon. Within a decade, the anarchist press was selling over ten thousand papers a week. Anarchist groups adopted names such as 'Hate', 'Dynamite', 'The Sword', 'Viper', 'The Panther of Batignolles' and 'The Terror of La Ciotat' as an indication of their aggressive stance towards bourgeois society. At the same time, anarchist theory was made more acceptable by proposing the 'commune' as the practical base for the organization of the new society, as opposed to the 'collective'; 'need' became the new criterion for the distribution of goods and services, which were to be freely available to all, regardless of the work each person had done; anarcho-communism was born.

All anarchist activity and propaganda was centred on the class struggle, which was especially bitter and violent up to the mid-1890s. A miners' strike in Montceau provoked the burning and pillage of religious schools and chapels, and ended in the dynamiting of churches and managers' houses. Many other strikes involved violent clashes with police or troops and occasionally coalesced into riots and looting. The anarchist belief in violent direct action, formulated in the policy of 'propaganda by the deed' (rather than by the word), reflected the particular bitterness of these struggles. Propaganda by deed was translated into action in three forms: insurrection, assassination, and bombing. The insurrectionary method, which had proved something of a fiasco in Spain and Italy in the 1870s, was not tried out in France. Instead, assassination became the principal weapon of revenge against the bourgeoisie and the figureheads of the State. The first wave of attempted assassinations was directed against political leaders throughout Europe: in the five years from 1878 there were attempts on the lives of the German Kaiser, the Kings of Spain and Italy, and the French Prime Minister. The killing of the Russian Emperor, Alexander II, by the 'People's Will' was, however, the only successful revolutionary execution of a reigning monarch.

There was a hiatus of ten years until the next batch of attempts on heads of State; in 1894 the French Prime Minister was stabbed to death, and the next decade saw the spectacular demise of a Spanish Prime Minister, an Italian King, an Austrian Empress and a President of the United States. In France, the gap between these two waves of political assassinations was marked by attempts on the lives of upholders of the ruling order in a more general sense. This time the victims were employers who had given workers the sack, a wealthy doctor, a priest, and brokers in the Paris Stock Exchange. The bourgeoisie began to be more than a little concerned when the anarchist 'propagandists by deed' began to use dynamite: in 1892 over one thousand explosions were reported in Europe. In Paris, bombs exploded in the Chamber of Deputies, a police station, an army barracks, a bourgeois café, a judge's house, and the residence of the Public Prosecutor.

It was ordinary workers rather than 'professional' activists who carried out these acts of propaganda, although such desperate measures were habitually praised in the columns of the anarchist press. The 'terrorists' of the early 1890s were mainly poor working class men—a cabinetmaker, a dyer, a shoemaker, for example—unable to get any work, often with a family to support, bitter at the injustice they had suffered, and sympathetic to anarchism. This was one aspect of the world into which most of the illegalists were born; Bonnot was in his mid-teens when the spectacular bombings took place, causing a panic among the bourgeoisie not to be repeated until he himself became France's 'Public Enemy Number One'.

As the anarchist desire for the abolition of the State was translated onto an immediate, practical level through individual acts of assassination and bombing, so the wish for the 'expropriation of the expropriators' was reduced to individual acts of 're-appropriation' of bourgeois property. This was the theory of *la reprise individuelle*, whose most celebrated practitioners were Clément Duval and Marius Jacob; the infamous Ravachol, who went to the guillotine in 1894 singing the scandalous anticlerical song *Père Duchesne*, was known more for his bombings than his burglaries.

Clément Duval, twice wounded in the Franco-Prussian War of 1870, spent four of the following ten years in hospital and was rendered permanently unfit for his trade as an iron worker. He was imprisoned for a year after having been caught stealing eighty francs from his employer, in order to buy desperately needed food and medicine for his family. On his release he threw in his lot with the hardened working class anarchists of 'The Panther of Batignolles' and began a short-lived life of crime. In October 1886 he set fire to the mansion of a wealthy Parisian socialite, having first burgled it of fifteen thousand francs, but he was caught two weeks later, despite wounding a policeman in the course of the arrest. In court, the judge refused to allow him to read his written defence, so he posted it to the anarchist paper *La Révolte*: "Theft exists only through the exploitation of man by man, that is to say in the existence of all those who parasitically live off the productive class . . . when Society refuses you the right to exist, you must take it . . . the policeman arrested me in the name of the Law, I struck him in the name of Liberty". The death sentence was later commuted to hard labour for life on Devil's Island, French Guiana.[1]

If Duval worked alone, the next anarchist burglars of note were leaders of gangs which became successively larger until the veritable federation of burglars organized by Marius Jacob. Vittorio Pini, an anarchist shoemaker on the run from the Italian authorities, began a series of burglaries with four other comrades in and around Paris that netted over half a million francs. They stole almost exclusively to support hard-up comrades or prisoners and to subsidize the anarchist press in France and Italy.

Léon Ortiz ostensibly dropped out of anarchist politics in order to begin a career as a professional burglar, with a gang of ten others. He too donated funds to the cause, but not as strictly as Pini had done. He and his men were the only ones convicted at the notorious 'Trial of the Thirty' in 1894; the nineteen anarchist propagandists went free.

Alexandre Marius Jacob was really in a class of his own. At thirteen he was working on a pirate ship in the Indian Ocean. At sixteen he was a known anarchist in prison for manufacturing explosives. At seventeen he pulled off a remarkable theft from a jewellers by posing as a policeman. And by the age of twenty he was successfully burgling churches, aristocratic residences and bourgeois mansions all along the south coast of France. In 1900, aged twenty-one, he escaped from prison after feigning madness and went into hiding in Sète. Here he concluded that his previous criminal efforts had been amateur and decided to set up a properly organized anarchist gang to finance both the movement and themselves; they adopted the name of 'Les Travailleurs de la Nuit' (The Night Workers).

Uniforms were acquired for the purpose of disguise, and research done into safe-breaking techniques, in order that the correct special tools and equipment be obtained. A list of potential targets was drawn up from 'Who's Who'–type books which gave the names and addresses

---

1   He escaped with half-a-dozen others in 1901 and reached New York, where he rejoined the anarchist movement, eventually dying at the ripe old age of eighty-five. His memoirs of his time in the prison colony is now available in English, entitled *Outrage: An Anarchist Memoir of the Penal Colony.*

of the rich. Then they set to work. They had no particular base, their field of operations being France itself; some of their more lucrative burglaries were the cathedral at Tours, an Admiral's mansion in Cherbourg, a judge's house at Le Mans and a jewellery factory in rue Quincampoix, Paris. Jacob checked out the cathedral of Notre Dame and the home of the Bayeaux Tapestry but decided to cross them off his list. He left notes signed 'Attila' condemning owners for their excessive wealth and occasionally set fire to mansions that he'd burgled. As the group expanded from its original dozen members, some comrades went off to form autonomous gangs, so that a sort of federation was set up involving anything up to a hundred members, but the composition became less and less anarchist.

Jacob escaped arrest in Orleans by shooting a policeman, but they caught up with him again at Abbéville. He was taken into custody after a brief shoot-out which left one policeman dead and another wounded. Under pressure, one man informed on the whole gang, in such detail that investigations took two years to complete, and the charges ran to 161 pages. At the Assizes of Amiens in 1905, he was accused of no less than 156 burglaries; outside, an infantry battalion surrounded the court, and some jurors, afraid of anarchist reprisals, didn't turn up. He was sentenced to forced labour for life and packed off to Devil's Island, where the Governor labelled him the most dangerous prisoner ever.[2]

All these leading anarchist burglars donated sums to the cause and defended their actions by saying that they had a 'right' to steal; it was a question not of gain or profit, but of principle. The 'natural right' to a free existence was denied to workers through the bourgeoisie's monopoly ownership of the means of production; as the workers continued to create wealth, so the bourgeoisie continued to appropriate this wealth, a state of affairs maintained ultimately only by force, but legitimized. It was the immoral bourgeois who was the real thief, both in history and in the present; the anarchist 're-appropriation' was 'superior in morality', it was part of a rightful restitution of wealth robbed from the working class, done with moral conviction and good intent to further 'The Cause'. As *La Révolte* commented: "Pini never conducted himself as a professional thief. He was a man of very few needs, living simply, poorly even,

---

2   He tried to escape seventeen times, and spent five years in solitary, including two whole years in chains. Pardoned in 1928, he returned to France and eventually took his own life in 1954. His autobiography is now available in English.

with austerity; that Pini stole for propaganda purposes has been denied by no-one".

Anarchist arguments in favour of *la reprise individuelle* had a long history. *L'Action Révolutionnaire* asked its readers to steal from pawn shops, *bureaux de change* and post offices, and from bankers, lawyers, Jews (!) and *rentiers*[3] in order to finance the paper. *Ça Ira* suggested that its readers set an example by applying themselves immediately to relieving the rich of their fortunes. *Le Libertaire* thought that the thief, the crook and the counterfeiter, in permanent revolt against the established order of things, "were the only ones conscious of their social role". In 1905, a contemporary wrote of *Père Peinard*, the most scurrilous of the anarchist papers, with the widest working class readership:

> With no display of philosophy (which is not to say that it had none) it played openly upon the appetites, prejudices, and rancours of the proletariat. Without reserve or disguise, it incited to theft, counterfeiting, the repudiation of taxes and rents, killing and arson. It counselled the immediate assassination of deputies, senators, judges, priests and army officers. It advised unemployed working men to take food for themselves and their families wherever it was to be found, to help themselves to shoes at the shoe shop when the spring rains wet their feet, and to overcoats at the clothier's when the winter winds nipped them. It urged employed working men to put their tyrannical employers out of the way, and to appropriate their factories; farm labourers and vineyard workers to take possession of the farms and vineyards, and turn the landlords and vineyard owners into fertilizing phosphates; miners to seize the mines and to offer picks to shareholders in case they showed a willingness to work like their brother men, otherwise to dump them into the disused shafts; conscripts to emigrate rather than perform their military service, and soldiers to desert or shoot their officers. It glorified poachers and other deliberate breakers of the law. It recounted the exploits of olden-time brigands and outlaws, and exhorted contemporaries to follow their example.

---

3   *Rentier*. A person living off a private unearned income.

Alongside this shining example of proletarian propaganda came the more 'intellectual' approach of the anarchist theoretician. Elisée Reclus put forward the logical argument for the *reprise individuelle*:

> The community of workers, have they the right to take back all the products of their labour? Yes, a thousand times yes. This re-appropriation is the revolution, without which everything still is to be done.
>
> A group of workers, have they the right to a partial re-appropriation of the collective produce? Without a doubt. When the revolution can't be made in its entirety, it must be made at least to the best of its ability.
>
> The isolated individual, has he a right to a personal re-appropriation of his part of the collective property? How can it be doubted? The collective property being appropriated by a few, why shouldn't it be taken back in detail, when it can't be taken back as a whole? He has the absolute right to take it—to steal, as it's said in the vernacular. It would be well in this regard that the new morality show itself, that it enter into the spirit and habit.

Men of 'high principle and exemplary life' such as Elisée Reclus and Sébastien Faure were so carried away by their convictions on the immorality of property that they were ready to condone virtually any kind of theft on purely theoretical grounds, but the abstract theoretical arguments put forward by these intellectuals were unconnected to their own daily practice.

Nevertheless, in the Trial of the Thirty in 1894, Faure, Grave, Pouget and Paul Reclus and others were charged jointly with the Ortiz gang with criminal conspiracy. The propagandists went free and the burglars went to jail, but for Jean Grave at least, it was a salutary experience and he determined henceforth to play no part in propounding theories of the validity of theft. The paper that he launched the following year called *Temps Nouveaux* was soberly written and gained a wide audience in 'fashionable' circles sympathetic to anarchism. Grave saw in crime a corruption that would make people unsuited for the high ideals of a free society. He objected in particular to the type of professional crook who, rather than being a threat to the system, was the mirror-image of the policeman, recognizing the same social conventions, with similar minds and instincts, respectful of authority. But "if the act of stealing is to assume a character of revindication or of protest against the defective organization of Society, it must be performed openly, without any sub-terfuge". Grave anticipated the rather obvious objection: "'But', retort the defenders of theft, 'the individual who acts openly will deprive himself thus of the possibility of continuing. He will lose thereby his liberty, since he will at once be arrested, tried and condemned'.

"Granted, but if the individual who steals in the name of the right to revolt resorts to ruse, he does nothing more nor less than the first thief that comes along, who steals to live without embarrassing himself with theories".

In fact, a new generation of anarchists, spurred on by the 'individu-alist' ideas of Max Stirner, were to take as their point of departure exact-ly what Jean Grave objected to, that the rebel who secretly stole was no more than an ordinary thief. The developing theory of 'illegalism' had no moral basis, recognizing only the reality of 'might' in place of a theory of 'right'. Illegal acts were to be done simply to satisfy one's desires, not for the greater glory of some external 'ideal'. The illegalists were to make a theory of theft without the embarrassment of theoretical justifications.

Saint Max

With the dawn of the twentieth century a new current arose within French anarchism: self-conscious anarchist-individualism. The main in-tellectual base for this new departure was the rediscovery of the works of the much maligned and neglected philosopher, Max Stirner. Karl Marx himself had not underestimated the radical nature of Stirner's challenge and in *The German Ideology* directed a most vicious polemic against him and his affirmation of 'egoism'. But Stirner's book, *The Ego and Its Own*,[4] although causing a great stir at the time, was soon forgotten. In France interest was only reawakened around the turn of the century due to a conjunction of two main factors: the current fad for all things Ger-man (rather ironic considering the relative proximity of the First World War), and the keen interest in individualist philosophy amongst artists, intellectuals and the well-read, urban middle classes in general.

One indigenous bourgeois individualist was Maurice Barrès, who wrote an acclaimed trilogy entitled *Le Culte de Moi*, in which, having

---

4   *Der Einzige und sein Eigentum* being the original German title.

observed that, "our malaise comes from our living in a social order inspired by the dead", depicted a new type of man who, in satisfying his ego, would help turn humanity into "a beautiful forest". Despite such apparent sentimentality, his individualism was based upon the privileged material position of the bourgeoisie, whose self-realization was only made possible by the subjugation of the desires of the masses. Barrès ended up in later years as an anti-semitic, Christian nationalist. Individualism gained more radical currency through Henrik Ibsen, the Norwegian writer, who produced critiques of contemporary morality in dramatic form. He developed the theme of the strong individual standing alone against *both* the tyranny of the State and the narrow-minded oppressive moralism of the masses. Ibsen's appeal lay in the fact that personal longing for independence existed at all levels of society, so anybody, regardless of their class origin, could identify with the individual who was opposed to the mass. But Ibsen's individualism addressed moral questions rather than economic ones.

In the fad for all things German, Friedrich Nietzsche was the most fashionable of the writers-cum-philosophers. He railed against the prevailing culture and ethos of his time, and especially against attitudes of conformity, resignation or resentment; he willed the creation of the 'Superman', who would break through the constraints of bourgeois morality and the artificiality of social conventions towards a rediscovered humanity of more primitive virtues. For the record, he was neither a nationalist nor an anti-semite. Nietzsche regarded Stirner as one of the unrecognized seminal minds of the nineteenth century, a recommendation which, coupled with the aforementioned vogue for German philosophy, resulted in *fin de siècle* publication of extracts of his work in *Le Mercure*, and in the symbolists' 'organ of literary anarchism', *Entretiens politiques et litteraires*.[5] In 1900, the year of Nietzsche's death, the libertarian publisher Stock printed the first complete French translation of Stirner's work, entitled *L'Unique et sa Propriété*.

Young anarchists, in particular, quickly developed a fascination for the book, and it rapidly became the 'Bible' of anarcho-individualism. Stirner's polemic was much more extreme than the well-worn ideas that had until then made up the stuff of revolutionary ideology. Anarchist thinkers had tended, like Proudhon, to conceive of some absolute moral

---

5   Symbolism was the avant-garde cultural movement of the time.

criterion to which people must subordinate their desires, in the name of 'Reason' or 'Justice'; or, like Kropotkin, they had assumed some innate urge which, once Authority was overthrown, would induce people to cooperate naturally in a society governed by invisible laws of mutual aid. The 'anarchism' of Tolstoy and Godwin was also thoroughly grounded in moralism, a throwback to their Christian backgrounds of, respectively, Russian Orthodoxy and English Dissent. Even anarcho-syndicalists such as Jean Grave had a 'revolutionary morality' which viewed the class struggle as a 'Just War'.

Stirner saw all 'morality' as an ideological justification for the repression of individuals; he opposed those revolutionaries who wished to set up a new morality in place of the old, as this would still result in the triumph of the collectivity over the individual and lay the basis for another despotic State. He denied that there was any real existence in concepts such as 'Natural Law', 'Common Humanity', 'Reason', 'Justice' or 'The People'; more than being simply absurd platitudes (which he derisively labelled 'sacred concepts'), they were some of a whole gamut of abstract ideas which unfortunately dominated the thinking of most individuals: "Every higher essence, such as 'Truth', 'Mankind' and so on, is an essence OVER us". Stirner perceived the repressive nature of ideologies, even so-called 'revolutionary' ones; he believed that all these 'sacred concepts' manufactured by the intellect actually resulted in practical despotism.

For Stirner the real force of life resided in the will of each individual, and this 'Ego', "the unbridled I", could not come to real self-fulfillment and self-realization so long as the State continued to exist. Each individual was unique, with a uniqueness that should be cultivated: the Egoists own needs and desires provided the sole rule of conduct. Differences with other individuals were to be recognized and accepted, and conscious egoists could combine with others into "unions of egoists", free to unite or separate as they pleased, rather than being held together in a party under the weight of some ideological discipline. Certain conflicts of the will might have to be settled by force, as they were already in present society, but these should be done without the need for moral justification.

Stirner saw desire as the prime motivating force of the will: "My intercourse with the world consists in my enjoying it . . . my satisfaction decides about my relation to men, and I do not renounce, from an excess of humility, even the power over life and death. . . . I no longer humble myself before any power". The realization of individual desires was to be the basis for the elimination of the State, for what was the State ultimately but the alienated power of the mass of individuals? If people re-appropriated their power, habitually surrendered to the State, then established society would start to disintegrate. In the struggle against the State, which every conscious egoist would be forced to engage in, Stirner distinguished between a 'Revolution', which aimed at setting up an immutable new social order, and 'rebellion' or insurrection, a continuous state of permanent revolution, which set "no glittering hopes on 'institutions'". Stirner's rebellion was not so much a political or social act, but an egoistic one.

Furthermore, in this battle with the State, Stirner felt that "an ego who is his own cannot desist from being a criminal", but this did not mean that a moral justification for crime was necessary. Discussing Proudhon's famous dictum "Property is theft", he asks, why "put the fault on others as if they were robbing us, while we ourselves do bear the fault in leaving the others unrobbed? The poor are to blame for there being rich men". He suggested that Proudhon should have phrased himself as follows: "There are some things that only belong to a few, and to which we others will from now on lay claim or siege. Let us take them, for one only comes into property by taking, and the property of which for the present we are still deprived came to the proprietors likewise only by taking. It can be utilized better if it is in the hands of us all than if the few control it. Let us therefore associate ourselves for the purpose of this robbery". He summed up: "To what property am I entitled? To every property to which I *empower* myself. . . . I do not demand any 'Right', therefore I need not recognize any either. What I can get by force, I get by force, and what I can not get by force I have no right to, nor do I give myself airs or consolations with my imprescriptable 'Right' . . . Liberty belongs to him who *takes* it".

Stirner proposed 'expropriation' not as the 'legitimate' response of a victim of society, but as a way of self-realization: "Pauperism can be removed only when I as an ego *realize value* from myself, when I give my own self value, and make my price myself. I must rise in revolt to rise in this world". Yet he seemed unsure as to whether a rebellious crime should be glorified or superseded: "In crime the egoist has hitherto asserted himself and mocked the sacred; the break with the sacred, or rather *of* the sacred may become general. A revolution never returns, but a mighty, reckless, shameless, conscienceless, proud CRIME, does it not rumble in distant thunder, and do you not see how the sky grows presciently silent and gloomy?" Elsewhere, in his less poetic moments, Stirner was more pensive: "Talk with the so-called criminal as with an egoist, and he will be ashamed, not that he transgressed against your laws, but that he considered your laws worth evading, your goods worth desiring; he will be ashamed that he did not despise you and yours altogether, that he was too little an egoist". These seemingly contradictory attitudes were later to be keenly felt by some of the illegalists.

The Ego and Its Own was a startling work, written from a point of view that might be called 'radical subjectivity', a work of an all-consuming passion best summed up in the egoist's battle-cry: "Take hold and take what you require! With this the war of all against all is declared. I alone decide what I will have!"

If socialists continually ignored the question of individual desires and the subjective element of revolt, then it must be said that Stirner made little effort to direct his attention to basic socio-economic questions and the need for a collective struggle of the dispossessed, which would realize each individual's desires. He saw 'the masses' as "full of police sentiments through and through" and reduced the social question of how to eliminate the State and class society, to an individual one to be resolved by any means. Still, he had at last made it possible for rebels to admit that their revolt was being made primarily for their own self-realization: there was no need to justify it with reference to an abstract idea. Those who claimed to be acting in the name of 'The People' were often sentimental butchers. Stirner stripped away the dead weight of ideology and located the revolution where it always had been—in the hearts and minds of individuals.

The force and vigour of Stirner's ideas appealed to many anarchistic spirits determined to live the revolution there and then. The long association of French anarchism with theoretical voluntarism and practical illegality, sympathy for working class criminality, and hostility to bourgeois morals and socialist politics, meant that Stirner's ideas were easily accessible to many anarchists not yet blinded by an ideologically 'pure' anarchism. In contrast to the latter, the new generation of anarchists felt it necessary to call themselves 'anarchist-individualists', although they saw themselves as upholding the banner of anarchism pure and simple.

This milieu, which emerged after 1900 and was largely Libertad's creation, was one that had already assimilated Stirner's basic ideas into the body of its theory by the time of the Bonnot Gang. It is quite possible that none of the gang had ever actually read *The Ego and Its Own*, but their actions and Stirner's theories were to have striking similarities.

A LIFE OF CRIME. Clément Duval (top left) and Marius Jacob (top right). Both were sent to Devil's Island for life. Max Stirner (bottom left) provided the theoretical framework for illegalism, which was vigourously opposed by Jean Grave (bottom right).

2. A New Beginning

Do with it what you will and can, that is your affair and does not trouble me. You will perhaps have only trouble, combat and death from it, very few will draw joy from it.
—Max Stirner (1806–56) on his book *The Ego and Its Own*

Libertad

AROUND THE TURN of the century, anarchist-individualist propaganda was centred on Sébastien Faure's weekly journal *Le Libertaire*—still in existence today as the organ of the 'Fédération Anarchiste'. This gave space to individualist ideas and was critical of syndicalism. One anarchist who worked for the paper was Albert Joseph, habitually known as 'Libertad', who founded the milieu within which illegalism was to flourish. Libertad was brought up in an orphan school, the abandoned son of a local Prefect[1] and an unknown woman, and went to secondary school in Bordeaux. A job was found for him, but he was soon dismissed and sent back to the children's home from which he absconded and took to the road as a *trimardeur* or tramp. This probably brought him his first contact with anarchists, as tramps often lodged at anarchist-run labour exchanges—the *bourses du travail*, where they might be given popular revolutionary song-sheets to sell on their travels at two centimes apiece. Some tramps would have been unemployed workers on the *viaticum* (that is, given journey money and supplied with coupons for free meals and lodging in the hope that they would find work). Many of them would have been workers sacked for syndicalist or revolutionary opinions. Some tramps lived parasitically off the *bourses du travail*, while others were more devoted to spreading anarchist propaganda on their travels around France and neighbouring countries such as Switzerland and Belgium. Many had decided to refuse regular waged work (or had

---

1 State administrator of a Département.

it refused for them) and lived hand-to-mouth, doing part-time work, selling cheap trinkets at local markets and doing the odd bit of thieving.

Libertad made his way north from Bordeaux and arrived in Paris in 1897 at the age of twenty-two. Marked down for his anarchist opinions, he had already been under surveillance for three years—over the next ten his police record was to accumulate paper to a thickness of three inches.

In the capital he stayed on the premises of *Le Libertaire* and worked on the paper for several years alongside Charles Malato and, occasionally, the syndicalists Pelloutier and Delesalle; he also collaborated on the pro-Dreyfusard daily *Le Journal du Peuple* launched by Sébastien Faure and Émile Pouget. He was not yet of the individualist persuasion, although it was probably here that he encountered individualist ideas.

In 1900 Libertad found work with a regular publishing company as a proofreader[2] and stayed there until 1905, joining the union, the Syndicat des Correcteurs. In the same year, after speaking at a public meeting in Nanterre just outside Paris, he met the individualist anarchist Paraf-Javal and in October of 1902 they set up the *Causeries Populaires* at 22 rue du Chevalier de la Barre in Montmartre, just behind the Sacré-Coeur. The location was somewhat appropriate, as this street was the old rue des Rosiers where two generals had been shot by Communards in 1871. The Sacré-Coeur itself had been built, quite deliberately, on the site of the old artillery park where the insurrection had begun; MacMahon, the Marshal in charge of the repression, had specifically ordered its construction, "in expiation for the crimes of the Commune". The basilica was still incomplete, however, when the *Causeries Populaires* were founded.

The church was meant to stand evermore as a psychological and material expression of the victory of the bourgeoisie. Dominating Paris, atop the working class neighbourhood of Montmartre, it was seen even by the esteemed novelist Émile Zola as "a declaration of war" and as a "citadel of the absurd". As a Christian church, it proclaimed the continued reign of suffering, both ideologically and in reality, and demanded resignation to that suffering.

Libertad had already had dealings with the place. Hungry, he had gone to receive Christian charity in the form of food doled out to the

---

2   A favourite job among Parisian anarchists, due to the relatively high pay and flexible hours.

poor each evening but first had to listen to the sermon. After suffering in silence for several minutes he could finally bear it no longer and sprang to his feet to denounce the priest's hypocrisy. A tumultuous scene ensued and Libertad was carted away and sentenced to two months' prison for insulting public morals.

Rapidly he accumulated further convictions—for vagrancy, insulting behaviour and shouting, "Down with the Army!", the latter deemed more serious than disturbing the *Pax Dei*, as he received three months in prison.

Now in his late twenties, bearded but already balding, Libertad began a dynamic proselytization in Montmartre that was an extraordinarily powerful affirmation of anarchist individualism. Crippled in one leg, he carried two walking sticks (which he wielded very skillfully in fights) and habitually wore sandals and a large loose-fitting typographer's black shirt. One comrade said of him that he was "a one-man demonstration, a latent riot"; he was quickly a popular figure throughout Paris. His style of propaganda was summed up by Victor Serge as follows: "Don't wait for the revolution. Those who promise revolution are frauds just like the others. Make your own revolution by being free men and living in comradeship". His absolute commandment and rule of life was, "Let the old world go to blazes!" He had children to whom he refused to give state registration. "The State? Don't know it. The name? I don't give a damn, they'll pick one that suits them. The law? To the devil with it!" He sung the praises of anarchy as a liberating force, which people could find inside themselves.

Every Monday evening a *causerie* or discussion took place in the best room of the rue du Chevalier de la Barre. It was a gloomy ground-floor room decorated in the 'modern style' with flower-patterned wallpaper; comrades would sit on the old decrepit benches or chairs pilfered from the local squares and bistros, the speaker (if there was one) would lean against an old rickety table while others would be flicking through the books and pamphlets piled up on a counter at the back of the room.[3]

By 1904, the *causeries* were proving successful enough in the working class quarters of the XVIIIth, XIVth and XIth *arrondissements*, in Courbevoie and the Quartier Latin, to enable a bookshop to be opened

---

3   What the comrades didn't know was that the police surveillance was kept on all these meetings from their very inception, the Third Brigade, otherwise known as the '*Recherches*' (Intelligence) followed one or two people home from every meeting, endeavouring to keep their list of subversives up to date.

in the rue Duméril and an annexe in the rue d'Angoulême in the XIth *arrondissement*.

Libertad's erstwhile cooperation with the syndicalist militants was now coming to an end. In 1903 he and Paraf-Javal had formed the Anti-militarist League in association with some leading syndicalists, but this alliance fell apart during the Amsterdam Congress of the International Antimilitarist Association (AIA) in June 1904. Libertad and Paraf-Javal saw desertion or draft-dodging as the best antimilitarist strategy, believing that if anarchists stayed in the army awaiting a revolutionary situation, they would very quickly all end up in military prisons or the African disciplinary battalions. The Congress, however, saw such a strategy as too individualistic, preferring soldiers to remain disaffected within their units so as to make the army as a whole less reliable. Despite the mutiny of the 17th Line Regiment in 1907 (when the Government rather stupidly sent local troops in to suppress the revolt by vineyard workers who were no more than their own kith and kin) the individualist strategy was probably more realistic, especially given the large number of men rotting in the African hard labour prisons.

As a result, Libertad and Paraf-Javal left the Antimilitarist League and stepped up anti-syndicalist propaganda. A whole series of articles appeared that year in *Le Libertaire* against participation in elections, unions and cooperatives: all participation in power structures, even 'alternative' ones, was seen to reinforce the hierarchical system of power as a whole.

Paraf-Javal put forward the individualist argument in an article entitled 'What is a Union?' and answered his question as follows: "It is a grouping whereby the downtrodden masses class themselves by trade in order to try and make the relations between the bosses and workers less intolerable. From the two propositions, one conclusion: where they don't succeed, then the union's task is useless, and where they do, then the union's work is harmful, because a group of men will have made their situation less intolerable and will consequently have made present society more durable". Further pamphlets rolled off the presses: *What I Mean by Anarchic Individualism, Anarchist Individualism in Practice*, pamphlets on Max Stirner, and Han Ryner's *Little Individualist Handbook*.[4] Libertad, however, was less a writer than an orator, preferring to intervene verbally.

---

4   *Le Petit manuel Individualiste* (1903) was written by Jacques Ner (1861–1938) aka Han Ryner. He later collaborated with Lorulot and Émile Armand.

In January 1905 the veteran Communarde, Louise Michel, died in Marseille, and the AIA called a meeting in Paris to organize a spectacular 'revolutionary' funeral. Libertad went along, but his attitude clashed with that of the militants. He told them that the whole ceremony was ridiculous, just as ridiculous as calling a woman well into her seventies 'the Red Virgin'. "She lost her virginity long ago", he proclaimed. The crowd became hostile and he withdrew, muttering, "You're all idiots". The funeral went ahead as planned, with tens of thousands lining the route and in the procession. The city was swamped with police and regular army units, and many bourgeois apparently fled fearing that revolution was imminent; some Catholics even locked themselves in their churches ready to defend themselves against the crowd. Despite police provocations, including the banning of songs and unauthorized flags, there were very few 'incidents'; by contrast, in Russia, the same day was to go down in history as 'Bloody Sunday'—the start of the 1905 Revolution.

The *Causeries Populaires* now had a regular audience, but it was still of minimal size, and the only hope of reaching a wider public lay in publishing a regular paper that could continue in print the discussions of the ideas of Stirner, Nietzsche, Bakunin, Georges Sorel (the theorist of revolutionary syndicalism) and others, as well as arguing for a new revolutionary practice based on the self-realization of the individual.

Libertad and his two lovers, the schoolteacher sisters Anna and Amandine Mahé, and Paraf-Javal, now put their combined energies into founding an anarchist-individualist weekly, so they wouldn't have to rely on *Le Libertaire* to voice their opinions. The first issue of *l'anarchie* appeared on 13th April 1905 and continued to appear every Thursday, without interruption, until it was suppressed with all the other revolutionary papers at the outbreak of war in 1914. Its title harked back to the first paper ever to adopt the anarchist label: Anselm Bellegarrigue's *L'anarchie: journal d'Ordre*, of which only two issues were produced (in 1850). His slogan had been, "I deny everything, I affirm only myself". Libertad ended his first article with the battle-cry, "Resignation is death. Revolt is life".

There was a print run of four thousand, although perhaps only half that number were sold (at ten centimes a copy, like the other anarchist papers); readership figures are unknown. Financially it was maintained by voluntary donations to supplement the small income from street and bookshop sales; it probably also benefited from the occasional *reprise individuelle*—thefts carried out by comrades.

The main contributors besides Libertad, Paraf-Javal and the Mahé sisters were René Hemme (aka 'Mauricius' or 'Vandamme'), André Roulot (aka 'Lorulot'), Ernest Lucien Juin Armand (aka 'Émile Armand'), and Jeanne Morand (one of another pair of sisters with whom Libertad had intimate relations). Anna Mahé was the nominal manager of the paper.

L'anarchie declared itself against resignation and conformity to the existing state of affairs, and particularly opposed vices, habits and prejudices such as work, marriage, military service, voting, smoking tobacco, drinking alcohol and the eating of meat. It exalted *l'en dehors*, the outsider, and the *hors-la-loi*, outlaws. According to Lorulot its purpose was to work sincerely for 'individual regeneration' and the 'revolution of the self'. *L'anarchie*'s view of society was essentially as follows: firstly there were not two opposed classes, bourgeois and proletarian, but only individuals (although there were those who were for, and those who were against, society as it was then constituted). The Master and the Slave were equally part of the system and mutually dependent, but the Rebel or *Révolté* could come originally from either category: their propaganda was addressed to anybody prepared to rise in revolt against existing society.

The *syndicats* or unions were seen simply as capitalist organizations which defended workers *as workers*; thus keeping them in a social role which it should have been the anarchist aim to destroy. To invest them with value only so long as they were workers had nothing to do with their own realization as individuals. The syndicalists were seen as unwitting tools of capitalism, whose practical reformism was only kept going by the myth of 'The Revolution', an ideology which furnished the unions with militants for their present-day battles. Only Georges Sorel had been shrewd enough to accept that the idea of 'The Revolution' was indeed a myth. But not only was such a myth necessary, it was in fact the whole essence of socialism, without which the struggle for the working class might collapse into despair. For Sorel, the present-day struggle was everything, and in this he had something in common with the politics of *l'anarchie*, though he was a believer in the mass rather than in the individual.

Sorel's realism was seen by the anarchist-individualists as further evidence of the bankruptcy of syndicalism; especially nauseating to them was the dry academic moralizing of Jean Grave, the 'Anarchist Pope', in *Temps Nouveaux*, while the May Day celebrations were regarded contemptuously, as nothing more than theatrical role-playing, mirroring the absurdity of the bourgeoisie's 14th of July (Bastille Day): it changed nothing.

The individualists' ideal was to live their lives as neither exploiter nor exploited—but how to do that in a society divided in this way? Their answer was for people to take direct action through the *reprise individuelle*, or in slang, *la reprise au tas*—taking back the whole heap.

A good part of 1906 was spent campaigning against the elections. Previously Libertad had stood as the 'abstentionist' candidate in the XIth *arrondissement*, but this time they relied on 'interventions', posters and the paper. At one large socialist gathering in Nanterre, on the outskirts of Paris, the Socialist Deputy[5] was almost thrown out of the window: many of the interventions by the anarchists ended up in fighting.

However, trouble was also brewing internally: Libertad and Paraf-Javal had argued, and the latter had taken control of the bookshop in rue Duméril, setting up a 'Scientific Studies Group' which announced itself for a 'reasoned social organization obtained by scientific camaraderie, methodically and logically obtained outside all coercion'. What this actually meant was not quite clear, except that Paraf-Javal was obsessed with science and logic, synonymous as they were in those times with the idea of 'Progress'. In February 1907 a police report noted that the two groups had fallen out and foresaw trouble in the future; the police were not to be disappointed.

For the time being, however, there was only trouble with the authorities. On May Day, Libertad, Jeanne Morand and another comrade, Marcel Millet, were arrested for evading fares on the Metro and assaulting a ticket collector and a policeman; Millet was also charged with carrying a knuckleduster. Libertad spent a month in prison, but within two weeks of his release there was more serious trouble when it was decided to hold a Sunday evening *causerie en plein air*. It was a warm summer night and soon a reported two hundred people had gathered in the rue de la Barre on the heights of Montmartre.

Some local traders complained about the noise and obstruction, and the police ordered the crowd to disperse. The anarchists refused and

---

5 The lower chamber of the French Parliament is the Chambre des Deputés, equivalent to the House of Representatives or the British House of Commons.

COMRADES EN PLEIN AIR. A forerunner of the renowned 'anarchist picnic' – a gathering of the *Causeries Populaires* sometime between 1905 and 1908. Libertad, on the left of the picture with walking stick and beard is flanked by his lovers, the Mahé sisters, Anna and Amandine.

when police reinforcements were called, a pitched battle ensued leaving several wounded. The street was left littered with bottles, broken chairs and the usual strange debris of people suddenly scattered.

After that affair things seem to have remained comparatively quiet for the next year, until the summer season of interventions got under way. Syndicalist meetings were often the target this time, and the anarchist-individualists were definitely *persona non grata*. On one occasion, Libertad asked for the right to speak but was refused and told that his group was not welcome. Fights broke out with the stewards and lasted for half an hour, until finally Libertad's group stormed onto the platform and sent the syndicalists fleeing; the meeting broke up in disorder without Libertad being heard.

The conflict between Paraf-Javal's group of 'scientists' and the *Causeries Populaires* comrades now came to a head. Paraf-Javal was already angry that his pamphlets were being sold at *causeries* and were not being paid for, when one of Libertad's group, Henri Martin (alias 'Japonet'), Amandine Mahé's new lover, stole some money from the bookstall at a meeting of the 'Scientific Studies Group'. At a subsequent meeting a brawl ensued between partisans of the two groups in which knives, knuckledusters and spiked wristbands were used. After this incident Paraf-Javal would only go out armed with a revolver and a dagger, but he preferred to stay at home writing a diatribe against Libertad's group. The pamphlet *Evolution of a Group under a Bad Influence* was greeted with anger and derision by anarchists everywhere and effectively isolated his small clique. At the rue de la Barre, however, Libertad was also on his own, having fallen out with both the Mahé sisters, Jeanne Morand and Henri Martin. The De Blasius brothers, who ran the print shop, had also had enough of the rue de la Barre, and at the instigation of Paraf-Javal they departed with some of the printing material and most of the pamphlets.

Just over two weeks later, on 29th September 1908, a detective of the Third Brigade included in his report the following: "a few days ago there was a fight between a well-known comrade, 'Bernard', and Libertad inside the *Causeries Populaires* in the rue de la Barre. Libertad gave Bernard a serious blow to the head, and, covered in blood, the latter ran out towards rue Ramey. During the fight, one of the Mahé sisters kicked Libertad in the stomach to try and put a stop to it". A week later he was taken seriously ill to the nearby hospital of Lariboisière and eventually died in the early hours of the morning of

12th November. There were rumours that he had died at the hands of the police on the steps of Montmartre, or that his death was due to 'natural causes', but it seems (and this is substantiated by a later editor of *l'anarchie*) that the true cause was that kick in the stomach by his one-time lover.

He had fallen out with his erstwhile comrades to such an extent that they refused to view the body or claim it for burial. After the statutory seventy-two hours it was taken to the École de Clamart medical school to be used in the furtherance of scientific research.

City of Thieves

By the end of 1908, *l'anarchie* was becoming the only anarchist paper which positively promoted crime and the theory of 'illegalism'. This theory differed from the *reprise individuelle*, not just due to its connection with the anarchist-individualist current, but because the illegalists stole not simply for the greater advancement of 'the cause', but for their own advancement, according to Stirner's line of argument. Or at least so they said: in practice, successful illegalism probably helped support the weekly paper and comrades who were in dire financial need. Yet there was not necessarily a contradiction here, for, as part of the movement, their own self-realization was reflected in the self-realization of other comrades: an egoistic gesture in revolutionary terms should also be an altruistic one.

Lorulot had already encouraged illegality because it involved "minimal risks and satisfactory returns", while Armand suggested that it was unimportant whether a comrade earned his living legally or illegally, but important that he live to his own profit and advantage. Illegalism was viewed favourably by many individualists in the *Causeries Populaires* milieu, not least because they engaged in petty-crime, or benefited from the crimes of others, like much of the populace of working class Montmartre. As Victor Serge later recalled: "One of the peculiar features of working class Paris at this time was that it bordered extensively on the underworld, that is on the vast world of fly-by-nights, outcasts, paupers and criminals. There were few essential differences between the young worker or artisan from the old central districts and the ponce from the alleys around Les Halles. A chauffeur or mechanic with any wits about him would pilfer all he could from the boss as a matter of course, out of class-consciousness".

In fact there were neighbourhoods in Paris more or less recognized as 'criminal', with their own traditions and way of life—principally the northern outskirts of the city; Pantin, St-Ouen, Aubervilliers and Clichy. A large number of Parisian criminals made their living from the thousands of tourists who, in the wake of the Great Exhibition of 1900, flocked to see the glittering capital of European civilization. There were plenty of professional beggars and pickpockets, as well as thousands of part-time prostitutes on the *boulevards* and in the *brasseries*—working class women forced to service 'gentlemen' in order to make ends meet.

There were also professional loan sharks, confidence tricksters, forgers, counterfeiters, and even some specializing in dog or bicycle theft. Parisian workers, if not part of this 'underworld', were usually sympathetic to it and naturally hostile to the police, and not averse to a bit of thieving themselves; the public in general sometimes seemed to have an almost ambivalent attitude to crime.

The anarchist viewpoint that was sympathetic to crime was probably received more favourably by many workers than Jean Grave's moral sermonizing that all crime was essentially bourgeois. One of the most popular working class heroes of the time was the anarchist Ravachol, who had declared that, "To die of hunger is cowardly and degrading. I preferred to turn thief, counterfeiter, murderer". If working class people were sympathetic to such a figure it was because they understood where he was coming from.

The hostility of employers to workers who expressed unsound opinions, or who were denounced to them by the police as 'anarchists' or 'troublemakers', meant that many hundreds of workers found it extremely difficult to find work and were virtually forced into criminality. Under capitalism, where a worker's only power is his or her labour power, which must be sold in order to survive, what can someone do when the employers refuse to buy, consequently denying the right to live? The illegalists answered this question through a reversal of perspective: through the physical power that is all a worker possesses, the means of survival have to be seized directly, without exchange, and, if necessary, by force.

The crossover in Paris between the working class, the underworld and revolutionary politics was a similar sort of phenomenon to the situation in Czarist Russia, but there, politics was much more firmly rooted, by necessity, in illegality. Paris, long a haven for Russian refugees, sheltered upwards of twenty-five thousand exiles, of whom the police estimated that no less than fifteen hundred were 'terrorists' and five hundred and fifty of them anarchists or 'Maximalists'.[6] The French Intelligence services tried to keep a close watch on the latter category, especially in their plans for 'expropriations' and also because they had links with French revolutionaries and Indian nationalists, whom they aided in the study and manufacture of pyrotechnics. The Social-Revolutionary 'Maximalists' who had split from the party in 1906 were well-known for their advocacy of a wider application of 'terrorism' than the regular SRs, including the incendiarism and pillage of estates, as well as individual assassinations. In Russia hundreds of country houses were burnt down and hundreds of policemen and civil servants killed. The Maximalists also carried out expropriations at home and abroad: one, discussed in rue St Jacques by the Maximalists, was planned for a branch of the Crédit Lyonnais in Paris but was rejected in favour of an attack on a bank in Montreux in Switzerland. In this bungled operation in 1907 four people were killed and both revolutionaries arrested.

A more spectacular action took place in the same year, carried out by members of the Bolshevik faction of the Russian Social-Democratic Labour Party. Led by Stalin's close friend Semyon Ter-Petrossian (aka "Kamo"), a brutal attack was made on the coach bringing funds to the State Bank in Tiflis, Georgia, leaving 40 dead in the central square, although netting the huge sum of 340,000 roubles. But the cash was mainly in 500 rouble notes with known serial numbers, and several revolutionaries were captured in Paris trying to exchange them. At the same time in Poland (then still a part of the Russian Empire) the Polish Socialist Party's Combat Organization, led by Jozef Pilsudski, were conducting raids on tax offices, ambushing Treasury vans, and assassinating Governors, policemen and officials (336 being killed in 1906 alone). The experience, often violent and clandestine, of the Russian revolutionaries was communicated by refugees to those western revolutionaries who were most sympathetic to both revolutionary ideas and direct action—the anarchists above all.

But if the Bolsheviks, for instance, engaged in expropriations, this was far from illegalism; such expropriations were only done for 'the Cause'—ostensibly to bring on the Revolution, but primarily to bolster

---

6 The headquarters of the Russian Social Revolutionary Party (The SRs) was in Paris, as was its nemesis, the Okhrana, the Russian secret police.

Party funds. The comrades responsible only received fifty kopeks a day to live on. Bolshevik illegality was simply a necessary tactic at the time for building the Party.

Nevertheless, the effect of armed expropriations, assassinations (an agent of the Okhrana was executed in a Paris hotel room in 1908) and bomb explosions (usually accidental, as when Vladimir Stryga stumbled and blew himself up in the Bois de Vincennes in 1906 and 'Svoboda' did the same in the Bois de Boulogne in 1908) provided anarchists with inspiration, and something to admire and sympathize with. Above all, the Russian Revolution of 1905 had sent revolutionaries everywhere into a state of great excitement, and the French syndicalist leaders in particular determined to face up to their responsibilities as the vanguard of the working class.

State of Emergency

By 1906 the Republican Bloc had successfully beaten off the challenge to its power of the extreme right-wing, a struggle which had lasted for ten years and which had been crystallized in the Dreyfus affair. Essentially, it was a showdown between the more 'progressive' capitalists who sought to usher France into the era of mass-production and the backward, pro-monarchical forces of the Catholic church and army, who still harked after the feudal traditionalism of the *Ancien Régime*. It was a struggle that French capitalism as a whole could not afford to lose, and, needless to say, clerical militarism was routed, the State took control of mass-education, and the 'Radicals' were at last left free to deal with the working class.

The CGT had largely stayed out of this fight between what they had correctly analyzed as 'rival factions of the bourgeoisie', although many anarchists were prepared to give grudging support to the 'Dreyfusards'. In 1906 the CGT emphasized their independence in the 'Charter of Amiens' which announced their autonomy from the parties of both Right and Left, and called for a general strike on 1st May in demand of an eight-hour working day.

This was the first ever general strike in France, but only two hundred thousand workers responded—a fraction of the industrial workforce, of whom only seven per cent were CGT members. Nevertheless, the 'Radical' Prime Minister Clemenceau (an ex-syndicalist) declared a state of emergency, arrested the CGT leaders, Pouget, Griffuelhes and Yvetôt, and proceeded to turn Paris into an armed camp: sixty thousand troops were mobilized to patrol the streets.

Faced with blatant repression by the Government and a lack of mass support, the strikers returned to work, but over a million days were lost that year, the highest ever. It was the crest of the revolutionary syndicalist wave, although the CGT continued to expand, doubling its membership to six hundred thousand by 1912. It was believed by the authorities that at least one hundred thousand would identify themselves as anarchists.

The 'Radical' Bourgeoisie, now dominant in the offices of the State, went on the offensive: not only was industrial action by 'civil servants' outlawed (a category which included teachers and railway and postal workers) but troops were sent in to break virtually every strike, with the result that dozens of workers were killed and hundreds wounded. A bitter strike by miners in the Nord was crushed in 1906. The protracted struggle of the vineyard workers of the Midi was finally overwhelmed in 1907, despite the mutiny of a whole regiment of troops sent in to break the strike. The strike of the Nantes dockers collapsed the same year. In 1908, fourteen striking quarry-workers were shot down (with two killed, including one teenage boy) by police inside the union office at Draveil and later in the same dispute some two hundred were cut down by dragoons, with four killed, at Villeneuve-St Georges[7]; at the same time, electricians plunged Paris into darkness in the hope of winning their dispute but were forced back to work just like the construction workers. The textile workers were defeated the following year, and an attempted strike by postal workers ended up as a fiasco, with the CGT leadership imprisoned again. Aided by this fortunate absence of the anarchist 'old guard', and pointing to the series of defeats as evidence of bad management, the reformists, led by Léon Jouhaux, captured the leadership at the end of the year.

Nevertheless, with the numerical strength of the CGT still growing, the employers attempted to vaccinate their workers against the syndicalist virus by recruiting them to company or Catholic-run unions—the 'Yellow' or 'Green' unions as they were known—or tried to bargain with more receptive union leaders on a local basis. Meanwhile the Government introduced social legislation, in the form of pension laws, which

---

7   There is a report on a contemporary French website, Paris-Luttes.info, that suggests both Libertad and Rirette Maîtrejean were present and injured at this demonstration. "30 juillet 1908: 'une manifestation qui a mal tourné,'" July 31, 2015, https://paris-luttes.info/30-juillet-1908-une-manifestation.

meant that workers had more to lose if they got the sack. As strikes became shorter in duration, involving fewer workers, strikers increasingly used 'hit-squad' tactics as a way of outmanoeuvring the police and army and directly damaging the employers. But workers' living standards as a whole continued to decline, despite the appearance of abundance given to Paris by the new era of mass-production, and more workers were pushed into 'marginal' and criminal activities in order to survive. Only one other legal resource was left to the working class by the bourgeois State: electoral politics. It was no surprise that as the number of working class defeats multiplied, so the socialist vote steadily increased.

But one group of proletarians, at least, was not prepared simply to resign itself to this dominant atmosphere of defeatism. Instead they invested their struggle with an even greater fury—rather than be exploited they would refuse waged work, rather than be forced into poverty they would steal, rather than vote they would riot, rather than 'make propaganda' in the army they would refuse to do military service altogether, rather than complain about their situation they would take immediate direct action to improve it. These were the sorts of attitudes expressed by the new generation of rebels who had responded to the theory and practice of anarchist-individualism. For if Libertad's propaganda had helped create a climate of defiance, it had also reflected a general mood.

THE INDIVIDUALISTS. Albert Libertad (top left), the first editor of *l'anarchie*, and his successor Emile Armand (top right). Paraf-Javal (bottom left), their rival whose threat to blow up the premises led to the move to the suburbs. André Lorulot (bottom right), vegetarian and naturist who could not stomach illegalism.

3. The Rebels

He who has no means of subsistence, has no duty to
acknowledge or respect other people's property, considering
that the principles of the social covenant have been violated
to his prejudice.
—Johann Gottlieb Fichte (1762–1814)

MANY OF THE principal characters involved with the Bonnot Gang (but not Bonnot himself) spent some time in Belgium in the couple of years prior to 1911, although some of them only became acquainted later, in Paris. Nevertheless, the Belgian experience was a formative one, during which they learned the ground rules of clandestinity and illegality. However, if these rebels served their apprenticeship in Belgium, their practice was to be firmly centred on Paris.

Brussels

Towards the end of August 1909, a nineteen year-old future editor of *l'anarchie* arrived in the French capital from Brussels. His name was Victor-Napoleon Lvovich Kibalchich, to become better known as Victor Serge, the pro-Bolshevik revolutionary and later critic of Stalinism. At this time though he was the fiery young anarchist who wrote for the Brussels anarchist weekly *Le Révolté* (The Rebel) under the pseudonym *Le Rétif*—'the Restless One'.

He had been born in the winter of 1889 into a poor Russian refugee family living in exile in Verviers in Belgium. His mother Vera was from an impoverished Polish noble family while his father Lev was a former cavalryman who had fled Russia in 1887 and was now a university lecturer. Victor's paternal uncle was Nikolai Ivanovich Kibalchich, the explosives expert for *Narodnaya Volya* (The People's Will) who made the bomb that killed the Czar in 1881. Victor's father had the walls of their abode adorned with portraits of executed revolutionaries, no doubt including his brother and the four others hanged with him. Victor's earliest memories were of adult conversations about "trials, executions, escapes, and Siberian highways, with great ideas incessantly argued over, and with the latest books about these ideas". Idealism and self-sacrifice were the reigning values of his parents' milieu, and, although Victor was determined to abandon self-sacrifice as a positive virtue, he never could nor would abandon the revolutionary idealism of the Russians.

While still very young he had his first major initiation into the ways of capitalism: his brother Raoul died of hunger because the family did not have enough money for food. When he was fifteen his parents split up. His mother, suffering from tuberculosis, left for Tiflis in Georgia perhaps in the hope of some clean air, with his elder sister Elena and her husband. His father then moved to Forest, a suburb of Brussels, with a new family, and so Victor was largely left to fend for himself. His earliest childhood friend was Raymond Callemin, born in Brussels in 1890, whose French father was a drunkard and an "old socialist disgusted with socialism" who patched shoes from morning till night. He disowned his son for keeping bad company. Together, Victor and Raymond read Zola's *Paris* and Louis Blanc's *History of the French Revolution* and at the age of fifteen, in 1905, they joined the 'Socialist Young Guards'. Neither of them went to school or college because, as Victor put it, "learning was life itself".

The Young Guards were the youth movement of the Belgian Socialist Party, yet there was often tension between the two. While the workers' struggles could be militant and violent (the last general strike was in 1902), the Party still held to an electoral policy, despite the property qualification that excluded most workers, as well as all women. The local secretary of their group was Jean De Boe, an orphan from Anderlecht and trained typographer, who later recalled that they became extremely close, and developed a more radical politics in opposition to most of their socialist comrades. According to De Boe it was the writings of the former Communard and journalist, Jules Vallès, who became the revolutionary role-model, for Victor, above all. At sixteen years old Victor gave his first lecture, on the 1905 Russian Revolution, which was by then in the throes of counterrevolution, and a cycle of revenge assassinations, deportations, hangings, bank robberies and lengthy prison sentences. Soon enough they were being labelled 'anarchists'.

According to Victor, after some French deserters brought them a "whiff of the aggressive trade unionism of the anarcho-syndicalists" they became revolted by electoral politics and abandoned socialism, as it did not demand that harmony between deeds and words, the personal and the political, that anarchism appeared to demand: "Anarchism swept us away completely because it both demanded everything of us and offered everything to us". Absolute liberty was at the same time a revolutionary method for the individual and a revolutionary goal for everyone, to be realized immediately. This was both the greatness and weakness of anarchism as each individual's method could be argued as valid due to the 'truth' invested in its extrapolated conclusion.

After reading Kropotkin's *Appeal to the Young*, Victor and Raymond decided to go and stay at a communitarian colony called *L'Expérience* ('The Experiment') at Stockel in the forest of Soignes just south of Brussels. Over the gate hung the slogan from Rabelais: "Do what thou wilt". Further on they saw a dilapidated white cottage, door falling off its hinges, impossible to heat, sitting under the trees. Victor recalled seeing in the yard "a tall black-haired devil with a pirate's profile, haranguing a rapt audience". This was the founder of the colony, Émile Chapelier, an ex–coal miner and ex-con; here they met a cobbler, a painter, some printers, gardeners and tramps, a Swiss plasterer, an ex-officer, Leon Guerassimov, from Russia converted to Tolstoyan anarchism, and Alexander Sokolov, a chemist from Odessa, the latter shortly to become infamous. One day a newcomer arrived, having been unable to find work due to his known anarchist sympathies. Édouard Carouy, born in 1883 at Montignies-les-Lens, had had a hard childhood, both his parents having died when he was only three years old. He had spent many years apprenticed to a metal-turner in Brussels and had subsequently worked in Malines, St Nicholas and the Dutch port of Terneuzen, where he'd pilfered from the docks. He too decided to make the colony his home. Although a good few years older than Victor and his friends, he was later to follow them all to Paris, but at this period he seems to have kept apart from their revolutionary group.

The teenage comrades quickly read their way through the series of pamphlets published by the French syndicalist confederation, the CGT; subjects covered included *The Crime of Obedience, The Immorality of Marriage, Planned Procreation, The New Society* and antimilitarist literature. For serious entertainment they read novels by Anatole France and poetry by the Belgian Émile Verhaeren or the Parisian Jehan Rictus, the latter famous for his *Soliloquys of the Poor* and use of the hard-style slang spoken on the streets.

In November 1906 the colony moved to nearby Boitsfort, and here Victor Kibalchich learnt to proofread, edit, typeset and print their irregular four-page journal, *Communiste*. The first edition was printed in June 1907, and sported the mottos "Truth will set you free" and "Freedom will make you good". It continued for seventeen issues. The skills learnt here were to sustain Victor and Jean throughout their lives.

In June 1908 under the heading "Illegalists" Victor Kibalchich wrote in support of Émile Armand who had been sent to prison in Paris for counterfeiting.[1] But, at this tender age, he drew a distinction between those militants who steal through conscious revolt against society, and those for whom theft is simply an act of cowardice or weakness, the act of "a brute too stupid to imagine better". The inherent difficulty with this approach was who was to judge, and by what criteria, if a theft was a conscious act of revolt or not? Was it fair to characterize a worker as a 'brute' just because he was not yet a conscious rebel? And if the act itself was the same, how could solidarity be given to one and not the other? Surprisingly perhaps, Kibalchich chose not to distinguish between those, such as Marius Jacob, who steal to fund 'the cause' and those who merely use the proceeds for their own ends.

The *Communiste*, unsurprisingly, did not endear itself to the socialists and it was banned from the *Maison du Peuple*, as were Victor, Raymond and Jean. After the collapse of the Boitsfort commune in February 1908 (variously blamed on personality differences, sexual conflicts and simple lack of organization) the three friends formed the Brussels Revolutionary Group, meeting every Thursday in Jean De Boe's home in Anderlecht with public meetings once a month. They issued their own 'Manifesto' for the May Day demonstration of 1908; distributed as a flyer it called not for "passive processions and noisy braying" but for expropriation of the capitalist class by direct action. A definitive break with the politics of the socialists and a clear statement of their anarchism.

In September 1908 the group transformed the *Communiste* into *Le Révolté* (The Rebel) the 'first' issue therefore being number 18; the format remained a small, four-page news-sheet, however. It was subtitled 'Organ of Anarchist Propaganda—appearing at least once a month'—later changed to twice a month. Although the back page was devoted to the 'Mouvement Social', the paper was hostile to trade-unionism,

---

1   Armand was later said (by Mauricius) to have suffered for another's crime. Being found in bed with a man's wife, the money was not in fact his, but he could not admit it. The perils of free love.

the more so as the Belgian unions were mainly controlled by the Socialist Party (unlike in France where the CGT was anarcho-syndicalist and quite distinct from the French Socialist Party). There were numerous occasions of anarchists being expelled from unions and being prevented from speaking at meetings. The conviction that theory and practice be unified in each individual's life led to *Le Révolté* adopting an approach very similar to that of *l'anarchie*; they sometimes printed reports from Paris and shed a tear for the passing away of Libertad in their obituary.

Victor Kibalchich became a principal contributor having already styled himself *Le Rétif*, denoting someone who is more disobedient than simply restless, a maverick. The very same month he was arrested for the first time on leaving an anarchist meeting that turned into a brawl with the cops. He was not charged but was put under police surveillance.

Victor wrote many articles for the paper, including some that make interesting reading in the light of his subsequent involvement with the 'Bonnot Gang'. In February 1909, under the title 'Anarchist-Bandits', he praised "our audacious comrades who fell at Tottingham [*sic*]" and expressed "much admiration for their unequalled bravery", which proved that "anarchists don't surrender".. The comrades in question were Paul 'Elephant' Hefeld and Jacob Lepidus,[2] both sailors from Riga in Latvia, who belonged to a cell of the clandestine revolutionary group called 'Leesma' or 'Flame'.

They had carried out a wages snatch on a Tottenham (North London) engineering factory, and in the course of a chase lasting for several miles had shot almost two dozen of their pursuers, three of whom died, one being a boy of ten. The two men committed suicide, but not before successfully passing on their haul to a waiting accomplice who was never caught.

Le Rétif continued his article: "Reader, I detect on your lips a sentimental objection: But those poor twenty-two people shot by your comrades were innocent. Haven't you any remorse?—No! Because those who pursued them could only have been 'honest' citizens, believers in the State and Authority; oppressed perhaps, but oppressed people who, by their criminal inertia, perpetuate oppression: Enemies! For us the enemy is whoever impedes us from living. We are the ones under attack,

---

2   Lepidus' brother was Stryga who had been killed by his own bomb in the Bois de Vincennes three years earlier.

and we defend ourselves". He characterized such 'noble bandits' as, in the existing social circumstances, "the vanguard of a barbarous army".

In the next issue a reader protested against the article, saying that there was nothing anarchist about the *reprise individuelle* and that anarchists couldn't be thieves in any circumstances. Victor Kibalchich disagreed. Not long afterwards a bomb was found in Brussels and claimed by the self-styled 'International Anarchist Group' to have been the work of their chemist. It had been destined for the ex-Minister of Justice, responsible for numerous expulsions of foreign refugees; the group also declared that it had recently carried out an expropriation of three thousand francs.[3] All this bravado led to the undoing of one of their members. Police in Ghent raided the house of twenty-two year-old Abraham Hartenstein, who was none other than Alexander Sokolov, the Odessa chemist from the old libertarian community of Stockel. At the sight of police uniforms he reacted as he would have done in Czarist Russia; he drew his revolver and shot two policemen dead. But he did not escape arrest.

Victor Kibalchich probably had a hand in drafting the statement printed in *Révolté* by the Brussels Revolutionary Group which lashed out at the 'honest' anarchists who criticized Sokolov on the grounds that the situation in Belgium bore no relation to that in Russia. The BRG was defiant and supported him unconditionally, declaring that "anarchists do not surrender . . . we are in permanent insurrection!" Sokolov was sentenced to life imprisonment. As no further word was heard from the so-called 'International Anarchist Group' it could be inferred that its existence was in fact Sokolov's own creation, in the tradition of Bakunin's 'World Revolutionary Alliance'; anarchists sometimes showed a surprising propensity for creating organizations.

During the summer of 1909, Kibalchich went to work in Armentières, just inside the French border, as a photographic assistant; he found lodgings in a small mining village outside Lille. One evening in July he attended an anarchist meeting in Lille and struck up a conversation with Mauricius who'd come from Paris and was at the time the principal speaker on the *Causeries Populaires* circuit. Victor was evidently attracted by Mauricius' companion and apparently whispered to him: "Who's that skinny little bird with you?"

---

3   At this time three thousand francs would have been a year's salary for a skilled worker. A clerical worker might expect to earn about eighteen hundred francs.

Henriette Maîtrejean, née Anna Estorgues, was better known as 'Rirette'; born in Tulle (Corrèze) in central France, she had come to Paris in 1905 in the company of her anarchist husband Louis whom she'd married at seventeen, a year after her conversion to anarchism. One day at the Sorbonne university, when she was nineteen, she met a 'scientific anarchist' whom she found more stimulating than her rather down-to-earth husband, the 'anarchist worker', and she began to while away her time with him in the Luxembourg Gardens. Although now only twenty-two years old, she already had two young children, Maud and Chinette, but she still had the looks of a girl in her teens. The 'scientific anarchist' in question was in fact Mauricius. During the course of the meeting in Lille, Victor argued against her but, far from impressing her, only made her think "What a poser!"

According to the Brussels *Gendarmerie*, Rirette and Victor were expelled together from Belgium in August 1909. In fact, a few months earlier Rirette had lent her papers to another anarchist to enable her to cross the Franco-Belgian border; this comrade happened to be expelled from Brussels for anarchist propaganda at the same time as Kibalchich. Victor's last article for *Révolté* was dated 7th August 1909; his status as a refugee put him at the mercy of the Belgian authorities and after the Sokolov affair they had obviously had enough of him. He went immediately to Paris.

Jean De Boe now took over the management of *Révolté*. Since falling out with the socialists he had been blacklisted for his anarchist opinions and imprisoned for a short time, supposedly in another's place, for anti-militarist articles; a 'Russian living in Brussels' had been the real author.[4]

Raymond Callemin, Victor's childhood friend, was now back from his travels in the Ardennes and Switzerland, and helping out at *Révolté* alongside Jean De Boe and Édouard Carouy. He began to write

---

4 Until this year, 1909, Belgian conscription was by the annual drawing of lots, for eight years military service followed by five years in the Reserve. The brutal activity of the Belgian forces in the Congo during this period was a matter of worldwide opprobrium. The Socialist Party's position was to call for annexation as a colony, as until 1908, it was no more than a personal fiefdom of Leopold II who lived with his mistress (originally a sixteen year-old French prostitute he had discovered in 1895) in luxury on the French Riviera. In another footnote of history, Leopold was almost assassinated by an Italian anarchist Gennaro Rubino in 1902. An estimated ten million people died in the Congo as a result of Leopold's policies. At his funeral procession in December 1909 crowds lined the streets to boo and shout obscenities at the cortège. He was a cousin of Queen Victoria.

occasional articles for the paper and in February 1910 was questioned by police about some antimilitarist articles that had appeared. He had previous convictions for theft in Charleroi and Seraing, and for fighting with police during the general strike; this time, however, he was released. The socialists also did not welcome his return to Brussels and ejected him from the *Maison du Peuple*.

Meanwhile, in the wake of the Sokolov affair, the collective at *Révolté* had split into two factions: the 'revolutionaries' and the 'individualists', with Raymond, Jean and Édouard being in the latter group. The individualists kept control of the paper and Jean De Boe wrote the major article in February 1910, outlining the troubles they had gone through. By this time, though, Édouard Carouy was in charge of the paper, as Jean was living outside Brussels.

In 1910, Édouard became acquainted with Octave Garnier, a handsome twenty year-old French anarchist and draft-dodger who was to become, alongside Bonnot, the prime founder of the 'Bonnot Gang'. Born in Fontainebleau, near Paris, on Christmas Day 1889, he later looked back on his life as a long struggle against oppression: "From my earliest years I rebelled against the authority of my father and mother, as well as that of school, before being old enough really to know why".

At the age of thirteen, he started work.

> Having attained the age of reason, I began to understand what life and social injustice was all about; I saw bad individuals and said to myself: "I must search for a way of getting out of this filthy mess of bosses, workers, bourgeois, judges, police and others". I loathed all these people, some because they put up with and took part in all this crap.
>
> Not wishing to be either exploited or an exploiter, I went stealing from shop displays, which didn't yield very much; at seventeen I was caught for the first time and sentenced to three months in prison. Through this I understood the meaning of 'justice': my companion, who had been charged with the same offence as me, as we were caught together, was only sentenced to two months, and that was suspended.
>
> When I got out of prison I went back to my parents, who reprimanded me with some violence. But having submitted

to what is known as 'justice' and prison had made me even more rebellious.

Garnier had worked previously in an office, and for a butcher and a baker. Knowing the latter trade quite well, he wished to return to it. Unfortunately, he was confronted with employers who demanded formal certificates from him, which of course he did not have, something which angered him even more. Having forged the required documents, he found himself working a sixteen or eighteen-hour day, seven days a week, for seventy to eighty francs. It was enough to satisfy his principal needs, but no more. It irked him that his boss was coining it while doing nothing but giving him and the other employees a hard time. Finally, fed up with doing repetitive tasks he chucked the job in.

"I really would have liked to educate myself, to know more about things, and develop my mind and body, in a word, to become a person able to run my own affairs in every way, at the same time having the least possible dependence on others". However, he was still tied down by the need to work in order to survive. He was interested in becoming a mechanic but found it impossible to find an opening, so he looked for a labouring job. Society began singularly to disgust him. He took part in strikes but soon became disillusioned and cynical about them. Most workers, rather than trying to change their miserable situation for the better, preferred to drink themselves into a stupor, so becoming more brutish, easily led and fooled. Even successful strikes didn't change anything: workers got a few coppers more, but prices went up, and soon enough they were no better off than before. The promises of the union leaders were no better than those made by the capitalists: Garnier saw both groups as manipulating the workers for their own ends. He left the syndicalist milieu for a brief flirtation with 'revolutionary politics' but found the latter almost identical to the former.

So I became an anarchist. I was about eighteen and no longer wanted to go back to work, so once more I began la *reprise individuelle*, but with no more luck than the first time. At the end of three or four months I was caught and sentenced to two months. I came out, and this time tried to work again. I took part in a strike, in the course of which there was a fight with the police, and I was arrested and sentenced to six days in prison.

As I was in frequent contact with anarchists, I came to understand their theories, and became a fervent partisan of them, not because these theories gave me any particular pleasure, but because I found them to be the most fair and open to discussion.

Within this milieu, I met individuals of integrity who were trying as much as possible to rid themselves of the prejudices which have made this world ignorant and barbaric. They were men with whom I found discussion a pleasure, for they showed me not utopias but things which one could see and touch. Moreover, these individuals were quite sober. When I discussed with them, I didn't need, as was the case amongst the great mass of barbarians, to turn my head away as they chatted to me, for their mouths didn't reek of alcohol or tobacco. I found them to be fair, and encountered amongst them great energy and strength of opinion.

My views were soon set, I became one of them. No longer did I want to go and work for someone else, I wanted to work for myself, although as to how, I didn't have much choice. But, having acquired some experience, and full of energy, I resolved to defend myself to the death against the stupid mass and the iniquity of present Society.

Horrified at the idea of joining the army, he left Paris in the middle of 1909, in the hope of delaying his call-up; he would be of military age on Christmas Day. It was not until May 1910, however, that Garnier began to work his way towards the frontier with Belgium—the traditional refuge of draft-dodgers, criminals and political refugees from France. His recruitment group was due to be called up at the end of September, for a period of two years (as fixed by the law of 1905), but Garnier was intent on joining the ever-increasing ranks of the seventy thousand draft-dodgers and deserters wanted by the French authorities, a number equivalent to two army corps. In the meantime, in July, Garnier was arrested for causing actual bodily harm. However, he was lucky enough to receive a sentence (two months) that would allow his release before his call-up papers arrived.

Out of prison once more, he worked for a few days as a navvy in order to get enough money to buy a ticket to the frontier. He only paid for part of the journey, as he needed the rest of his money for food.

He was spotted by the Station Master sneaking out of the station at Valenciennes but managed to talk him out of calling the police. He did another labouring job for a week before telling the boss to get stuffed, then committed two burglaries and successfully crossed the frontier into Belgium. Around the 6th October he arrived in Charleroi, found some work, and met up with the local anarchists. It was quite possibly here that he first met Édouard Carouy, Raymond Callemin and Jean De Boe, although these three were still concerned with *Révolté*, which was based thirty miles away in Brussels. In the first week of November, he was arrested and held for eight days on an unknown charge but released for lack of evidence. His mother made a special trip to Belgium to see him, but was apparently rather disturbed at finding that her son had become a hardened and uncompromising anarchist. She returned to Paris with a heavy heart, worried about what was to become of him.

Octave, meanwhile, had begun a liaison with a married woman, Marie Vuillemin, who was the same age as him. She abandoned her husband, a housepainter to whom she'd only been married for one month, and ran away to Brussels with Octave. She was completely devoted to her newfound lover, and Octave in turn was in love with her.

The comrades Octave had met in Charleroi, and with whom he'd carried out a few burglaries, had already preceded them to the Belgian capital. Here, he was further initiated into the art of house-breaking by Édouard Carouy, who carried out the odd burglary to supplement his meagre income from a part-time job as a fitter in a garage (or it might have been the other way round). Octave also learned the art of counterfeiting, in association with Louis Maîtrejean, the separated husband of Rirette, and his friend Alphonse Rodriguez, an anarchist and professional crook from Lyon.

Raymond, however, seems to have kept out of such activities, being engaged in a sort of courtly romance with a young Russian refugee called 'Macha', of whom he later had fond reminiscences:

> I had just joined the revolutionary movement; I believed fanatically in universal brotherhood, in the reign of justice, soon to be inaugurated, in the equality of the sexes, in all the glowing and bountiful utopias that can overwhelm a young man who eagerly wants to burn up all that energy that he feels inside.

It was at that time, in our favourite meeting-place, that I met a newly-arrived young Russian exile girl, who was totally ignorant of French. With her I spent the happiest hours of my life. The (platonic) intimacy of two young people talking together about the goodness of humanity, building idyllic castles in the air, was something so sweet and good. I can still picture the poor, neat little garret where she lived, the tiny table over which our heads always touched and our hair mingled, as we felt each other's hot breath; our hands never stopped meeting, and our cheeks brushed lightly, and in this way we experienced pleasures that were sweet and entirely innocent.

We had stormy discussions about which methods should be used to change the face of the world. And she would often talk to me of that far-away place, her distant, dark homeland, and as she did so, furtive glances would dart from her soft eyes. But these bursts of well-founded revolt were moderated, in an almost comic way, by child-like feminine emotions. Each time she knocked over a cup of tea, she couldn't help shouting "Mama!"

We were two true friends, one of whom wore a dress. Sexual equality was no longer even discussed between us . . . yet she retained the most charming modesty sometimes; when she was getting dressed to go out, she forced me to look out of the window, which I always obediently did.

But this tender friendship did not last. I departed one fine day for fresh experiences, and new adventures. We wrote to each other a few times, then life's course separated us altogether.

Paris

After Libertad's death at the end of 1908 there were three factions competing for control of *l'anarchie* according to police reports: one based on an alliance of the Mahé sisters and the De Blasius brothers, one around Léon Israel and friends, and the 'Go Barefoot' brigade. The arguments were calmed, however, by giving the editorship to a fourth party—Armand, a thirty-six year-old Parisian who had progressed from the Salvation Army, through Tolstoyanism, to individualist anarchism, having read Max Stirner the previous year.

By the time of Victor Kibalchich's arrival in Paris, Lorulot had taken over the editorship of *l'anarchie* from Maurice Duflou, who had returned to the basement to supervise the running of the print shop. Mauricius was still handling the bulk of the *Causeries Populaires*, although Rirette sometimes gave talks on subjects such as 'the Psychology of Love', 'the Role of Women amongst Anarchists' and 'Can One Love?', the sort of topics generally left to women speakers. Traditional masculine and feminine roles still exerted a pervasive influence, regardless of the anarchist belief in free love.

Rirette had just returned from a trip to Italy with Mauricius after getting meningitis in Rome; back at the *Causeries Populaires* she re-encountered Victor and they realized that their initial hostility was based on mutual attraction. He had originally found work as a draughtsman in a machine-tool shop in Belleville, and after finishing his ten-hour shift would go to the Sainte Geneviève Library on the Left Bank and try and read politics. However he soon found himself too exhausted by work to do anything in the few 'free' hours left to him, so he quit and rented a little garret in rue Tournefort, near the library, behind the place du Panthéon. Here he tried to support himself by teaching French to the numerous Russian exiles and students, amongst whom he discovered a seventeen year-old Baron's son who enjoyed smoking hashish and inhaling ether, and who was prepared to pay Victor two hundred francs a month. But this stroke of good luck soon came to an end.

Victor and Rirette began to spend time together strolling and chatting together in the Luxembourg Gardens; sometimes they would go to the woods of Saint Cloud, or talk of music and poetry as the sun set over the River Seine. Rirette and her two girls moved in with Victor.

One day in the Luxembourg Gardens, Victor introduced Rirette to a shy young anarchist called René Valet. She found him of an extreme sensibility and rather sad, something like Poil de Carotte, the poor ginger-haired kid who suffered at the hands of his family in Jules Renard's semi-autobiographical novel of the same name. René was from a 'good' middle class home but still faced the problem of military service; he lived there until his call-up papers came, then left for Belgium, where he became briefly acquainted with Octave Garnier. Back in Paris he collaborated on *Le Libertaire* and became secretary of the anarchist 'Revolutionary Youth'. He lived near Denfert-Rochereau, not far from Victor's place, and had set up a small locksmith's workshop there. He and Victor became good friends and 'discussed everything together'. Occasionally they would attend anarchist *soirées* in the rue Montagne Sainte Geneviève where there was music, singing and recitals in poetry and prose. René was often bursting to stand up and recite some of the many passages of prose and poetry that he knew by heart but felt too inhibited even amongst comrades. Finally, however, his day came and he recited some of Jehan Rictus' verse with such feeling that he had the same stunning effect on his audience as had the author when he first stood up in a Left Bank café and made a name for himself overnight. The last line of the poem ran: *"Quand c'est qu'on s'ra vengés?"*—"When will we be avenged?"—the profound emotional intensity which showed itself on these occasions was destined to find other outlets.

On his arrival in Paris at the end of August 1909, Victor made contact with the anarchist-individualist group at the rue de la Barre and immediately began writing for *l'anarchie*. Under his old pseudonym of *Le Rétif* he had an article or letter in virtually every issue from September onwards. Almost at once he found himself at odds with the editor, Lorulot, who felt that Kibalchich's rhetoric was excessive and too inflammatory. Kibalchich glamorized the death of Adolph Fischer, one of the four Haymarket martyrs, whose last words were reputedly: "Today is the most beautiful day of my life". *Le Rétif's* rhetorical question concerning the anarchist martyrs was "Aren't they better and more lived than the pacific theoreticians?" In fact the men were themselves propagandists who had had nothing to do with the bomb-throwing for which they were made scapegoats and judicially murdered by the State. In reasoned opposition to Kibalchich, Lorulot felt that even the most brave and fierce were obliged to compromise if they didn't wish to be immediately suppressed by the power of the State. Such a message didn't sell papers, however, and *Le Rétif's* bravado was more to the young anarchists' tastes. In February 1910 Victor, now turned twenty, got his first front-page article entitled 'Anarchists and Social Change'. He was clearly destined for greater things.

Meanwhile, social ferment, if not social change, was in evidence on the streets of Paris.

Blood on the Streets

On 13th October 1909 the world first heard the news of the death of Francisco Ferrer, the pacifist libertarian educationalist who had founded the *Escuela Moderna* in Barcelona, as well as the syndicalist journal *Solidaridad Obrera*. Accused, despite being in England at the time, of having incited the popular uprising of the *Settimana Tragica* in Barcelona, he was executed by firing squad in the moat of the Montjuich fortress. In Paris, a spontaneous movement brought thousands of workers onto the streets, including Victor Kibalchich and René Valet, who met up in the Latin Quarter and followed the crowds as they headed for the Spanish Embassy in the VIIIth *arrondissement*. Throughout the city, people were drawn to the Embassy to express their disgust with the Spanish Government, arguably the most appallingly brutal and reactionary regime in Europe.

The Prefect of Police, Louis Lépine, had ordered the barricading of all the entrances to the boulevard Malesherbes, where the Embassy stood, and was there in person to supervise the disposition of his troops. Push and shove soon turned to fighting, and subsequently to night-long rioting, in this prosperous district of banks and aristocratic residences. Victor and René joined a mixed group of comrades from *l'anarchie*, *Libertaire* and *Guerre Sociale*, and at one point one of their group took a pot-shot with his revolver at Lépine, who was standing only a dozen yards away.[5] The Radical Government, who had won their own fight against clerical militarism, which was still triumphant in Spain, happily authorized a legal demonstration which took place two days later, half a million strong, led by the Socialist Party leader, Jean Jaurès.

Another Parisian riot took place on 1 July 1910 over the fate of the young worker, Liabeuf, who had been condemned as a pimp simply because he had a loving relationship with a prostitute. His officially provided defence counsel did not bother to turn up for the hearing, and the judge quickly declared him guilty and sent him to prison. On his release, humiliated and in search of vengeance, he put on some spiked wristbands, armed himself with a revolver, and went out and shot four policemen. The Prefect of Police, Lépine, had demanded the death sentence, which was duly pronounced, but Miguel Almereyda, founder of *La Guerre Sociale*, appealed to the working people of Paris to stop the execution by force.[6]

Hundreds of workers responded to the call and gathered on the boulevard Arago outside the prison of La Santé. Victor, Rirette and René

---

5   The devious nastiness of Lépine, the ex-Governor of Algiers, can be gauged from the fact that he once ordered policemen on strike duty to beat up pickets, intervening personally to stop it, in order to curry favour with workers.

6   Almereyda was said to be an anagram of "y'a la merde" (there's shit); his real name was Eugène Bonaventure Jean-Baptiste Vigo, father of the French filmmaker Jean Vigo. He was killed in prison in 1917.

Valet were all there; occasionally, René thrust his hand into his pocket and clutched his Browning pistol, but he did not make use of it. As the wagon carrying the guillotine arrived, rioting erupted which lasted all night. At dawn the blade fell, but in exchange for Liabeuf, the rioters had left one policeman dead.

These riots certainly testified to the combative, if desperate, mood of Parisian workers. In his memoirs, Serge saw "working class attitudes, aggressive and anarchic, pulled in opposite directions by two antagonistic movements, the revolutionary syndicalism of the CGT and the shapeless activity of the anarchist groups". Doubtless, many workers could quite happily accommodate both attitudes and actions, and even vote socialist as well. The new CGT leadership, though consciously reformist, determined to carry on the militant tradition with an organized attack on the industrial front. The revolutionary syndicalists, for all their ideas, did not have a monopoly when it came to the question of practical militancy.

Strike!

The year 1910 saw more strikes—one and a half million of them—than in 1906, with more workers involved and more days lost than in any of the previous three years. It was to be the last desperate burst of militancy in the fight to halt declining living standards and arrest the employers' offensive, before the oncoming storm of the First World War. The key strike was that of the railway workers.

Their last major victory had been almost twenty years earlier, when they had won the right to cut the working day to twelve hours. Discipline was vigorous: there was an elaborate system of fines for insubordination, drunkenness or being late, while dismissal merited the forfeiture of one's pension rights. Accidents were common: on the Nord railway there had been one accident every day for the previous ten years; forty-three per cent of a sample of retired railwaymen had suffered at least one accident at work, and compensation was negligible. To add insult to injury, their real wages had dropped consistently since the turn of the century, so that Permanent-Way men got less than ordinary navvies.[7]

---

7   P-Way men were full-time employees who maintained the track and were essential to the safe running of the railways. Many accidents on the privatized railways were the result of cost-cutting in this area. Navvies were ordinary unskilled labourers hired and fired at will, but who could earn more than employees for a short period.

The national railway strike lasted only two weeks. The 'Independent Socialist' Minister, Aristide Briand (another ex-syndicalist) went one further than simply calling in the army and arresting two hundred leaders. As it was a strike by 'civil servants', and consequently illegal, he proclaimed a State of Emergency and mobilized every railway worker into the army; any worker failing to report for duty would be arrested and tried under military law for desertion before a court martial. The strikers responded with hundreds of acts of sabotage: 'hit squads' of twenty to thirty strikers attacked and stopped trains in the outer suburbs, on their way to or from Paris; signal cables were cut, signal boxes burnt out, points sabotaged, and gunshots exchanged with the army. Forcibly sent back to work, the railwaymen worked to rule and misdirected goods, but it was all in vain—after two weeks, the strikers had been bludgeoned into submission, three thousand dismissals followed and troops were used to smash sympathy strikes by dockers and electricians. The general atmosphere in France in the run up to war was one of working class defeat.

In some areas of Paris, young Victor Kibalchich encountered a "terrifying world of utmost poverty, spiritless degradation; the borderline of humanity under the rubble of a great city. There, a tradition of total, overwhelming defeat had been kept up for at least ten centuries". He saw Paris as "an immense jungle where all relationships were dominated by a primitive individualism" (rather than an anarchist one). "To be yourself would only have begun to be possible once the most pressing needs were satisfied".

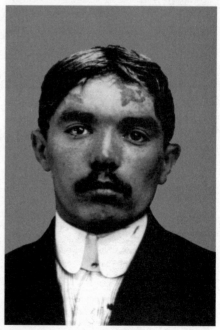

THE REBELS. Victor Kibalchich (top left), son of exiled Russian revolutionaries, who embraced individualist anarchism. Raymond Callemin (top right), his childhood friend. Édouard Carouy (bottom left), metal worker, professional burglar and anarchist sympathizer, shown here in his early thirties. Jean De Boe (bottom right), organizer of the Brussels Revolutionary Group.

4. Anarchy in Suburbia

Instead of wasting time chatting . . . it would be better to start the revolution inside oneself and realize it according to the best of our abilities in partial experiments, wherever such an opportunity arises, and whenever a bold group of our comrades have the conviction and the courage to try them.
—Luigi Galleani (1861–1931)

The Move

THE ANTAGONISM BETWEEN the *l'anarchie* comrades and Paraf-Javal's Scientific Studies Group had subsided in the wake of Libertad's death, only to be replaced by a quarrel with *Le Libertaire*. In November 1909 fighting broke out between the two factions and one winter evening the windows of 22 rue de la Barre were smashed in. The rupture between the individualists and the other anarchists was becoming more and more violent, and the mainstream anarchist and syndicalist journals— *Temps Nouveaux*, *Le Libertaire* and *Guerre Sociale* were declaring their intention of getting the *Causeries Populaires* group off their backs once and for all.

In the summer of 1910 the old quarrel with Paraf-Javal flared up again. One night, Lorulot and Dutilleul surprised Maurice Duflou the ex-editor, trying to steal away with most of the printing equipment from the basement of number 22. They threw him out and said that his furniture and belongings would be kept until he returned the two thousand francs' worth of printing material that he'd taken. Two comrades, Lorenzi and Laheurte were put on guard.

At six in the morning on Sunday 8th May, two trucks drew up outside 22 rue de la Barre; in them were Paraf-Javal, his son and a dozen other men. They jumped out of the trucks and broke into the ground floor of the building; fighting ensued on the second floor and shots were fired by the defenders, leaving one of Paraf-Javal's group dead and another seriously injured. The attackers withdrew and summoned the police, who arrived and arrested the five comrades inside: Lorulot, Lorenzi, Laheurte, Dutilleul and Bunin. They, in turn, demanded that Paraf-Javal, Duflou and the others be arrested for theft, housebreaking and aggravated burglary, but the police were unmoved. In retaliation for their dead comrade, the Scientific Studies Group now threatened to blow up the premises. The owner thought that such a threat was not to be taken lightly and gave the *l'anarchie* group notice to quit before the start of July. Meanwhile, the *l'anarchie* five were charged with affray and released on bail to appear before the Seine Assizes in October. After an article by Paraf-Javal appeared in *Le Matin*, the conservative daily, Lorulot gathered up forty comrades to enforce his demand for a right of reply. At one in the morning the editor felt it might be unwise to refuse their request, and a reply duly appeared.

There was still the problem of having to move, however, and the threats of retaliation. Lorulot felt that it might be better to leave Paris altogether, and came up with the idea of moving to the suburbs, which appealed to him as a lover of nature. And so in the last week of June 1910 the seat of *l'anarchie* was transferred to 16 rue de Bagnolet in the leafy suburb of Romainville, east of the city.

Victor Kibalchich had managed to keep out of the internecine strife between the warring anarchist factions, despite being a reasonably prominent figure in the individualist milieu: he had a front-page article in *l'anarchie* the week after the affray and chaired a meeting on 'Idealism' at the rue de la Barre in June. Fortunately he lived some distance from Montmartre and so avoided the trouble that plagued the Montmartre premises. When Lorulot and the others departed for Romainville, Victor stayed on in Paris to organize a *Causeries Populaires* group in the *Quartier Latin*. *La Libre Recherche* (Free Enquiry), sociological study circle of the Latin Quarter first met in September 1910 in the Café Dubourg in the rue des Carmes. Victor, alongside Lorulot, now took over from Mauricius as the main speaker on the *Causeries Populaires* circuit.

Rirette introduced Victor to an eighteen year-old grocer's boy she'd met in a bar frequented by anarchists in the Latin Quarter. Victor described him as "a perfect example of the crushed childhood of the back-alleys. He grew up on the street: TB at thirteen, VD at eighteen". He was later to become infamous as "the man with the rifle", but for the moment he was just the shy, nervous and pale-faced André Soudy, who liked taking Rirette's two daughters for walks in the Luxembourg

ROMAINVILLE. The house at 16 rue de Bagnolet became an anarchist commune and the new seat of *l'anarchie* where free love and vegetarianism were the order of the day. Here the 'scientific individualists' led by Raymond-La-Science evolved into 'illegalists' dominated by Octave Garnier.

Gardens. His father was a plasterer and ex-innkeeper in Beaugency (Loiret), who had sent André to work at eleven as a grocer's boy in a local store. At sixteen he was working a fifteen-hour day in Orleans, despite the fact that he had tuberculosis and was beginning to spit blood. The French suffered from TB more than any other European nation, and the incidence was especially high in northern France; in poor areas up to twenty-five per cent of all schoolchildren suffered from it, and the death rate was eighty per cent higher than average. Kibalchich recalled: "Even the bitterest joking helped to keep him living, convinced as he was that he was not long for this world, 'seeing the price of medicine'". Even his friends called him "Pas de Chance" (Not a Chance).

As soon as he turned eighteen, in February 1910, André departed for Paris, where he found a little room in the rue des Bourdonnais next to the huge market of Les Halles. He eventually found a job at the socialist grocers' cooperative Égalitaire in the rue Mouffetard, not far from Victor's and Rirette's lodgings. Occasionally he would pass boxes of lobsters to comrades, or give housewives double-measures, just so that he could see the surprised looks on their faces.

While *l'anarchie* had moved outside Paris, other comrades continued the 'interventions' within the city. Royalist, syndicalist and Christian-Democrat meetings were all seen as legitimate targets. The anarchists would form a 'battle-square' in one corner of the hall and demand the right to speak: such a demand being habitually refused, heckling, jeering and whistling would commence. Such interventions normally ended up in fighting with the Catholic or union stewards or the royalist *Camelot du Roi* thugs. Victor Kibalchich, René Valet, and André Soudy often went along to these meetings together. Rirette recalled André standing at the back of the balcony at one meeting and shouting out: "You're a nutter!", as the first politician came up to speak. There was laughter from those in the balcony. When the next speaker stood up Soudy cried: "You're another nutter!" More hilarity from the audience. By the time the third speaker had risen, only to be insulted, the whole audience was crying: "Nutter! Nutter!"

On 10th October 1910 the trial of the five comrades from the rue de la Barre, indicted with affray and lesser charges, began at the Palais de Justice on the Île de la Cité. The defence lawyer was Gustave Hervé's secretary,[1] Boucheron, who made his name on such trials. Amongst the defence witnesses were some who were to figure in later events surrounding the 'Bonnot Gang' affair: Mallet, Collin, Fromentin and Dubois; of the latter two, the first was the reputed anarchist 'millionaire' and philanthropist, the other was a car mechanic with a garage at Choisy-Le-Roi. The case lasted three days. Laheurte and Lorenzi got five years, Bunin three months for carrying a prohibited weapon (a 9mm Browning semiautomatic) and Lorulot and Dutilleul were acquitted. Paraf-Javal's

---

1   Gustave Hervé (1871–1944) was radicalized during the Dreyfus affair around the turn of the century and became a strident anti-militarist advocating insurrection to prevent war. He was seen as the far left of the socialists and edited the weekly newspaper *La Guerre Sociale* (The Social War). Boucheron, his secretary and lawyer, made his name defending socialists and anarchists, and was the lead lawyer at the later trial of the surviving members of the Bonnot Gang.

crew had never been charged, and it was suspected by some that he had used his influence as a freemason to get all the charges dumped on the rue de la Barre group. Two weeks after the trial the *l'anarchie* comrades staged an intervention at a Freemasons' conference, which resulted in uproar. Victor Kibalchich defended their actions in an article in *l'anarchie* entitled 'Shut the Mouths of the Red Jesuits': he was for the systematic obstruction of speakers at public meetings, and for more combative interventions generally. Lorulot, on the other hand, was against too much aggression as it tended to prevent their ideas getting across.

In January 1911 events in the East End of London, namely the siege of Sidney Street, attracted the attention of the anarchist-individualists. Members of a Latvian revolutionary cell (part of the Leesma network which carried out the Tottenham hold-up in 1909) were engaged in an expropriation of a jewellers in Houndsditch when they were discovered by the police. They shot their way out, leaving three policemen dead and two wounded, but in the confusion accidentally shot one of their own comrades. This mishap led to two of them, Fritz Svars and William Sokolov, being traced to 100 Sidney Street. Rather than surrender, the two men did battle with seven hundred police and dozens of soldiers, dying only when the house caught fire and burnt to the ground. Victor Kibalchich felt it necessary to comment *in extenso* on such resistance to the State in (so the old myth went) socially pacific England; his article was entitled simply 'Two Men'.

> In the ordinary sense of the word we cannot and *will not* be honest. By definition, the anarchist lives by expediency; work, for him, is a deplorable expedient, just like stealing.
>
> He chooses the methods of struggle, according to his power and circumstance. He takes no account of any conventions which safeguard property; for him, force alone counts.
>
> Thus, we have neither to approve nor disapprove of illegal actions. We say: they are logical. The anarchist is always illegal—theoretically. The sole word 'anarchist' means rebellion in every sense.
>
> We want total rebellion; our logic, free from the last traditional sophisms, tells us that the rebel will only be impeded in the economic field if he accepts the legal and moral considerations he rejects elsewhere.

> Determined people accept the risk; the thought of reprisals renders them at one and the same time more wary, more audacious and more decisive in persevering to the finish. Reprisals, when they do occur, spread combativity.
>
> The magnificent resistance of the Russian comrades killed in London has stirred the enthusiasm of rebels everywhere. It constitutes an example of courage and determination from which all the tramps have drawn strength, and all the undisciplined will draw profit.
>
> They did well to defend themselves until death. They acted as every rebel should act in the same circumstances.
>
> It can never be repeated too often: the slightest blow delivered against an individual legitimates, on their part, the use of all methods of struggle.
>
> Peace-loving, well-intentioned people, you will see again this nightmare: a thousand brutes hurling themselves against two men! You will see again often, more and more often, the numberless pack of police and soldiers hunting the rebels, being held in check by a few lone individuals.

His use of the future tense was indeed to be prophetic; the battle-lines were being drawn. The Paris Préfecture de Police[2] wholeheartedly supported the action of the English authorities—"The means adopted for the reduction of such redoutable bandits to impotence are the only ones that ought to be employed". The socialist response was varied; *Humanité* called them bandits whose mentality was 'capitalist'; the Russian Social-Democratic Labour Party agreed with English democracy in denouncing them as 'criminal hooligans'. One socialist who did eulogize the resistance at Sidney Street was a contributor to *Pagine Libere*—Benito Mussolini.[3]

Victor continued to stay in Paris and chaired meetings with Lorulot, 'Against Socialism', 'On the Eve of War', and 'Anarchism and the old Parties'. Some were held at the *Universités Populaires* with the singing of revolutionary and popular Montmartre songs, and theatre group

---

2 The Paris Préfecture de Police, created by Napoleon, was independent of the general French police authority, the Sûreté Générale, and answerable directly to the Minister of the Interior. It controlled the municipal uniformed police and the detective service (the 'PJ', the Police Judiciaire).

3 Article entitled 'Hors Ligne!' 1 January 1911.

performances. The anarchist-individualist milieu was quite lively with groups being dotted about all over France, and information about them appearing on the back page of *l'anarchie*.

The Romainville Commune

L'anarchie was now being published by comrades living in a large detached house in the suburb of Romainville, two kilometers northeast of Paris. It could be reached quite easily by tram from Concorde, Opéra, République or Bastille, or by train to the station which stood almost opposite. The house itself had a basement, ground and two upper floors; there was a courtyard and an extensive garden with fruit and lilac trees. The rent had been settled at eight hundred francs for the first year and a thousand francs thereafter. Romainville had the atmosphere of a country village and still retained some of the charm that had led Victor Hugo to describe it as a place "where young lovers went to gather lilac in April".

Romainville was soon to become the home of the comrades from Brussels: Victor Kibalchich, Raymond Callemin, Jean De Boe, Édouard Carouy, and the French draft-dodger Octave Garnier. Jean De Boe was first to arrive, at the end of 1910, via Switzerland and Marseilles, where he'd been wrongly arrested for theft. Raymond arrived in February 1911, although he had visited previously. Édouard, Octave and Marie seem to have turned up, maybe together, in April. There were Belgian arrest warrants out for both men for their suspected involvement in a burglary in Charleroi the month before, during which a gendarme had been shot.

In Romainville, Édouard met up with a small, dark-haired Italian anarchist, Jeanne Belardi (née Botelli), during one of those pleasant Sunday afternoon open-air meetings at rue de Bagnolet. She was "cultivated but temperamental", according to Rirette. Married to Brutus Benardi or Belardi, who was doing a five-year stretch in Melun prison for forging ten-franc pieces, Jeanne came to *l'anarchie* to find companionship, and support for her four year-old daughter: she found both in strong, muscular Édouard Carouy.

René Valet also came to live in Romainville in the spring or summer of 1911 with his companion, Anna Dondon, a twenty-six year-old from Decize (Nièvre). She was on parole from Rennes prison after a second sentence (five years this time) for circulating false ten-franc pieces. She had come to Paris with her brother and met the comrades of *l'anarchie*, among them René Valet. Her daughter, however, was still being looked after by her parents in Decize.

Victor and Rirette moved into 16 rue de Bagnolet in the summer of 1911, bringing the two children, Maud and Chinette, with them.

Amour libre—free love—was certainly practiced in anarchist circles as part of the struggle against the dependence and slavery of bourgeois marriage. Victor, Édouard and Octave were all consorting with married women, two of whose husbands were in prison for counterfeiting (a popular practice amongst anarchists), and three of whom had children by their previous relationships. Still, despite the much-proclaimed demand for female emancipation, Rirette could say that "amongst the anarchists, rarely is the woman's opinion asked". Whether bourgeois, worker or 'rebel', the activity of the man was still very much the focus of attention.

The editor of *l'anarchie*, Lorulot, was also consorting with a married woman, Louise Dieudonné (née Kayser), nicknamed 'the Red Venus'—a play no doubt on Louise Michel's moniker 'the Red Virgin'. She was married to a cabinet maker from Nancy, strong, moustachioed Eugène Dieudonné, an anarchist ever since, at the age of fifteen, he had seen his best friend clubbed into the gutter by police during a strike. Eugène had done his military service, unlike the other comrades at Romainville, but had spent half his time in prison for insulting his superior officers and for making antimilitarist propaganda. When he was demobbed in 1907 he married Louise, and a child, Jeannot, was born the following year. He was happy enough in his work, but Louise desperately wanted to see Paris and convinced him to leave Nancy in provincial Lorraine.

In the spring of 1909 they found a flat near Bastille and he began work in the Faubourg St Antoine. Louise loved the city, but it did not suit Eugène at all. To her he now seemed rather ordinary compared to the vigorous young rebels, or the more thoughtful intellectual types, that she met at the *Causeries Populaires*. An affair developed between her and Lorulot, and, after some anguish, she left Eugène to live with Lorulot in Romainville. He felt helpless faced with the power of love and his anarchist principles. On 6th June he returned to Nancy and took his infant son to his mother's.

In Romainville, *matinées* and *soirées* were held in the garden virtually every other Sunday, especially after spring had come and the weather was fine. There would be discussions, eating, drinking and lazing about on the grass, and the habitual singing of revolutionary and popular folk songs, or the reciting of passages of prose and poetry.

The principles of communal life at rue de Bagnolet revolved around *la vie naturelle*—the natural life. It was a common enough idea at the time and found expression in such groups as the 'naturists', the 'savages' and the 'nomads', all living out their particular interpretation of *la vie naturelle*. Living in libertarian communes, or life on the road, sometimes travelling in groups of over a hundred people were part of the experience of many anarchists. Large groups of 'bohemians' travelled around central Europe and France in convoys up to sixty caravans strong. They lived partially by stealing, 'altering' stolen horses in much the same way as Bonnot was to 'ring' stolen cars. They were forbidden to stay in towns and were constantly harassed by the authorities, just like the Romany community; occasionally the police would round up a whole group, arrest and photograph them, and note down their names, which were almost certainly aliases. They'd then be released and told to move on.

Lorulot, Libertad and Zo d'Axa all praised this marginal existence as anti-capitalist. Victor, Raymond and Édouard had belonged to the colony in the forest of Soignes, and Lorulot had lived for some time with the libertarian commune at St Germain-en-Laye just outside Paris: apparently one of his favourite activities was wandering naked through the woods. In Romainville, however, *la vie naturelle* was given a 'scientific' basis. Raymond, Octave, Édouard, René and presumably their female companions, Marie, Jeanne and Anna adopted a diet akin to Lorulot's, but based on scientific rather than 'natural' principles. The communal table was often spread with 'cuisine Lorulot': a typical meal being brown rice or maize porridge, a milky soup, scraped vegetables and macaroni cheese, all highly flavoured with herbs. 'Antiscientific' substances such as salt, pepper and vinegar were never used. Some vegetables were home-grown in the back garden by an ex-con called Huc, who also looked after the chickens and pet ducks and rabbits. Vegetarianism was the order of the day, while some comrades also experimented with fruitarianism. As for beverages, tea and coffee were avoided in preference to water, and alcohol was completely shunned. Besides tuberculosis, the other killer disease of the working class was chronic alcoholism. The anarchist attitude was that alcohol dulled the senses of workers to their exploitation and was therefore another weapon in the arsenal of capitalism; alcoholism was a sort of materialized form of the Christian-induced attitude of resignation to suffering.

Keeping fit was seen as important both for general health reasons and in case of brushes with the police. Tobacco smoking was definitely out. Comrades took up the latest Swedish exercises and also went for long walks and cycle rides. Louise, Rirette, Raymond, Édouard, Marie and Octave would get up early on Sunday mornings and cycle down to the River Marne at Nogent. There they would hire a boat or two and drift along, while Louise sang Édouard's favourite sentimental old love song. An old romantic at heart, Édouard liked to buy caged birds and set them free: he hated the idea of imprisonment of any creature, human or not. As they lazed about on the river, Octave and Marie were obviously unaware that destiny would bring them back to this place under rather different circumstances.

At the time it was very à la mode in anarchist circles to possess a Browning semiautomatic pistol: they were quite easily obtainable, being manufactured at the Fabrique Nationale d'Armes de Guerre in Herstal, Belgium. The new 1910 model came in two versions, the more powerful 9mm and the smaller calibre 7.65mm; easy to disassemble and clean, they were light and perfectly balanced. The Browning had such cachet that even the playwright Alfred Jarry carried two and gave one to Picasso. The poet Apollinaire occasionally brought his out when drunk and fired it into the ceiling at the infamous Montmartre bar, the *Lapin Agile*. They were rarely used in anger, however: comrades simply tended to be picked up for carrying a prohibited weapon and given three months in jail.

This didn't deter Octave, Édouard and René Valet from conducting target practice in the back garden at Romainville—something which, coupled with their nocturnal activities, made Lorulot extremely anxious and led to several arguments.

One major topic of discussion was the 'importance of science'. It was held that science, by teaching that it was possible not just to comprehend but also to change one's environment, could counter the dominant attitude of resignation to the current order of things. At the time, a belief in the impartiality of science was bound up with the old idea of 'Progress' and the general climate of discovery, experimentation and change that had accompanied the expansion of capitalism.

Some anarchists suggested that 'scientific law' should regulate the whole life of the 'new Man' to the exclusion of irrational sentiment, emotion and idealism. 'Reason' was to replace 'Faith', much as the old nineteenth century *philosophes* had suggested, but this time the discoveries of science would allow more practical, material applications of 'Reason' to everyday life. The ideas of Buchner, Haeckel and, above all, Félix Le Dantec were discussed incessantly. Le Dantec was a determinist, biologist, and philosophical rationalist in the tradition of the great biologist Lamarck, but his ideas were marked by an extremely mechanistic conception of life. He had published books on sexuality and atheism, which put him in favour with the individualists, and in 1911 he brought out a volume entitled *Egoism—Foundation of All Society*. He declared: "Life is an absolutely egotistical act, and the living being is in struggle against the entire universe. It is enemy of everything outside of it". Words rather reminiscent of Stirner.

Victor Kibalchich, however, grew annoyed at the direction these discussions were taking: "Taine and Renan's blind cult of science, here reduced to almost algebraic formulae by fanatical populizers, became the catechism of the individualist revolt . . . the doctrine of 'comradely living' slightly counteracted the unpardonable isolation of these rebels; but out of it was emerging a constricted *coterie* equipped with a psychological jargon demanding a long initiation. I found this coterie at once fascinating and repellent". Nevertheless, Kibalchich himself was not totally averse to using 'scientific' argument in his polemics: at the end of one article in 1911 he suggested that anarchists "destroy by all means that science has provided".

Raymond was said to be the leading light of the 'scientific individualists' and acquired his nickname—Raymond-La-Science—from the way that he habitually began sentences, "La Science dit . . ." or "La Science affirme . . .". This *coterie* cannot have been very unified however, as Victor and Rirette were not part of it, and Édouard apparently used to get irritated and tell Raymond to shut up; René seems to have said little, and Octave just put up with him.

Unfortunately, Lorulot, although he could quite happily share their scientific diet, could not stomach their illegalist ideas and—more to the point—their actions. Already concerned about the target-shooting, he was worried that sooner or later some of their burglaries would be traced back to *l'anarchie*. Rirette said later that Lorulot was never an illegalist in words or deeds. After several arguments he decided to return with Louise to Paris and there set up his own magazine, but as nominal editor of *l'anarchie* he would need a replacement.

Victor Kibalchich was the obvious choice: he was an old friend of the scientific-cum-illegalist group from Brussels, with whom he shared ideas (or so it seemed in print), and he was a regular contributor to *l'anarchie* and a leading speaker at the *Causeries Populaires*. In fact, it was Rirette's name that appeared on the front page as the nominal editor; perhaps Lorulot felt that making her liable for the contents of the paper would have a calming effect on some of the fiery young men who were being rather too careless with their words and actions.

On 13th July 1911, the first issue appeared bearing Henriette Maître-jean's name on the cover. Two weeks later it was explained: "Our situation is very precarious"; there was no money coming in and a malaise reigned amongst their friends. Lorulot, it was said, had left "for personal reasons" but would continue to help.

The Romainville commune now consisted of the four couples—Octave Garnier and Marie, Édouard Carouy and Jeanne, Victor and Rirette, Anna and René Valet, the three children, Huc the gardener and Raymond Callemin. A frequent guest was Marius Metge, a friend and associate in crime of Édouard's. He was a draft-dodger who had escaped to England and may have had a hand in the antimilitarist manifesto from London that appeared in the pages of *l'anarchie*. He was nicknamed *Le Cuisinier* ('Cookie' or 'the Cook') as he'd been an assistant cook in Paris before his call-up papers had arrived; burglary was now his chosen profession. Nicknames were traditional amongst criminals and were adopted by anarchists for much the same reasons: to avoid being traced or identified by the police or their informers. Thus Octave Garnier was *Le Terrassier* (the navvy), Édouard Carouy was *Le Rouquin* ('Ginger'), Victor *Le Rétif*, Raymond *La Science*, Metge *Le Cuisinier*, and Marie *La Belge*; the other women were simply *La Belardi* (Jeanne) and *La Dondon* (Anna) after their surnames.

While Victor scribbled away writing and translating, Raymond was made treasurer and also helped Jean De Boe with the typography. Jean, however, soon left to help Lorulot with his new magazine. Garnier and Carouy lived on the first floor and worked the printing press. Octave also helped Huc in the garden and baked most of the bread. The four women seem to have done most of the cooking: Rirette alone of the four did translations, wrote articles and chaired meetings. The three children were taken care of in communal fashion. René Valet helped out generally in the print shop. On the second floor were a large shower room and a graffiti-covered room for travellers—in keeping with the anarchist ethic of obligatory hospitality for comrades in need, no questions asked.

Causeries continued to be held in the garden at 16 rue de Bagnolet on Sundays in July and August; Victor talked on 'Individualism and the Social Question', and there was a discussion on 'The Freedom of Love'. On 20th August there was an excursion, starting from the Gare du Nord at seven in the morning, to Enghien for an anarchist picnic. Still, despite these comradely affairs and Lorulot's departure, new tensions arose amongst the comrades living at Romainville.

Collapse of the Romainville Commune

The first murmurings of discontent came over the question of communal eating and the ideological correctness of one's diet. Some consternation was caused by Victor and Rirette's refusal to give up tea and coffee; they grew irritated by the salt and pepperless vegetarian diet and sat at the communal table less and less frequently. Soon the two of them were dining separately and were declared by some of the others to be "insufficiently evolved". There were disagreements over the contents of the paper: Victor refused, as *de facto* editor, to insert an article by Garnier entitled 'Salt Is Poison' and was annoyed at alterations made to articles by Raymond. As illegalism increasingly became an article of faith for Octave Garnier and Édouard Carouy, their denunciations of Victor as a do-nothing intellectual and armchair anarchist became more virulent.

One day, in the last week of August, Édouard Carouy suddenly disappeared from Romainville. He had apparently been denounced to the police as an accomplice in an attempted burglary in the suburb of Maisons-Alfort on the night of 23rd–24th August, in the course of which two men had been arrested. Jeanne gathered up their belongings and herself left two days later. Eight days after this, in the first week of September, Octave and Marie, René and Anna, as well as Raymond all decamped for equally mysterious locations, but presumably back to Paris. This left just Victor, Rirette, her two daughters and Huc the gardener.

Édouard Carouy was obviously worried that if he stayed he might be picked up for the Maisons-Alfort job, and if his real identity was discovered he would also face extradition to Belgium for the attempted murder of the policeman in Charleroi. He had tasted prison life and was determined not to return there under any circumstances.

Édouard and Jeanne rented a small, typically suburban *pavillon* from a teacher in St Thibault-les-Vignes, further west of Romainville on the River Marne. He rented the place in the name of Raoul 'Leblanc'—after Maurice Leblanc, the author of the Arsène Lupin novels that may have been based on the exploits of the anarchist burglar Marius Jacob.

The other comrades departed from Romainville encouraged by the arrests of certain of Octave's friends in July and triggered by the hasty departure of Édouard. Besides this, they were evidently not getting on too well with Victor and Rirette. Victor was still close to René, and Raymond was an old friend, but it seems that they were both now under the powerful influence of Octave and his mentor, Édouard. In the wake of the latter's departure, and given his dislike for Victor, it seems most plausible that it was Octave Garnier who suggested that the rest of them leave; he also had other schemes in mind.

In his memoirs, however, Victor Kibalchich recalled a split on theoretical lines. He claimed that, as a condition of his taking up the editorship of the paper, "the previous editing and printing staff, whose leading light was Raymond, should get out and . . . I should be allowed to recruit my own colleagues. Nevertheless, for a month two staffs coexisted: the old one and mine". He had wanted to give *l'anarchie* a new emphasis, "in the form of a turn from individualism to social action" (whereas it could be said that those who had left were to make a turn from individualism to antisocial action). It has even been suggested that he began to lead some sort of campaign against illegalism, which he said was a theory that had "emerged out of Armand's spluttering".

In fact, Armand had very little to do with illegalism, despite having written a play called *The Illegalists*. He had edited *'L'Ère Nouvelle (New Era)* for the previous ten years—a mainly Tolstoyan, pacifist journal, since turned to individualist anarchism. He had lived in Orleans for over a year (a town much favoured by criminals banned from living in Paris, due to its proximity to the capital) from where he was about to start publication of a new magazine called *Hors du Troupeau* (Outside of the Herd). He had written a few casual justifications of illegalism, but then so had most anarchist individualists, including Victor himself. The latter's later disagreements with Armand seem to have clouded his memory somewhat.

Further problems with Kibalchich's story are raised given the following article which appeared on the inside pages of *l'anarchie* between the time of Carouy's disappearance and the departure of the other five comrades. It was entitled 'Considerations on the Present State of Anarchist Propaganda and Action' and its author was Lorulot. He came out firmly against illegalism as some sort of anarchist panacea that could remedy social injustice. He suggested that in its "pride, brutality and lack of intelligence", the mentality of the illegalist could be no more than a mirror image of the mentality of a stupid cop. Comrades full of pride, vanity and 'perverted temperaments', doing everything to profit themselves, were bad propagandists and bad comrades. He was against 'swindling, exploitation and laziness' and for 'reason, education and conscience'; some comrades were guilty of such vile acts as defrauding comrades and parasitism. Yet they presented the illegalist alone as a 'true anarchist' and boasted of their exploits, unaware that this 'playing to the gallery' and loose talk could easily put the police on their trail and endanger others. Lorulot saw their individualism as 'perverted' with a tendency to *embourgeoisement*; the same impulsiveness which can make rebels can also make them unsuited for real comradeship. "For my part, I would not want to assume the responsibility of leading naive youths to do acts for which they are unprepared, and who, tomorrow, would be victims of their own stupidity and my own blindness".

It's not hard to see why Lorulot left Romainville; he must have had violent arguments with Garnier, Carouy and their supporters, although he kept his strongest words until after he was back in Paris. Nevertheless, it was up to Kibalchich as *de facto* editor to see that the article went in, although it would have been difficult to refuse space to the former editor. The article was obviously directed against the comrades in Romainville, and its insertion in *l'anarchie* must have led to further recriminations between them and Victor Kibalchich, despite the fact that he did not agree with the contents. Indeed, he welcomed a reply written by 'Levieux' (probably a pseudonym) that treated Lorulot's article as verging on the hysterical and compared his argument to the pro-legality line put forward by Jean Grave in *Temps Nouveaux*. Levieux denied that everything illegal was presented as an anarchist act by the illegalist comrades and described imprisoned comrades as victims of the law, not of illegalism. The risks of resignation were as great, if not worse, than the risks of revolt. By October, Lorulot was calm enough to accept that illegal actions were a necessity imposed by society, but that illegalism could only be a last resort.

The surprising thing about all this is that Kibalchich later put himself in the role of Lorulot, as leading a campaign against illegalism and for 'social action', something which forced a split between him and his erstwhile comrades. On the evidence (or inferences from such) this story seems untenable. There was no turn from individualism to social action. *Le Rétif* was consistent in his articles from the time of *Révolté* until his arrest the following year: he fiercely defended the actions of comrades who had taken up arms against the State and society. What is certain, however, is that Kibalchich never committed any burglaries or acts of armed resistance; he remained an intellectual, and it was probably this, combined with his 'unscientific diet', which caused the hostility between him and the illegalists. After Carouy's departure, the insertion of Lorulot's article was the final straw, and, under the dominating influence of Octave Garnier, the others quit *l'anarchie*.

Paris Again

Soon, a new disaster overtook *l'anarchie*: there was an accident with the Marinoni printing press that reduced the 14th September issue to only one page. Within a couple of weeks the machine had packed up almost completely, and it was not known whether the fault was repairable. There was no money to go to another printers to print a proper issue, and publication of Victor Kibalchich's *Against Hunger* and Levieux's antimilitarist pamphlet would have to be postponed. The crisis was serious enough to warrant a special meeting the following Sunday to discuss the whole question of the future of the journal. On top of this, the bookshop, a principal source of income, was selling less and less; being stuck out in suburbia it was losing them both financial and physical support. With the press broken, it was decided that the situation in Romainville was hopeless, and it would be better to return to Paris.

Rirette scouted around for somewhere suitable and came up with a small place in the rue Fessart, near the Buttes-Chaumont, which overlooked Paris from the north-east. The first edition of *l'anarchie* sporting the new address came out on the 19th October 1911. A week later the bookshop was moved to Paris as well.

In the capital, however, the atmosphere was stifling. The revolutionary movement was deadlocked, the organized section of the working class having been bludgeoned into temporary submission since the defeat of the railwaymen's strike. Kibalchich wrote: "We breathed the oppressive air of the prelude to war". Imperialist squabbles ran their course towards the impending catastrophe of the First World War: the Agadir incident, the partition of Morocco, the massacre at Casablanca, the Turkish-Italian war, the Austrian annexation of Bosnia, the build-up to the Balkan wars, and the feverish arms race between the great powers. The 1911 revolutions in China and Mexico were greeted with enthusiasm but simply highlighted the sense of impotence of revolutionaries in seemingly tranquil Europe.

At *l'anarchie*, however, life went on, despite some fuss with the building's proprietor over the mail. Three new pamphlets were printed: one on *Free Love*, Kibalchich's *Against Hunger* and Mauricius on *The Social Role of the Anarchists*. The *causeries* went on as usual with Lorulot, Kibalchich and Mauricius as the main speakers. Lorulot announced that the first issue of *Idée Libre* would appear on 1st December. Few, if any, of the old comrades visited Victor and Rirette at rue Fessart; Marius Metge popped in occasionally and André Soudy made a reappearance. The tuberculous young Soudy had had some very bad luck: while in hospital in 1910 he'd let a friend use his garret, and the friend had subsequently given his address when caught thieving. The place was searched and stolen goods found—Soudy was taken from his hospital bed and charged with receiving. His sentence was eight months in prison and five years exile from Paris: his previous convictions for insulting police, resisting arrest and distributing leaflets in the course of a strike at the big grocery stores were taken into account. He was released on 24th August, and went to the new premises of *l'anarchie*.

Soudy enjoyed taking Maud and Chinette for walks in the pretty little park on the Buttes-Chaumont, where, with the few centimes he had, he would buy them sweets. The kids called him *Le Béchamel* (white sauce), due to his very pale complexion. He was still ill but could not afford to go to the seaside health resort at Berck-sur-Mer where he sometimes went for a cure. Instead, Rirette booked him into the Parisian sanatorium of Brévannes under the false name of 'Columbo', because he was officially forbidden to be resident in the capital.

Édouard Carouy had meanwhile dyed his hair from red to black and was living off the thirty to forty francs a week that he made by selling fake jewellery and trinkets in the suburban markets. On his travels, he also kept his eyes open for places that could easily be burgled: in his little hand-cart he had a secret drawer containing the necessary tools of the trade. His main partner-in-crime, Marius Metge, had hired a small detached house in Garches in the western suburbs where he lived with his girlfriend, Barbe Le Clech, an illiterate Breton from the wilds of

Morbihan, who knew some of the illegalists from Charleroi. Together, Carouy and Metge got to know both the eastern and western suburbs of Paris and, over the two months following *l'anarchie*'s departure from Romainville, they burgled houses in Alfortville, Pavillons-sous-Bois and Rueil-Malmaisons, a shop in Chatou, the Société Electro-Industrielle and the post office in Romainville.

Carouy also found some part-time work with an anarchist locksmith, Louis Rimbault, who ran a garage in rue Bolivar, Pavillons-sous-Bois. He was a friend of Victor Coissac, later to be the organizer of the well-known and long-lived commune *L'Intégral*. Rimbault himself had just come, in the summer of 1911, from the Bascon libertarian colony near Chateau-Thierry (Aisne) having failed to drum up any enthusiasm for his Proudhonist-inspired plans for the workers in the region. He was thirty-four years old.

Octave Garnier and his companion Marie were now staying at his mother's house at 42 rue des Laitières in Vincennes. Raymond-La-Science, René Valet and Anna were staying with various friends in Paris, sometimes with their old comrade from Brussels and Romainville, Jean De Boe, who was working with Lorulot on his new magazine. Louise Dieudonné was still with him, but in August Eugène arrived to try and convince her to come back to him and their child. He talked to the other comrades, who, being at odds with Lorulot, were sympathetic to him, but he soon returned to Nancy, promising to come back again later in the year. Whether Octave, Raymond, René and the others visited him there is unclear. In Paris they often went to the theatre together, or to concerts (Raymond especially loved Chopin), but in general their activities remain obscure.

Garnier continued to work as a navvy and on the construction of a second railway line between Pontoise and Dieppe. As a card-carrying CGT member he was involved in strikes at Chars, Marines and Cergy, where he worked on the Poissy-Vauréal tramline. He was sentenced to a few weeks in prison for assault, insulting behaviour and incitement to murder during a construction workers' strike. He worked next at Achères, then at Maisons-Lafitte, leaving suddenly after the death of a scab named Merck on 13th November. In his memoirs, scribbled in school exercise books, Garnier recalled these as days when, "we didn't have much money; we carried out burglary upon burglary, of which I can mention the principal ones which were those in the months of August, September and October 1911".

"In August we did several which each brought in three hundred or four hundred francs, a post office which brought us seven hundred francs, and a villa in Nantes which got us four thousand francs. But besides those we did several others which didn't bring in much.

"In the two months of September and October, our principal burglary was that of the post office in Chelles in the *Département* of Seine-et-Marne, which brought in four thousand francs, and a few others of lesser importance. Lastly, towards the beginning of November, we did another one in Compiègne, which got us three and a half thousand francs. It was a good haul, but this money was soon spent, as many of our comrades, having been hassled by the police or other people, had been given financial help".

Clearly, Octave was dissatisfied. During that autumn, he, René and Raymond "discussed together ways of making the cry of our revolt be heard more strongly than ever". Garnier wanted to do something on a much bigger scale and had already arranged the renting of several safe houses. He admired Carouy's cool professionalism but felt that he lacked imagination; Raymond and René could be relied upon to back him up, but it was he, Octave, who would have to come up with a plan. For once, Raymond was right: they must put science at the service of their revolt. They must have the best tools, the best weapons and a fast car, then they would be prepared to make their attack upon society.

They had the know-how to steal a car, but only Octave had had a few lessons: "I looked for a mate to act as driver, but in vain. I had learnt to drive, but not yet being very good at it, still hesitated to rush out and steal a car in order to pull off a job that would keep us free from want for a good time. At this point I became acquainted with Bonnot".

 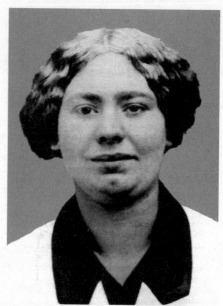

 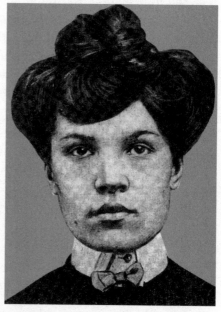

YOUNG PARISIANS. Octave Garnier (top left), with the piercing eyes, who always shot first. Marie Vuillemin (top right), his lover who stayed with him to the end. René Valet (bottom left), the sensitive young poet who joined the gang out of solidarity. Anna Dondon (bottom right), his lover who may have played an active part but did not face trial.

5. Bonnot

The criminal type is the type of the strong human being under unfavourable conditions.... His virtues have been excommunicated by society: the liveliest drives within him forthwith blend with the depressive emotions.... He has to do in secret what he does best and most likes to do.
—Friedrich Nietzsche (1844–1900)

The 'Little Corporal'

BONNOT'S CHILDHOOD AND youth, if not particularly extraordinary, were nevertheless unique. The known facts would seem to be as follows. He was born on 14th October 1876 in the small village of Pont-de-Roide (Doubs), which nestled into the foothills of the Jura mountains, not far from the Swiss border. It was an area traditionally associated with anarchism: Proudhon was born in the same *Département*.

Bonnot's mother died when he was five, and his grandmother took care of his upbringing to the best of her abilities. His father was a metal-caster (smelter) at a local factory and an alcoholic. At school the teacher found young Jules to be "an intelligent pupil but lazy, undisciplined and insolent"; he left aged twelve and went to work at the same factory as his father. Two events marked his adolescence: his father remarried and Jules gained some half-brothers and sisters, and his fifteen year-old brother Justin committed suicide by throwing himself in the River Crochère after his girlfriend didn't turn up for a date.

As a teenager, Jules began to frequent the evening dances in Montbéliard, the local town, and occasionally got into a fight: in 1895 he did ten days for actual bodily harm. At the factory he was accused of stealing copper shavings, and was forced to find a new job in the forges of Pont-St-Vincent. His father and the in-laws went to work in Neuves-Maisons, while Jules moved on to Nancy in north-east France. There, after a brawl in a café, he was imprisoned for three months for obstructing and assaulting police, and for insulting behaviour. On his release he went to see his father, who, however, would have nothing to do with him and shut the door in his face. Bonnot was now twenty-one and obliged to do his three years' military service—perhaps a spell in the army would sort out this 'insolent' and occasionally violent young man.

In November 1897 Bonnot was called-up into the 133rd Line infantry regiment garrisoned at Belley (Ain) some sixty miles east of Lyon. He was attached to the sapper company and learned to repair and drive the regiment's new lorries. For the whole three years he was the rifle shooting champion of his company: the army had taught him skills that were to come in handy in later life. There were no recorded offences against army discipline and he finished his service as a corporal first class. Bonnot enjoyed his life in the army, the camaraderie, the shooting, and learning new skills; he took a new pride in himself and forgot about some of the anarchistic ideas that had partly gained his attention as a youth. He also met his first sweetheart during this time. On manoeuvres in 1899 he was billeted in a farmhouse in Vouvray, where he took an instant liking to the eighteen year-old seamstress, Sophie-Louise Burdet, who lived there with her mother. They corresponded until he was demobbed in 1900, and became engaged. Jules Bonnot's simple ambition at the time was to marry Sophie, settle down and raise a family. He was to be cruelly disappointed.

In Search of Work

In August 1901, Jules and Sophie were married in Neuves-Maisons just outside Nancy, where Jules' father was working in a foundry. Sophie's mother gave the couple her house and went to live in Geneva. Jules found work at the Marien factory in Bellegarde, and within a few months Sophie was pregnant. Everything seemed to be going well, but at the factory there was the usual friction between the workers and the bosses. Bonnot made friends with some anarchists there and was marked down as an agitator. He was sacked in the spring of 1902, with Sophie four months pregnant. Bonnot could find no other waged work, and so in desperation the couple threw themselves on the hospitality of the bride's mother in Geneva. In August a daughter was born but died only four days later; not long after that, Bonnot was expelled from Switzerland, almost certainly for his anarchist views.

For a time they managed to stay at Neuves-Maisons with Bonnot's father and sister, but still being without work, the couple decided to try

COMRADES IN ARMS. Jules Bonnot, left, in his early twenties, sits with two unknown comrades during military service. Bonnot enjoyed the camaraderie of army life. He also learned how to shoot.

Geneva again. This time Bonnot got a job building motorcycle engines with Moto-Sacoche, but he was sacked again in June 1903. Sophie was now pregnant for the second time, and a son was born in February 1904; he was named Justin after Bonnot's dead brother, and his father adored him. Work was still a problem, however. Sophie suggested that Bonnot visit a man she had met called Besson who was secretary of the Mechanics' Union in St Etienne. He helped Bonnot get a job for a time with the Société-Automoto there, and at Panhard et Levassor, a famous early French car manufacturer.[1] Both men then moved on to the Rochet-Schneider factory in Lyon, at the time one of the most respected luxury marques—everything was handcrafted, the beautiful brass fittings, polished wood and high quality leather trim. Sophie returned from Geneva with baby Justin and the family lived together in Lyon.

But Bonnot was sacked when the company found out that he had hit his previous boss at the Panhard factory with an iron bar, and was known as something of a troublemaker. Then Bonnot contracted tuberculosis and had to go to hospital. Besson meanwhile had grown more than fond of Bonnot's wife, and taking advantage of Bonnot's hospitalization, the two of them ran off to Dijon leaving the baby with Sophie's family. Despite several pleading letters, Sophie refused to return to her husband. Bonnot went to Geneva to take back his son, but his brother-in-law refused to let him in, then denounced him to the police as responsible for a theft at the main railway station there. Again he was forced to leave Switzerland. Bonnot declared he would only agree to a divorce if given custody of Justin: Sophie declined the offer. At an impasse Bonnot had no option but to go back to Lyon in his continual quest for work.

The Illegalist

Over the next three years Bonnot continued to work in Lyon, the main hub of the new French car manufacturing industry. First the Pilain works, then the Berliet factory, took him on as a mechanic. In September of 1907 he got his first driving licence. The following year, after he'd left Berliet, he began to associate more and more with local anarchists, who happened to be of the individualist variety, and partisans of the *reprise individuelle*. Bonnot took out a subscription to *l'anarchie*.

---

1   The first company to put the engine in the front of the vehicle.

An ex-chemistry student, David Belonie, introduced Bonnot to the art of counterfeiting. He was working in Lyon under a false name as there was a warrant out for his arrest. Expelled from Switzerland and Belgium, he had spent six months in prison for draft-dodging in Lille, where he had come into contact with another professional counterfeiter named, Alphonse Rodriguez. He was later to be the friend of Louis Maîtrejean, Rirette's husband, who would be introduced to Octave Garnier in Brussels. Rodriguez was an anarchist of no profession except counterfeiting; he had notched up ten convictions in various countries for counterfeiting, carrying prohibited weapons and insulting public morals—namely defending the assassination of the Empress Elizabeth of Austria in Geneva in 1898.

Bonnot also made the acquaintance of two Italians—Platano (aka Sorrentino) and Rusca. The former was an anarchist who had recently been arrested for flyposting antimilitarist posters, and who was currently working in a bakery; he and Bonnot began to work together forging ten-franc pieces and carrying out minor thefts and burglaries. David Belonie acted as their receiver, as he had contacts in Paris and Marseille. Platano and Bonnot burgled the Singer company, a cathedral and several post offices and private houses in the Lyon area; they also began to operate further afield into the Rhône Valley area and Switzerland. With the aid of Bonnot's knowledge of auto-mechanics, they progressed from motorbike to car theft and specialized in the stealing of luxury cars—landaulets and double-phaetons. Still, without documents, a quality car might only fetch three to four hundred francs.

Nevertheless, the men were stealing enough to be able to rent a garage in the false name of 'Renaud', and within a couple of years they had no less than four lock-up garages stacked with stolen goods. Bonnot rented an *appartement* at 245 Avenue Berthelot which ran along the south side of the old cemetery of La Guillotière on the right bank of the Rhône. Here he met the twenty-one year-old Judith Thollon, the woman who was to become the love of his life, but who was married to the keeper of the cemetery. According to David Belonie he was passionately in love with her, and after closing the heavy wrought-iron gates at night, they would wander together amidst the graves under the moonlight. Her husband knew of the affair but did not seem to be troubled by it. In 1910 Bonnot decided that he would try and amass enough money to retire with Judith to another country, and to this end he started to take lessons in English and German.

Jules Bonnot aged thirty-three, taken by the police in Lyon. Within three years he was to become perhaps the most infamous of all French anarchists.

He began to visit the houses of rich lawyers, posing as a businessman new to the area in search of advice on company law or other such matters. He would carefully 'case' the house, noting the entrances and exits, who lived there, where they slept, and most importantly the location of the safe. He stole some oxy-acetylene torches for use in safecracking.

In July 1910 he pulled off a neat job at a rich lawyer's house in Vienne. He and Platano drove there in a stolen car, having chosen a night when the rain was heavy enough to muffle the sound of any noise they might inadvertantly make. They cut through the wooden shutters, broke a pane of glass, and quietly slipped into the ground floor study. Bonnot spent twenty minutes at the safe cutting a hole thirty centimetres in diameter, and pulled out thirty-six thousand francs.

With his newfound wealth, Bonnot's friends began to refer to him wryly as *Le Bourgeois*. He was always well-dressed and had a concern for his appearance that he had kept from his army days. He would never travel without a little leather bag containing his toiletries, spare collars and cuffs and two small hand towels. He liked to see himself as a 'Master of Crime', a professional who did his work with a minimum of fuss, without leaving traces, and, even more importantly, without the need for bloodshed.

The Lyon comrades now went their separate ways: Platano returned to Italy, and Bonnot decided to visit London to see Belonie and Esteguy, another old acquaintance from Lyon. Rodriguez was apparently already in England but had been arrested for counterfeiting and sent to do hard labour in Dartmoor prison. Sorrentino was also in prison awaiting expulsion from France as an 'undesirable'. Belonie had left Lyon only shortly before; he had been working for a local firm that sold cash registers, and had sold all his stock, pocketed the money, and skipped the country. Bonnot turned up in London only to find that Esteguy was in Brixton prison and Belonie was nowhere to be found. There is a story, probably apocryphal, that Bonnot worked for a time as a chauffeur and was employed by Arthur Conan Doyle, the author of the Sherlock Holmes stories.[2] Bonnot went back to Lyon.

In 1911 Bonnot met a mechanic for Berliet called Henri Petitdemange, who was neither a professional criminal nor an anarchist, and who had been working in Paris. Bonnot suggested that they open up a garage together, and promised to guarantee his former wage. It seems that Petitdemange did not realize that his partner was a professional crook. Bonnot continued to steal cars, which would then be appropriately altered at the garage. In Vienne he stole a luxury olive green eighteen-horsepower La Buire from a local industrialist. In July 1911 he

---

2 A friend of Doyle's, Ashton Wolfe, was later to believe he recognized Bonnot's portrait on a visit to the Lyon Criminal Museum. However, the Conan Doyle Society have a full list of all his chauffeurs and say the rumour is untrue.

sold a car that he'd taken from behind the Lumière factory in Lyon to a contact south of Paris.[3]

This contact was a mechanic called Jean Dubois, who had a small garage on some waste ground at Choisy-Le-Roi. He was one of the anarchists who had been called as a defence witness in the affray case involving *l'anarchie* in 1910. He was born in Golta in the Ukraine, into an old French Huguenot family and had served in the French Foreign Legion, subsequently settling in France. Now aged forty-one, he had recently left his wife and four children, who lived in Courbevoie, after doing time in Fresnes prison for the burglary of a church. Bonnot spent some time with him in late July 1911; Dubois managed to sell the car that Bonnot had stolen to a man in Breuillet-Villages, and the two of them also stole a car from Blois and equipped it with new number plates and a paint job. The neighbours grew accustomed to Bonnot's loud singing as he washed and shaved from a basin out back; he would work out on a gymnastic trapeze, and then play with Dubois' Alsatian dog. After a few weeks Bonnot went back to Lyon, little guessing that events would ultimately lead him back to his rendezvous with fate at Dubois' garage in Choisy.

Accidental Death of an Anarchist

One morning in October 1911, two men passed by Bonnot's garage at 23a Route de Vienne, and were surprised to see two small Terrot motorcycle side-cars that they recognized as coming from the Weber factory where they worked. As honest workers, they immediately told their employer, Madame Weber, who in turn informed the police. Bonnot was out when the police arrived, and on his return was told by a neighbour that they had arrested Petitdemange and were looking for him also. Bonnot ran round to one of his secret garages, started up the La Buire and drove off to Paris. The police, meanwhile, were searching the house of Judith and M. Thollon, where they unearthed some correspondence between Bonnot and Dubois.

In Paris, Bonnot met up with Platano, who'd gone there on his return from Italy, where apparently he'd come into a considerable inheritance. Bonnot stayed in the Hotel Grand Turc and frequented some bars in Montmartre where he was introduced through Platano

---

3   The largest photographic factory in Europe. Louis Lumière was the first person to show motion pictures commercially.

Giuseppe Platano (1883–1911), Italian anarchist and Bonnot's partner in crime for several years. Whether he died by accident or design is still unclear.

to Garnier and a few other comrades. After a visit to Rodriguez, now back in Lille, and his sister in Longwy, he checked into the Hotel du Chemin Vert under the name of his brother-in-law, 'Comtesse', and received mail under this name *poste restante* rue Réamur; he wrote to Judith as 'Mme. Magaud' *poste restante* Lyon. At the end of November he decided that he must visit Judith whatever the risk, and persuaded Platano to accompany him. He and Judith met secretly at night in the cemetery, surrounded by the snow-covered tombs of the dead; it was to be their last meeting.

It was too dangerous to stay long; they said goodbye to Rusca at midday on 25th November, and Platano and Bonnot set off back to Paris in the small hours of the 26th, Bonnot at the wheel, well wrapped up against the cold; it was snowing as they said farewell to Lyon. By daybreak they were at Châlons. The La Buire was not running too smoothly, and, despite the rain, Bonnot had to stop to let the radiator cool down. They spent the night at a small hotel in Joigny. Next day Bonnot bought a few things for the car, then they set off again on the main route north, the N5.

At Logettes they were delayed by a puncture. While Bonnot fixed it, Platano began to inspect his new Browning pistol. What happened next is a matter of conjecture. It seems that as Bonnot took the gun from Platano for a closer look, it accidentally went off, shooting Platano behind the right ear and leaving him fatally wounded, though still breathing. Bonnot thought he was almost certainly going to die and decided that it would be more merciful to give him the coup de grâce and clear out as fast as possible. He put another bullet in his brain, emptied his pockets, threw his clothes into nearby bushes, and left the body in a ditch by the side of the road. Then he sped off.[4]

On the edge of the forest of Sénart, south-east of Paris, the petrol tank of the La Buire ran dry and Bonnot abandoned the car, taking his overcoat and bowler hat, his little leather bag and the gun from the back seat and leaving behind his mackintosh, cap and goggles. The place was, coincidentally, almost exactly the same spot as the notorious hold-up of the Lyon stage coach during the French Revolution. Certainly it was a good spot for an ambush, and perhaps Bonnot noted the fact in his memory for future reference as he walked the two kilometres through the forest to Lieusaint station. He had a snack in an inn opposite, then caught the 2.32 pm train to the Gare de Lyon. The winter snow was falling.

News of Platano's apparent murder reached Lyon the following day and so shocked Rusca that he went straight to the police and told them

---

4 Regardless of his motive, this was still murder. The fact that witnesses heard the two shots a short time apart possibly adds credence to his account.

that Bonnot was the man they were after, convinced as he was that Bonnot had murdered him for the forty-thousand-franc inheritance that Platano had on him from Italy.[5]

On 2nd December 1911, the police searched the Thollons' house again and this time found what they were looking for. In the cellar they uncovered three hiding places: two in cupboards on either side of the chimney behind loose sections of skirting board, and the third behind a loosened brick where a hole had been dug behind the fireplace. Stashed there were rolls of forged five-franc coins, a pair of binoculars, map measurers, calipers, various chemicals, mechanical precision tools, eight oxy-acetylene torches, oxygen cylinders, pressure gauges and perforators, a flask of nitro-glycerine and two handbooks—*How to Use the Blowtorch* and *Revolutionary Manual for the Manufacture of Bombs*. Last, but not least, there was a small box, inside of which were twenty-five thousand-franc notes. Judith and her husband were taken into custody, and a warrant put out for Bonnot's arrest on a charge of murder.

Bonnot's dossier in the Lyon police files stated: 'Bonnot, Jules. Known to be of very violent character. Always armed. Very dangerous in case of arrest. Operate by surprise. His friendships are suspect, his behaviour most dubious. His resources seem to be theft and counterfeiting'.

Bonnot could obtain the Lyonnais dailies at the Gare de Lyon in Paris. On 1st December the *Progrès de Lyon* announced: "At last Platano's murderer is known. It's Bonnot. Now it's only a matter of his arrest!" His photo appeared alongside the headline. But fortunately for Bonnot the Paris papers ignored the story. However, Bonnot now knew that not only was he wanted for murder, but the 'nest egg' of twenty-five thousand francs that he'd set aside for him and Judith to start a new life together had been seized. Judith herself, his only true love, was in custody. Now he had nothing but his wits, and a few thousand francs to count on. Clearly he needed to pull off another job like the Vienne one, to bring in enough money for him to disappear, maybe to England or Germany, where Judith could join him later. But for this he would need the help of the Paris comrades.

5　Seventy years later it is difficult to determine whether this inheritance really existed, whether Platano was actually carrying it, and if so, precisely what happened to it.

Judith Thollon (top left). Her loyalty to Bonnot ultimately cost her her life. Henri Petitdemange (top right), possibly innocent, who Bonnot tried to clear in his last note. David Belonie (bottom left), an old associate from Lyon to whom Bonnot entrusted the task of selling the bonds from the rue Ordener robbery. Jean Dubois (bottom right), former member of the French Foreign Legion who Bonnot knew he could count on if he was in a tight spot.

6. The Gang Forms

Do you want a name for this world? A solution of all its
riddles? A light for you too, you who are the best concealed,
the strongest, the most midnightly of men? This world is the
will to power and nothing else besides. And you too are that
will to power and nothing else besides.
—Friedrich Nietzsche

A Meeting of Egoists

THE FIRST THING Bonnot did on the afternoon of his arrival in Paris was look up his old mate, David Belonie, who was working as a laboratory assistant in a pharmacy in St Lazare, and who had returned two weeks earlier from a trip to London. He was lodging in an *appartement* at 45 rue Nollet, Batignolles, in the XVIIth *arrondissement*. The landlady, widow Rollet, knew him simply as 'Monsieur David'; Bonnot gave his own name as 'Monsieur Comtesse'. He told Belonie about the death of Platano, and Belonie suggested he'd better explain the affair fully in front of the other comrades, especially those, like Garnier, who had known him; the last thing Bonnot needed was the hostility of other comrades. A meeting was therefore arranged in a little top-floor garret in Montmartre, possibly Gorodesky's flat at 6 rue Cortot in Montmartre just behind the church of the Sacré-Coeur.

Garnier, Carouy and Callemin were there for sure, and possibly Belonie, Valet, De Boe and Dieudonné (on a two-week holiday from Nancy) and Gorodesky himself. Bonnot managed to acquit himself well, angrily denying that he'd killed Platano for his inheritance, as the current rumour had it. Anyway, he was now short of money and proposed that they do a few jobs together if anybody were interested. Octave Garnier realized that this was the man he was looking for, a good driver and mechanic, a professional with a certain degree of *sang-froid* and ten years' experience behind him. Édouard Carouy, however, being more or less of the same age, saw him as a rival and was still uncomfortable about the circumstances surrounding Platano's death. Raymond was neutral and dismissive of some of their schemes for making money: hadn't they had enough of those miserable little thefts and burglaries, getting rid of a few fake coins, or doing some disgusting menial job under the eagle eye of the foreman? It was time to think big, like robbing a bank for instance.

In fact, two armed men had attempted a robbery only a few days before. On 29th November, the two had tried to rob a bank messenger of thirty thousand francs as he left the St Denis branch of the Banque de France. They were chased through the streets by a band of honest citizens, and, despite firing at their pursuers, were arrested. Garnier held the view that if the men had killed one or two of these stupid citizens, then they might have got away. Raymond simply suggested that they didn't approach the problem 'scientifically.' Bonnot saw the cause of their failure more prosaically: they didn't have a get-away car.

Octave and Raymond were keen to work with Bonnot, but Édouard Carouy was not so sure, he was content to stick with 'miserable' but safe burglaries with his partner, Metge. At the time, Édouard had problems with his lover, Jeanne, who had temporarily left him to stay with Rirette and Victor at rue Fessart. They had been denounced to the police for having counterfeited money on the premises and were raided on the 26th November, but nothing was found. Jeanne had subsequently moved to a place in Bobigny, north of Romainville, the home of M. and Mme. Dettweiler; the latter being a laundress to whom Carouy had occasionally brought washing. The Dettweilers had moved there with their three children in October. The rue de l'Harmonie was still little more than a track across open land, on either side of which a few houses stood. Georges Dettweiler, an anarchist mechanic from Alsace, had just put the finishing touches to his scarcely built garage.[1]

In December, things got hot for Carouy: the police raided his place at St Thibault-les-Vignes looking for counterfeit coins. Again nothing was found, despite the fact that Carouy's lodger Léon Berger was a professional anarchist counterfeiter wanted by the court in Mantes, and both were under surveillance by Xavier Guichard's Third Brigade (Intelligence); Carouy, however, was only known to them as 'Raoul Leblanc' aka 'Aigny'. Nevertheless, he needed no further prompting, and

---

1   His father was said to have fought in the 1848 revolution and later transported for his revolutionary ideas.

so on 10th December, having made up with Jeanne, he cleared out. He borrowed Louis Rimbault's old lorry and, with the help of four mates, moved his gear by night to Dettweiler's place in Bobigny.

Carouy and Dettweiler sold a presumably stolen automobile to two socialist militants in Lagny for a knock-down price. The buyers, the Magisson brothers, had placed an advert in *Guerre Sociale* in October on behalf of the Chevalier couple, who were looking for a child to adopt. Following the sale, Édouard and Jeanne agreed to put Jeanne's four year-old daughter in the care of the Chevaliers in Thorigny, on the opposite bank of the Marne from St Thibault-les-Vignes.

Science on the Side of the Proletariat

Meanwhile, Bonnot, Garnier and Raymond-La-Science were thinking about their 'big job'. They all had the favoured weapon: the 9mm Browning, which, although not as accurate as the Mauser, was virtually half the size and was less than half the weight. A semiautomatic with a seven-round detachable magazine, it had an effective range of forty metres; five clips could be fired off per minute. It was a handgun that was easily concealable. And the police at the time were unarmed.

The next problem was to steal the appropriate car. They had visited the rich areas on the fringes of the city and noted down a few possibilities, but Garnier was determined that they should steal the best, to make the 'cry of their revolt' felt more strongly than ever: a revolt endowed with a Nietzschean sense of the aesthetic and a Stirneresque sense of mocking the sacred. The automobile that Garnier found was a superb 1910 model Delaunay-Belleville limousine belonging to a rich *bourgeois* in the fashionable suburb of Boulogne-sur-Seine (where the theorist of revolutionary syndicalism, Georges Sorel, also happened to live, and reflect on violence, amongst other things).

With its powerful six-cylinder, thirty-horsepower engine and distinctive circular radiator, the Delaunay-Belleville was regarded by many as the best car in the world until 1914. It was usually chauffeur-driven, and was much favoured by French Presidents and foreign royalty, including the Russian Czar, Nicholas II. They cost over fifteen thousand francs apiece from the luxury shop at 42 Champs Elysées, or from similar showrooms in Nice and Biarritz. The owner of the St Denis factory was one of the most important industrialists in France; Monsieur Louis Delaunay-Belleville was a progressive capitalist—his factory had instituted the 'English Week', a ten-hour day with a half-day Saturday and Sunday off, and was regarded as an 'excellent example' by the syndicalists. Of course, no single worker there stood a chance of ever owning what he produced. The name 'Delaunay-Belleville' had further connotations: Delaunay was the name of the assassin of the second-in-command of the Sûreté (the equivalent of Scotland Yard) in 1909, while Belleville was the name of the renowned working class suburb in Paris's East End. Joined together, the two names now signified one of the most prestigious of all capitalist commodities. The theft alone of such a car was, for the illegalists, a radically conscious gesture.

On the night of 13th December 2011, Bonnot, Garnier and Callemin took a trip to Boulogne-sur-Seine to expropriate the automobile. They hid behind some bushes, until all the lights in the house had gone out. The garage door was well locked, so they scrambled over the garden wall and crowbarred the door on that side. Then they came upon a second door which made a horrendous noise when forced; it was a still, cold night and they waited, tense and expectant, hoping that nobody had woken. All remained quiet, and they went into the garage.

They found the radiator still warm—Monsieur and Madame Normand had just been chauffeured back by their driver, Albert, from a night at the Opera; Bonnot examined the car by flashlight and briefly explained to Garnier how it worked, then he emptied the petrol into the tank from a can he'd brought along just in case. In the garage they found plenty of full petrol cans, tyres, tools and clothes, which they threw onto the back seat. Raymond knocked over a bucket, and they all froze, but again nothing happened. Octave and Raymond then argued as to how to open the main door; Bonnot soon had it open—he must have been conscious of working with amateurs. The three of them slowly pushed the car outside and shut the door. Garnier yanked the starting-handle a couple of times, but it didn't start; instead, a light came on at one of the windows, so they hurriedly pushed the car round the corner. Bonnot discovered a mechanism that hadn't been disengaged; he turned the starting-handle and the engine burst loudly into life. They were away.

As they sped through the night alongside the River Seine, Bonnot familiarized himself with the car. They passed the silent Renault factory at Billancourt, then crossed the fifth bridge they came upon to the south bank. With the windows down and the cold air blowing in their faces, they felt exhilarated; Bonnot began to sing. He skirted the southern fortifications of the city, then turned south towards Choisy-Le-Roi. In the early hours they arrived at Jean Dubois' ramshackle old garage; the dog began to bark, but quietened down on recognizing Bonnot. Dubois offered his apologies, but said that he couldn't risk hiding it for them as the police had recently been snooping around. The only thing they could do was take it over to where Carouy was staying and leave it in Dettweiler's garage. They quickly changed the number plates, then drove off over the waste ground and headed north to Bobigny. Their noisy arrival there an hour later set a dog barking and woke up some of the neighbours, who were naturally curious at yet another late-night arrival in three days. The car disappeared into Dettweiler's garage.

Looking for a Target

The gang now had the automobile, the guns and a couple of safe houses, so it was a question of finding the most lucrative target. Garnier later recalled in his scribbled memoirs: "We had two really big jobs to do; in the middle of October I'd bought an oxy-acetylene torch, and we had to have an automobile to transport it. There were two safes to get through in this job. As I knew how to use the oxy and Bonnot was a good driver, we decided, in consultation with the other comrades, to attempt the operation as soon as possible". Obviously, they were hoping to repeat the sort of success that Bonnot had had in Vienne a year and a half earlier. Nevertheless, in the third week of December, he and Garnier had also cased a bank in the neighbourhood north of Montmartre, so they had two possible jobs lined up, "in case one miscarried, the other might succeed".

Between meetings, life went on much as normal: Octave and Marie were still staying with his mother in Vincennes, Carouy and Jeanne remained with Dettweiler and the Delaunay-Belleville in Bobigny; Bonnot continued to lodge in rue Nollet, telling the proprietress that he was an industrialist from Belfort, and Raymond hung around at another comrade's place, often visiting Louise. Recently, Lorulot's relationship with Louise had begun to deteriorate, and Raymond provided her with a sympathetic ear, as a friend who still hoped that their relationship might become more of an *amitié amoureuse*.

Eugène Dieudonné had promised to return to Paris for Christmas in a final attempt to persuade Louise to return to him. On the evening of 18th December he collected a two hundred and forty-two-franc wage packet from his employer in Longlaville, and went to see his mother in

Nancy. The next day he received a telegramme: "We anxiously await you. Come at once. Raymond". This was later to be used as evidence to implicate Dieudonné in the gang's first major crime, despite Raymond's assertion that he sent the telegramme at the instigation of Louise, who was now willing to get back together with her husband.

On the evening of the 20th, Bonnot, Garnier and Raymond-La-Science and maybe another comrade, perhaps René Valet or Jean De Boe, made their way over to Dettweiler's garage in Bobigny for the last time. Garnier paid off Dettweiler, and then they hit the road. It was one o'clock in the morning of the 21st. On the way they stopped to pick up the oxy-acetylene gear which had been left in the safekeeping of a friend. "We were four mates in all", wrote Garnier, but the question remains, who was the fourth man? It seems unlikely to have been Eugène Dieudonné, despite the apparently cryptic telegramme sent by Raymond. It would have been possible for him to have got to Paris by the 20th, and maybe his restless state of mind as regards Louise could have lent itself to joining in a sort of cathartic exercise such as this. However, it seems more likely that Édouard Carouy would have accompanied them from Bobigny, or that Valet or De Boe came with the others from Paris. Whoever the fourth man was, he sat in the back alongside Raymond, and did not take an active part in the proceedings.

For the burglary they had in mind, Bonnot had demanded that it must be pouring with rain, so that the sound would cloak the noise of the oxy-acetylene torches. They waited and waited, but the clouds seemed very reluctant to release their liquid contents. Finally, at about 'half-three, they set off again and returned the oxy-acetylene gear to their friend. They decided to go for the job that Bonnot and Garnier had cased a few days before, a robbery that was at once simple, innovative and incredibly daring. It was to be a daylight attack on a bank messenger for the Société Generale, the largest of the Parisian banks, and rivalled on a national scale only by the famous Credit Lyonnais.

It was agreed to strike in an area that they knew well, in the Quartier des Grandes Carrières which lay to the west of the Butte de Montmartre and extended to the outer *boulevards*. The ambush would take place just before the messenger deposited his money in the local branch of the Société Générale in rue Ordener. The messenger had a regular routine, and would even be wearing the bank's uniform so he would be easily recognizable; there was also the hope that he might be carrying more money, as it was only a few days before Christmas. The use of the stolen limousine as a get-away vehicle was to be their trump card—and it was something that had never been done before, anywhere in the world—and it would cut down the possibilities of pursuit to a minimum. There were other plus factors: not only was the rue Ordener close to some of the main exits north from Paris, but the roads would hopefully be a lot clearer than usual as the seven thousand taxi drivers were still on strike after more than three weeks. If by any chance there were serious attempts to stop them, then they would have to be prepared to use their Browning semiautomatics.

It was a very bold plan, one that was rather out of keeping with their normal style of quiet nocturnal burglaries. It was a plan that certainly had style. But why had they settled on a plan of such audacity? One that, according to Garnier, was full of traps?

Bonnot, for one, must have felt that he had nothing to lose: he faced the guillotine for the murder of Platano, or transportation to French Guiana for his numerous other crimes. A fugitive in the metropolis, with only one real friend, David Belonie, to aid him, and with his lover, Judith, in prison, he must have felt that decisive action was necessary. His new comrades-in-arms, Octave Garnier and Édouard Carouy, were wanted for attempted murder in Charleroi, while the former was possibly involved in the death of a scab in Maisons-Latitte, and the latter was suspected of circulating false coinage and had been under surveillance by the Third Brigade. Only Raymond was not wanted by the police, but his disgust with bourgeois society and with spurious opposition to it, led him to agree with Octave's wish for 'intense living'. He did not have that particular penchant for criminality that the others possessed, but he wanted to partake in grand gestures rather than paltry, insignificant transgressions. So Raymond threw in his lot with Garnier and Bonnot in order to commit a crime of which Stirner might be proud—"mighty, reckless, shameless, conscienceless". Only Édouard Carouy decided not to join this 'union of egoists', although he was welcome to come along for the ride.

They went over the plan a few times, but they weren't in particular agreement as to how exactly to carry out the robbery, as it would be taking place at nine o'clock in the morning in a busy street in a quite densely populated neighbourhood. For the next few hours they drove around the deserted Paris streets, too tense to sleep. Garnier took the wheel, in order to get better acquainted with the art of driving; he already felt confident enough to take quite dangerous bends at high speeds, besides, as Garnier explained, "you really need to have two drivers in case one of them is wounded, so that at least somebody is able to shake off any pursuers". Sometime after daybreak, Garnier passed the steering-wheel back to Bonnot.

That morning, two papers hit the streets: *L'Auto* and *l'anarchie* each carried announcements on their respective front pages. The first read: "500 francs to whoever finds the Delaunay-Belleville limousine, 10-14 HP, model 1910, green and black trim, licence plate no 783-X-3, motor no 2679V, tyres 820/120; stolen 14th Dec. Contact M. Normand, 12 rue de Chalet, Boulogne (Seine)". The announcement in *l'anarchie* that the first two weeks of December had been financially disastrous was followed by an appeal for friends and comrades to make collections: "We just need to make an effort. We'd like to believe that this appeal will be heard and that the anarchist movement still has enough vitality in it to come up with the goods". By the end of the day, both Monsieur Normand and M. Kibalchich were to be poring over the evening editions with incredulity.

Not long after eight o'clock in the morning, the gang's luxury limousine was parked in rue Ordener. "We were fearfully armed", recalled Garnier, "I had no less than six revolvers on me, of which one was butt-mounted with a range of eight hundred metres; my companions each had three, and we had about four hundred rounds in our pockets; we were quite determined to defend ourselves to the death".

7. The Birth of Tragedy

The highest feeling of power and security finds expression in that which possesses GRAND STYLE.
—Freidrich Nietzsche

The First Ever Hold-up by Car

THE REGULAR BANK messenger for the rue Ordener branch of the Société Générale had been ill for the last four days, but his replacement, Monsieur Caby, did not alter the normal routine. At eight o'clock he went as usual to the main branch in the rue de Provence and picked up cash, cheques and correspondence for his local branch. In the company of another messenger, on a similar mission to St Ouen, he boarded a tram at the place de la Trinité for the twenty-minute journey to the Championnet stop on the corner of rue Damrémont and rue Ordener, where his bodyguard, Monsieur Peemans, would be awaiting him.

Despite the cold and the continuous rain it was still a fairly busy Thursday morning in rue Ordener, but not too busy for an inquisitive butcher not to miss the luxury limousine parked across the street from him outside number 142. It had been sitting there since shortly after eight o'clock, and was still there twenty minutes later, with the curtains drawn, the motor still running and the chauffeur, in a dark grey coat, grey cap and goggles, sitting patiently at the wheel beside another man, similarly attired, but with his dark grey cap pulled down almost over his eyes. Perhaps the curious butcher wondered why such a beautiful limousine should have so much mud clinging to the wheels and running board. Whatever the reason, Bonnot could not help but notice the man's rather over-interested gaze, and decided to move on. He slowly cruised up to number 148.

In the back, Raymond, wearing a black bowler and large overcoat was on the edge of his seat with nervous tension, next to the mysterious fourth man. They sat in silence, with only the almost noiseless patter of the drizzle as company. Octave exchanged a few words with Jules and glanced at his watch: it wouldn't be long now. His eyes were fixed on the corner of the street, where he soon expected to see his victim appear.

A few minutes later, Octave spotted the thirty year-old bodyguard walking out of the bank and past them towards his point of rendezvous with the bank messenger on the corner of the street. He stood there and waited. The grating of the wheels on the steel rails and the clanging of the bell heralded the approach of a tram. As it ground to a halt at the Championnet stop, a handful of bowler-hatted gents got off, but only one was given a firm handshake by the bodyguard.

Monsieur Peemans turned, and they both headed down the street towards the bank. As they approached, Octave fingered his 9mm Browning: it was now or never, and they had already covered fifty yards. Octave turned to Raymond and declared: "Let's go!", stepping out of the car as he did so. With his cap pulled down, his shoulders hunched and his hands thrust in his pockets, he fixed his gaze on Caby and marched straight towards him, with Raymond a few paces behind him to his right.

Twenty yards from the bank and six feet from the messenger and bodyguard, Raymond and Octave whipped out their guns and thrust them in their opponents' faces—M. Peemans covered his face with both hands and ran past them to the bank, as Octave pushed Caby to the ground and grabbed the small satchel. Raymond seized the briefcase, but Caby would not let go and was dragged along the street for a couple of yards. Octave shot him twice in the chest (a third shot missed) and ran to the car which Bonnot had brought alongside, and which he was already beginning to turn to the left. Octave jumped into the front seat next to Bonnot, but Raymond dropped the briefcase in the gutter, hurriedly retrieved it, threw it in the back and then scrambled in, as Bonnot executed a screeching U-turn into the rue des Cloys. Raymond managed to slam the door while Garnier fired a few parting shots over the heads of some of the foolhardy pursuers before the car swung a sharp right up the rue Montcalm; Bonnot swerved to avoid a bus and a scab-driven taxi—both drivers receiving warning shots—and then turned another sharp right into the rue Vauvenargues, where a few exhausted pursuers finally lost all sight of them. Five minutes later they sped through the Porte de Clichy—without stopping at the customs barrier[1] and then headed north-east towards St Denis. At the time, wrote Octave, "we

---

1   Paris of 1911 was still something akin to a medieval town, surrounded by fortifications, and with customs men on each of the twenty or so city-gates. Duty was still levied on various goods entering the capital.

didn't really know where we were heading for. Eventually we took the road to Le Havre, but not directly, we made several detours".

After racing through Pontoise some time after eleven o'clock, they stopped in order to check on the extent of their haul; they were counting on getting a hundred and fifty thousand francs in cash. Octave ripped open the small satchel and pulled out just five thousand five hundred in bills; he divided the sum quickly between the four of them. Then Raymond opened the larger case, only to find it stuffed full of cheques and bonds to the value of a hundred and thirty thousand francs. For a while they were rather despondent, but they perked up a little when one of them suggested that they could sell the bonds, or, as Octave pointed out, they could simply try again. They did not know that the bank messenger, Caby, had been carrying a wallet attached to the inside of his jacket, containing twenty thousand francs in cash.

Garnier took the wheel, and the gang set off through the driving rain for Beauvais. Raymond began sorting through all the bonds, putting to one side any cheques made out to a named person. He flung the empty wallet out of the window. Garnier soon got lost around Gisors, increasing the general sense of irritation. Doubtless Bonnot was wishing that they'd done the burglary—daylight robbery wasn't exactly his forte, and it hadn't even paid well. The dark grey sky glowering overhead reflected their mood as they made for Beauvais to stop for petrol. On the outskirts, a customs official signalled them to stop, but Garnier just pressed his foot hard down on the accelerator: "We abandoned the common courtesies; he was even stupid enough to try to run after us, then he just stood and stared in amazement; doubtless this 'ignoble brute' had never seen anything like this before!"

A quick stop was made to purchase some bread and chocolate, before they set off for Rouen, Bonnot driving. Just outside the town they halted once more, this time to get some oil; they were also lost again. The four of them stood in the street arguing about which direction to take, and what to do with the car; Raymond was for dumping it in the Seine, but it was evidently agreed to dump it over a cliff near Le Havre. By this time it was dusk, and in the darkness Garnier lost his way again, and they ended up in Dieppe some time just before seven o'clock.

As it was almost out of petrol, they agreed to abandon the car in a deserted street. Octave chose the rue Victor Hugo, and drove, unwittingly, onto the beach. The motor conked out and the luxury limousine spluttered to a halt. It was only when Octave stepped out of the car and sank up to his knees that he realized they were stuck in the mud. They succeeded in tearing off the false number plates, 668-X-8, and chucked one towards the sea, and the other into the Casino garden behind them; Bonnot stopped Garnier from setting fire to the car as it might attract some unwelcome attention. As they hurried to the railway station a stiff sea breeze whipped off Octave's hat and sent it spinning in the direction of the cold winter sea; it wasn't his lucky day.

By one in the morning, all four of them were safely in Paris, having arrived on one of those somnolent boat-trains carrying a sprinkling of drowsy passengers from England. Hopefully, the police would think that the gang had taken the night boat to Southampton. At Gare St Lazare, Raymond eagerly bought a copy of the right-wing *La Patrie* which sported the following headlines: "The Audacity of Parisian Brigands—A Bank Messenger Attacked in Rue Ordener", "Bold Attack in Broad Daylight". Their crime took precedence over that of a banker who'd embezzled no less than one million francs—two hundred times as much as the illegalists had got away with. The robbery had already been re-enacted for film, and the very next day was being shown as part of a musically-accompanied newsreel at local cinemas throughout Paris.

That day, the Société Générale offered a substantial reward for the bandits' capture, as did New Scotland Yard; it was assumed that the gang had indeed fled to England aboard the night boat 'Alma', which sailed at one o'clock.

La Presse reported the robbery as "without precedent in the history of crime", and called them "*les bandits en auto*"—the motor car bandits, for as yet it was unknown for criminals to use cars in such a manner.[2] The press slated the police for allowing such a thing to happen, especially as it was discovered that of the eighty-four cops assigned to the *quartier*, there were, at any one time, only eighteen effectives, of whom only one was on the beat. The right-wing *Gaulois* declared that the police had to cope with no less than two hundred thousand bandits in Paris (out of a population of three million) and were therefore obviously under strength at twenty thousand. The London *Times*, however, suggested a different reason as to why the police might be losing the 'war against crime': "The Press notes with increasing concern that at the moment when thieves and other pests of society are daily resorting to more dar-

---

2 The first similar type of hold-up in the USA, reported in Britain in *The Times*, appears to have taken place on 23rd September 1912, almost nine months after the 'rue Ordener outrage'.

A contemporary artist's image of the rue Ordener robbery. Images such as this helped sell newspapers and give the gang notoriety.

ing methods, the police are being more and more diverted from their primary duties in order to mount guard over strikebreakers and others who, in normal circumstances, ought not to require special protection". In this sense the class struggle was their ally, just as they were a part of the class struggle, despite their 'individualist' consciousness. Garnier, Bonnot and Raymond-La-Science had certainly made the cry of their revolt be heard; the only worrying thing about the press reports was a sentence tucked away at the end of the column in a couple of Parisian dailies: "The police think there may be a connection with the anarchist 'Mandino' killed at Châtelet-en-Brie".

Crime Doesn't Pay

As they had so much in the way of bonds and negotiable cheques, Bonnot suggested that they try and sell them in Amsterdam, the best place for such transactions, because the law there tended towards leniency, laxity even, for 'fences'. Bonnot knew of a contact there, through Rodriguez, named Vandenbergh, who might be willing to buy. Raymond went off to find Jean De Boe to act as interpreter, while Bonnot went to meet Belonie to arrange for his things to be picked up from rue Nollet: he certainly didn't intend to go back there himself. Octave went to see Marie, promising to meet them later.

It seems that on the Friday night they stole a car and immediately set off for Amsterdam, arriving late on Saturday 23rd December. Vandenbergh, however, had bad news for them: the bonds might be of great nominal worth, but at the moment they were the hottest property in

A luxury Delaunay-Belleville motor vehicle that only the very rich could afford, and the poor could only dream of, or steal. The exhilaration of driving such a vehicle at top speed through the streets of Paris can well be imagined.

Europe, and their serial numbers would already have been telegraphed everywhere. It would be better to wait a few months and then try cashing them outside Europe, in South America perhaps. Until such suitable time, the bonds would remain in his safekeeping; he would get in touch in two months. Neither could he suggest a buyer for the car, so they dumped it in a canal and caught a train back to Paris, arriving at the Gare du Nord on Christmas Eve.

Raymond expressed a desire to visit Victor, and headed off to Belleville accompanied by Octave, while the others went their separate ways. Sometime after nine o'clock Raymond knocked lightly on the door of 24 rue Fessart, and was let in by a somewhat surprised Rirette.

They took off their bowler hats and seated themselves near the fire; they both looked worn-out, Octave was sullen and laconic, and Raymond seemed awkward. Raymond confirmed what Victor and Rirette had guessed, but dared not voice: that they were the authors of the rue Ordener robbery. Victor pointed out that they'd taken a risk turning up there, as the premises of *l'anarchie* were habitually under surveillance, something which did not alleviate Octave's sense of unease. Rirette asked them to talk softly as the children were asleep, and offered them some warm milk, which they both humbly accepted. At midnight the church bells rang out, heralding the start of Christmas Day and, coincidentally, Octave's birthday—he was just twenty-two. As Raymond made a sort of last confession to Victor, his childhood friend, a mass of god-fearing Catholics confessed to the priest, and ate the flesh and blood of Christ.

In the dimly lit room, the conversation died; the atmosphere was strained, and as the local church clock struck one, Octave finally announced that they must be going. Victor felt a chill as he looked into those penetrating black eyes, those eyes which Caby would never forget, and which, along with the large moustache, were the most salient features of the description of his attacker. Garnier was someone who would never feel any remorse for what he had done, or any hesitation in doing what he felt needed to be done. He was so different from the almost babyfaced Raymond, who was too cynical really to believe in what he was doing, yet who had thrown in his lot with Garnier's revolt. They buttoned up their large black overcoats, put on their bowlers, shook hands with Victor for the last time, and slipped out into the cold night air.

Meanwhile, the hunt was on to find out where the Delaunay-Belleville had been kept in the week prior to the robbery. The neighbours opposite Dettweiler's place had been suspicious of the nocturnal comings and goings for some time now, and having read about the robbery, determined to report their suspicions to the authorities. The beadle at the local town hall received them cordially and promised to inform the appropriate people. In fact, thinking that he might be able to make a fast franc out of it, the beadle telephoned a journalist at the *Petit Parisien*, a popular daily. The result was that three days after Christmas the *Petit Parisien* informed its readers that the car used in the 'rue Ordener outrage' had been kept in the garage of an Alsatian mechanic in Bobigny. The police were, not unnaturally, furious, and although at six o'clock the next morning the Chief of the Sûreté,[3] Hamard, and a score of detectives raided the place, Édouard Carouy had flown. Georges and his wife were taken into custody, as was Édouard's lover Jeanne, when she turned up, to her misfortune, at six that evening. The detectives could find no material clues, however, and so they concentrated their efforts on their three captives. Finally, it was revealed that the second man was Carouy, already known to the police as Leblanc, alias Petitgris, alias Aigouy, and wanted by the Belgian authorities. Both he and Dettweiler were known anarchists: it was obviously time to turn to Xavier Guichard's 'Intelligence' for information on such people. In the meantime a warrant was put out for his arrest, and his photo released to the press; he was named as the author of the robbery. The police suspected that the gang might be in Amsterdam.

As soon as Édouard had realized that a journalist had been sniffing around and asking awkward questions about the car, he cleared out and went to stay with his partner in crime, Marius Metge. He was living at the time with Barbe Le Clech in a small bungalow called 'Holly Oak' in the western suburb of Garches. Édouard was extremely aggrieved that he'd been named as the principal author of the rue Ordener job, especially as he'd specifically decided not to get involved with Bonnot and Garnier. Dubois had been wise enough not to let them keep the car in his garage, more's the pity! And he, Édouard, had interceded with Dettweiler to allow them to hide the motor at his place—although of course, at the time he'd no idea of what they'd use it for. He was annoyed to think of the grilling that Jeanne would be getting at the hands of those bastards at the Sûreté. Still, they couldn't pin anything on her. As he shaved off his beard and thought about dyeing his hair black, he saw the face of the most wanted man in the country reflected in the mirror

---

3   The Sûreté Nationale can be considered as similar to the Federal Bureau of Investigation (FBI) in the United States; responsible for serious crime, espionage, threats to the State, and internal surveillance for the whole territory.

before him. It was time to show the comrades that there were easier ways of stealing a few thousand francs.

On 2nd January, he and Marius made their way across the southern suburbs of Thiais near Choisy-Le-Roi. It was an ideal job: a wealthy ninety-one year-old *rentier*, Louis-Hippolyte Moreau, had lived off his unearned income for the past thirty-five years in a large, old, detached house, which few people came near. His only companion was the seventy-two year-old housekeeper who'd been in his service for twenty-two years. It was a cold, foggy night as they walked up to the house in their espadrilles. They clambered onto a zinc-covered shed and dropped noiselessly into the garden, leaving their footprints in the snow. In no time at all, they were inside the house, searching for the old man's renowned fortune.

Exactly what happened next we shall never know, but it seems that the housekeeper and the old man were disturbed. The intruders stabbed the *rentier* and clubbed him with a hammer; the old woman was silently strangled. Which one of the pair (or perhaps it was both of them) committed these dreadful deeds is unknown. Victor Kibalchich later wrote that Metge, alias 'Cookie', "paid for another's crime", but, given that by

Victor Kibalchich's article 'Les Bandits' from the 4th January 1912 edition of *l'anarchie* which seriously undermined his later defence at trial.

then Carouy was dead, he could just have been doing Metge a favour. Neither of them admitted their guilt. They left the premises at four in the morning with five thousand francs in gold louis and an equivalent amount in bonds. Metge also took an umbrella and some earrings as gifts for Barbe. A week later, on 10th January, Carouy grew suspicious that they were being watched, and they all cleared out to no-one knows where.

On 12th January 1912, Xavier Guichard took over as head of the Sûreté, following the announcement on New Year's Day that Hamard was to be made Head of Intelligence. It was thought that Hamard would "clear up the rue Ordener affair first", but, when he failed, it was left in the hands of his deputy, Louis Jouin, who was busy keeping Rimbault's place in Pavillons-sous-Bois under surveillance. Jouin himself had some hopes for promotion, but his working class origins, the fact that he'd only been an NCO in the army, and lived unmarried with his common-law wife, all told against him. He could hardly match the impeccable bourgeois credentials of the authoritarian Xavier Guichard, an ex-Marine officer who'd served in New Caledonia, son of an eminent appeal judge, and whose brother just happened to be head of the Parisian municipal police.

As head of the Third Brigade, Guichard was already well-hated by the anarchists: his methods tended to be provocation and harassment. The 12,500-franc reward having enticed nobody, and his informers having signally failed to provide any useful information, he decided, much against the advice of Jouin (now officially 'Vice-Chief'), to begin a series of raids on the addresses of known anarchists and their meeting places. Guichard ordered his subordinates to restrict all reporting to the press. The searches began in the working class communes of Bobigny, Pantin and Aubervilliers, then moved out to Pavillons and Lagny and back to Bobigny in the hunt for Carouy. These 'trawling' operations revealed little, despite threats and minor charges being slapped on some comrades to encourage them to talk. In one raid, on a dance in Belleville, no less than twenty-nine of the fifty people present were found to be illegally carrying firearms, and were so charged.

At rather a loose end, Guichard accepted Jouin's advice to release Jeanne Belardi in the hope that Carouy would attempt to contact her. Carouy did not fall for the bait. On Friday 19th January, detectives arrested Louis Rimbault and found him in possession of firearms from an armoury burgled the previous November. There had been two significant arms burglaries since then: one in the early hours of Christmas Eve at Foury's, 70 rue Lafayette[4] and the other on the night of 9th January at the Smith and Wesson armourers, 54 boulevard Hausmann. From the latter were stolen seventeen revolvers, six hunting rifles, two Parker shotguns, two Harrington revolvers and, most worryingly for the police, nine Winchester repeating rifles. For most anarchists, carrying a revolver was simply a matter of image, they were rarely ever fired in anger, except at each other. But given the reckless nature of the bandits they were currently pursuing, it would be a matter of extreme anxiety if such lethal weapons were to fall into their hands.

While Monsieur Gilbert, the investigating magistrate, questioned Rimbault, Guichard took a Saturday morning off to attend the invitation-only execution of Renard, the worker from La Villette who had shot and killed a policeman in August 1910. Bourgeois justice was done in the cold light of dawn and the body taken to Ivry for burial in an unmarked grave.

Two days later the police raided the premises of *L'Idée Libre* in Passage de Clichy, and found Marie Vuillemin there. Intensive questioning revealed that she'd been living with a certain Octave Garnier in Vincennes, but a search of 42 rue des Laitières turned up very little beside a few burglar's tools. However, when a mugshot of Garnier was shown to Caby, still in hospital, he almost had a seizure: "It's him! It's him!" he cried, admitting he'd made an error in identifying Carouy. The photograph was released to the press, and the police confidently announced that his arrest was now "only a matter of hours".

Jeux sans Frontières

Octave Garnier had left the rue des Laitières with Marie on New Year's Eve, after hearing of Dettweiler's arrest. They spent a few days at his brother's place in rue du Plateau, while Octave arranged for René Valet to rent a 'safe house' somewhere. Posing as a *correcteur* (proofreader) for *L'Illustration*, he rented a small unfurnished sixth-floor garret in, of all places, rue Ordener, no doubt supposing that this was the last area the police would ever think to look for them. On 8th January, René and Anna moved in, bringing with them a bed, a table and a couple of chairs. Octave slept sometimes at Gorodesky's in rue Cortot, but now more often

---

4   In remembrance of the Bonnot Gang, this armoury was pillaged by autonomes after a demonstration for the release of Basque political prisoners in 1974.

at René Valet's. Marie went to stay for a while with Lorulot at *L'Idée Libre*. Louise Dieudonné had abandoned Lorulot around Christmas, after several heart-rending meetings with her husband Eugène in the cafés of Montmartre. Eugène had arrived in Paris from Nancy just before Christmas and arranged, through David Belonie, to take Bonnot's old room in rue Nollet. Belonie told the widow that 'Monsieur Comtesse' was away on extended business in the Côte d'Azur, and introduced her to 'Monsieur and Madame Aubertin' who moved in on the 26th or 27th of December. Bonnot, meanwhile, had contacted Rodriguez, now back from his custodial sojourn in England, with a view to disposing of the stolen bonds: he arrived on the 18th January, the day before Rimbault's arrest, and checked into a hotel near Barbès-Rochechouart in the name of Alphonse Lecoq. Belonie meanwhile was staying in Sotteville, on the outskirts of Rouen.

The illegalist comrades now decided to increase their range of operations to Belgium, in places that Garnier and Callemin knew well, or had knowledge of second-hand through Carouy and De Boe. On the day after Marie's arrest, Bonnot, Garnier and Callemin took a train to Ghent, and that night broke into the garage of a local doctor. Bonnot drove the stolen landaulet de luxe to Amsterdam, where they sold it for eight thousand francs. On the way back to Paris they stopped off in a town in the Nord and successfully burgled the house of an aged *rentier*. However, bad news awaited them on their return: Octave discovered that Marie was in custody and that his photograph had been splashed all across the main Parisian dailies—it was too late to turn back now, even if he wanted to. Only Raymond was as yet not suspected of any involvement in the rue Ordener hold-up, although it could only be a matter of time before his name cropped up. That same day, 26th January, Marius Metge, Barbe Le Clech and Arthur Mallet were arrested in St Cloud and taken to police headquarters for questioning. Both the men were found with loaded revolvers in their possession.

Following this, Bonnot and Garnier dashed down to Lyon to see the Thollons' lawyer to find out if there was any possibility that Judith might be bailed. Unfortunately, the lawyer explained, Judith was in a rather worse position than Jeanne or Marie for instance, because she was charged with receiving stolen goods, and was unlikely to be bailed given her association with one of the most wanted men in France. On the other hand, they might release her from custody in order to try and trap him; more than that, he could not say. The two men caught the train back to Paris, and after meeting with Callemin, set off again for Ghent.

On the town's outskirts, they found a promising garage with two cars inside. While Bonnot was trying, unsuccessfully, to get the cars to start, the chauffeur turned up by chance. He refused to start one of the cars when ordered to do so by Bonnot, either through obstinacy or his lack of understanding of French. Angrily, Garnier picked up a log and brought it crashing down on the chauffeur's head, killing him with one blow. As they ran off, they were challenged by a night-watchman, who was gunned down by Garnier for his pains, although he lived to tell the tale. Seeking a quick means of escape they tried another garage, but they were disturbed there also, and were forced to walk a few kilometres to the station at Wetteren to await the first train. In Antwerp they met up with Jean De Boe, and the four of them set off for Amsterdam to see if there was as yet any possibility of negotiating the rue Ordener bonds. Again, the result was negative. Still, in Holland they managed to steal a car, even if it did break down halfway across Belgium, forcing them to return to Paris by train.

When they got into the Gare du Nord, they found the press carrying reports that the police were looking for a gang of five, based around the north-eastern outskirts of the capital, who made their living from burglary, car-theft and forgery; beside the report were three photos—those of Bonnot, Garnier and Carouy. It was said that they plotted their *coups* in cafés on the boulevard Clichy. The anarchist link was now firmly established.

Victor's Dilemma

After Raymond and Octave had left rue Fessart in the early hours of Christmas Day, Victor felt that he had to do something to show Raymond, at least, that he was not abandoning him. There may have been no love lost between Victor and Octave, and Bonnot was unknown to him, but Raymond was his oldest friend. Victor had never engaged in criminal acts in the past, and would not do so now, but he had always vigorously defended the actions of revolutionaries when confronted by the repression of the State, or the reactionary hysteria of public opinion. As a propagandist, as *de facto* editor of *l'anarchie*, it was his duty to support his erstwhile comrades, in print at least.

The first edition of *l'anarchie* for the New Year appeared on Thursday 4th January 1912, and contained an article entitled 'The Bandits' signed by *Le Rétif:*

To shoot, in full daylight, a miserable bank clerk proved that some men have at least understood the virtues of audacity.

I am not afraid to own up to it: I am with the bandits. I find their role a fine one; I see the Men in them. Besides them I see only fools and nonentities.

Whatever may result, I like those who struggle. Perhaps it will make you die younger, or force you to experience the man-hunt and the penal colony; perhaps you will end up beneath the foul kiss of the guillotine. That may be! I like those who accept the risk of a great struggle. It is manly.

Besides, one's destiny, whether as victor or vanquished, isn't it preferable to sullen resignation and the slow interminable agony of the proletarian who will die in retirement, a fool who has gained nothing out of life?

The bandit, he gambles. He has therefore a few chances of winning. And that is enough.

The bandits show strength.

The bandits show audacity.

The bandits show their firm desire to live.

Only two sentences detracted slightly from this laudatory article: "Their acts are the effects of causes situated over and above their personalities. Causes which will only disappear with the dissolution of the social order". In other words, banditry existed only as a response to, in this case capitalist, society. This part of the article implied that the 'Bonnot Gang' were merely the agents by which this recurring phenomenon was now being carried out. The individuals involved were not masters of their actions, they were simply playing out roles. Or perhaps he just meant that despite the vigour of their action, they remained ultimately constrained by circumstances of time and space not of their own choosing: a truism.

Victor developed his arguments in notes made for two *causeries* to be held over the weekend of 27th to 28th January 1912. The first talk, 'The Individual against Society', was to be held at the *Université Populaire* in the Faubourg St Antoine, the second, entitled 'The Bandits' and billed with a *matinée artistique* was guaranteed to draw a good crowd to another *Université Populaire* in the rue de Tretaigne in Montmartre on the Sunday.

Kibalchich argued that Society was the enemy of all individuality through its laws of social conservation and conformity, which deformed individuals into stunted, although 'socialized', beings who could do little more than conform to a role. He was under no illusions about social progress, and fatalistically suggested that things would always be pretty much the same. As he repeated in a reply to a letter critical of his article, he considered the actions of the bandits, "logical, inevitable, even necessary". Victor felt that he had justified rather than eulogized the bandits, although, "Among us, they are *the only ones who dare to assert their right to life*". He wrote a second article called 'Anarchists and Criminals' which appeared in the next issue of *l'anarchie*, in which he emphasized this: "Outlaws, marginals, bandits—they alone dare like us to proclaim their will to live at any price. Certainly they live far from us, far from our dreams and our desires", but he had as much sympathy for them as he had for, "honest folks who've either made it or missed the boat".

The police, of course, were convinced that the bandits were not at all far, either physically, or ideologically, from *l'anarchie*. This milieu had been under almost constant surveillance: *Le Rétif* himself was first noted by the 'Anarchist Brigade' in July 1910, while Guichard was still in charge. They even had a letter from the Brussels Gendarmerie, dated 12th September 1911, which listed fifteen anarchists known to frequent France, amongst which were: 1 Carouy, Édouard . . . (dangerous, always carries a Browning pistol), 2 De Boe, Jean . . . with his mistress Barthelemess, Ida, 3 Lecot, Henri-Charles,[5] 4 Callemin, François-Raymond", and, ninth down the list, "Kibalchich, Victor". It was noted that they all frequented 16 rue Bagnolet in Romainville, the home of *l'anarchie*. Other names cropped up on the back page of the paper itself, in a column headed 'Three Words to our Friends': besides Rirette, Lorulot and *Le Rétif*, there were messages for Carouy, De Boe and Callemin (aka Raymond C), 'Platane of Lyon', Dieudonné, Rusca, Rodriguez, Belonie, Mallet, and others, as yet not introduced into the story—Élie Monier, Sazy, Reinart, Baraille, Bill, Ducret and 'Victor Grango'. In other words, it seemed that *l'anarchie* was the link between the group from Lyon and the group from Brussels: they were all a part of the same political milieu, of which Victor Kibalchich was the most outspoken theorist. Police informers and plainclothes detectives kept a constant watch on the meetings of the *Causeries Populaires*, and one reported that "the people at rue Fessart seem happy with the rapid increase in banditism". Of the 'illegalists' it was said that, "one lot became illegal through following through their theories;

---

5   Henri-Charles Lecot was an acquaintance of De Boe's.

the others covered their deeds with theory", and it was added that "many *Causeries Populaires* old-timers since the days of Libertad have left this milieu completely, finding them too compromising". Durupt and Israel were given as examples.

At last, Guichard ordered a raid on rue Fessart for Wednesday 31st January, a day when many comrades would be there getting the paper ready for distribution. Young Chinette heard the knock on the door at six in the morning and ran down the stairs to open it; in walked Louis Jouin and dozens of detectives. Victor later recollected that Jouin spoke to him amiably, "of the ideas of Sébastien Faure whom he admired, of the deplorable way in which the outlaws were discrediting a great ideal. He seemed neither malicious nor hypocritical, only a deeply distressed man doing his job conscientiously". All the eleven people taken in for questioning were released without charge.

But Victor was not to be let off the hook so easily. The following Tuesday, at seven in the morning, rue Fessart was raided again by armed detectives, who took away a handful of letters, some postage stamps, and, rather more seriously, two Browning 9mm semiautomatic pistols. That afternoon Victor was arrested and taken to the headquarters of the Sûreté, where he and Rirette were charged jointly with handling stolen goods, namely the two pistols, which both originated from the rue Lafayette armoury burgled that Christmas Eve, 1911. It was Rirette who later admitted that she had, somewhat thoughtlessly, bought them from 'a comrade' for herself and Victor. The coincidence in the timing of the burglary and the visit of Octave and Raymond to rue Fesssart late the same evening lends itself to the possibility that Victor and Rirette foolishly accepted the guns from the pair, perhaps out of solidarity.

Kibalchich was now in a rather invidious position: Rimbault, Metge and Mallet, known associates of Carouy, had all been found in possession of the same type of gun, albeit from different burglaries, and the bullets fired in the rue Ordener hold-up also emanated from a 9mm Browning. It was quite conceivable that the guns found at rue Fessart could link Victor directly to the *auto-bandits*.

Jouin talked amiably, but frankly, to Victor about these matters. Maybe things would be easier for him if he helped the police with their enquiries; after all, they both knew that he knew exactly who the bandits were. Perhaps Victor could supply them with some valuable information? Victor, however, remained silent. Jouin continued to talk, again about how the bandits were discrediting the anarchist ideal; he could understand how one ought to remain loyal to one's friends, but those articles he'd written didn't look good in the light of the charges against him, they might even be used against him as evidence of a conspiracy. Victor, clearly irritated by such a suggestion, repeated that he'd had nothing to do with the rue Ordener robbery, and knew nothing of the whereabouts of any of the people involved.

The Vice-Chief of the Sûreté tried a different tack: Marius Metge was in custody charged with having burgled the Romainville post office the previous autumn; Carouy was also suspected; stamps from the post office had been found at the rue Fessart that morning. The obvious explanation was that stamps had been bought when *l'anarchie* was still at 16 rue de Bagnolet, and they'd simply been taken with everything else during the move back to Paris. But Carouy and Metge regularly stayed at rue Bagnolet, and perhaps still visited Victor and Rirette at rue Fessart. Did Victor by any chance know of the whereabouts of these two men on the night of 2nd January? He had no idea. Jouin then casually informed him that Metge was being charged with the bloody murder of the old man and his housekeeper. Victor refused to believe that either of them could have had anything to do with such an appalling crime but was told that the police had incontrovertible proof: his fingerprints were found inside the house. Jouin pressed home his advantage—yes, it was an appalling crime, even by anarchist standards; could such men be still considered anarchists? Was it fair that such men should besmirch the anarchist ideal? Could he not see that by fully cooperating with their enquiries, Victor would not only be helping himself, he would be doing the anarchist movement as a whole a great favour? And to show him that he was a man of honour, and had faith that Victor would see reason, he would order Rirette to be released on bail.

As he was taken down to the cells, Victor dwelt upon his dilemma: it was impossible for him as an anarchist to say anything to the police; it was impossible for him as Raymond's friend to say something that might lead Raymond to the guillotine; yet to be associated with such things as the bludgeoning to death of an old man, and the gunning-down of an, albeit 'miserable', bank-clerk, and all in the name of anarchy, was very hard to swallow. And Rirette was liable to re-arrest at any moment if he did not speak. Still, he knew what his anarchist duty was, and that was to remain silent.

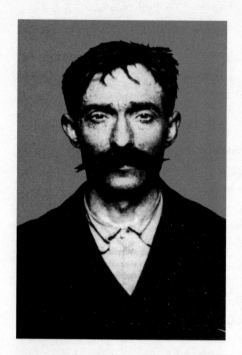

Georges Dettweiler (top left), anarchist mechanic, the first to be arrested. Marius Metge (top right), the anarchist cook and burglar who was later sent to Devil's Island. Louis Rimbault (bottom left), from libertarian colony of Bascon who feigned mental illness and so avoided trial. Alphonse Rodriguez (bottom right), formerly of HMP Dartmoor, who fingered Dieudonné and as a consequence was the only man acquitted.

8. Kings of the Road

*Believe me, the secret of reaping the greatest fruitfulness and
the greatest enjoyment from life is to live dangerously!*
—Friedrich Nietzsche

Drivin' South

DETECTIVES AT THE Sûreté were quietly confident that they would soon
be able to track down the rue Ordener bandits. Full descriptions with
photographs had been published in the national press of three of them;
the milieu from whence they came was riddled with informers and under considerable surveillance, and it was almost certain that they were
still somewhere in the capital. Scores of letters were still pouring into
the Sûreté suggesting who the robbers might be and where they were to
be found. People wrote down their wildest suspicions in the desperate
hope that they might share in the substantial reward offered by the Société Générale. It meant a lot of fruitless work for the police, but occasionally a letter might seem worth pondering over. One, dated 23rd January 1912, contained the following extract: "From rumours circulating
amongst the anarchists, the assassin of rue Ordener is a certain Eugène
Dieudonné, originally from Nancy, where he has doubtless returned to
his parents. The others are three Belgians known as Ortane, Remond
and Deboit; there's also Bonnot (from Lyon)".

Whether the police made any real use of such information of course
cannot be determined. Jouin believed that normal detective methods,
painstaking research and patient surveillance, would soon enough yield
results. Unfortunately for him, his superior, Guichard, was not an especially patient man, although for the time being he would let Jouin play
it his way. The problem was, that if the bandits remained free, not only
would they commit more crimes, but others might be tempted to imi-
tate them. Indeed, a 'copy-cat' robbery had taken place the very day of
the first raid on *l'anarchie*. A Société Générale bank messenger from the

boulevard Sebastopol branch was robbed of fifty thousand francs in the
rue de Meslay by an armed assailant sporting a thick, black moustache.
But there was no motorized getaway: it was not the *auto-bandits*.

Meanwhile, the illegalists were taking some 'scientific' precautions
against the possibility of recognition. Raymond obtained a flask of tinc-
ture of silver nitrate from David Belonie, who was still working in the
pharmacy, with which to lighten the colour of their hair; Bonnot was
especially partial to a blond tint. Their moustaches had long since been
shaved off. Garnier, of course, could do nothing about his deep penetrating eyes, and Raymond felt it necessary to remind him to look down
whenever somebody approached him. Bonnot suggested that they dress
well to allay suspicion, and dispensed new collars, shirts and cuffs that
he'd bought in Holland.

Despite their notoriety, Bonnot and Garnier had no thoughts of lay-
ing low or leaving the country. Rather, the chase spurred them on to
widen the range of their activities, while keeping Paris as their base.
Raymond and Octave even kept in contact with Rirette, meeting once
in a restaurant on the rue de Bretagne, and once in the rue du Temple,
despite the strong possibility that she was being followed.

In order to extend the range of their activities, Bonnot, Garnier and
Callemin made use of Jean De Boe and Eugène Dieudonné, who could
supply them with useful contacts in the south and east of the country.
Bonnot, Garnier and Dieudonné went to visit some of the latter's acquaintances in and around Nancy; they stayed with a factory worker,
Charles Reinart and his wife in Liverdun on the Moselle, and frequently
saw the Bill brothers, Charles and Émile (the former being engaged to
the Reinarts' daughter, Madeleine). Bonnot and Garnier spent their time
scouting locations for potential *reprises*.

De Boe and Callemin meanwhile made contact with Élie Monier,
aka 'Simentoff', who was living in Alais, with a view to setting up a job
in the south of France.

Monier was, like Garnier, an *insoumis*—a draft-dodger—who had
similarly made his way to Belgium to escape call-up, and had made
contact with the Brussels anarchists. Originally from the small town of
Estagel in the eastern Pyrenees, by the age of sixteen he was already under surveillance by the police for his anarchist opinions and for keeping 'bad company': his parents' house was searched after he had been
accused of theft in Carcassonne, and he was convicted of an unrelated
assault.

At eighteen, Monier left home and the small libertarian group in Estagel, and went to work as a gardener in and around Alais and Nîmes in the *Département* of the Gard. He spent long periods in Belgium after his call-up papers arrived in August 1909, and acquired a false *livret militaire* (which at the time had much the same function as the current *carte d'identité*) enabling him to travel back to France. In 1910, Jean De Boe visited him in St Étienne, after his expulsion from Switzerland, and later that year Monier wrote to *l'anarchie* briefly describing an anti-syndicalist intervention by comrades in Arles. They opposed the speech of Léon Jouhaux from the CGT who was encouraging people to make revolutionary propaganda in the army, by declaring that the best tactic was simply not to join at all. To do what Jouhaux suggested was simply to invite comrades to sacrifice themselves to the full brutality of military repression—hardly surprising that the 'disciplinary battalions' were currently full of committed revolutionaries.

In 1911, Monier worked in the Gard as a travelling salesman and burglar, in the company of Joseph Renard. Renard was also a draft-dodger and anarchist who believed in *la reprise individuelle*, and, at the time he was suspected of involvement in the rue Ordener hold-up because he was an acquaintance of Garnier and Carouy. As a member of the 'Estampes' gang he had committed a series of burglaries in and around Paris and Orleans, but his last attempted theft had come to grief. On 31st January 1912 he was caught burgling Orleans station with a companion, who promptly shot himself rather than submit to the police. Their haul was only a hundred and forty-three francs (which the police said was destined for the railway workers' orphanage), some stamps and a few copper tokens. Renard gave the name Oscar Wilde to his captors, and said he'd been born in Canada. Questioned about rue Ordener the police realized that he was not involved. He knew Garnier from Belgium, where he had worked on *Germinal*, the Verviers anarchist magazine, in 1910.

In November 1911, Lorulot had introduced Renard and Monier to Paul Sazy, a worker for the railway company PLM (Paris-Lyon-Méditerranée), and also the anarchist-individualist contact for Alais and the surrounding area. In February 1912 it was to Sazy and Monier that De Boe and Callemin went with a view to setting up a job in the south of France.

On 15th February a superb Peugeot limousine was stolen in Béziers from an industrialist and driven northwards towards Paris. At nine o'clock the next morning, however, it got a flat at Arnay-le-Duc. The occupants, five well-dressed men, managed to get a lift from a garage owner as far as Beaune. After lunch there they caught a train to Paris, arriving at 6.15 pm. Nobody was ever charged with this theft, but Bonnot and his associates were definitely suspected.

Four days later the press announced that the hunt for Garnier was taking place as far away as Chemnitz and Berlin, but the gang's next 'outrage' soon made them realize just how close to home the men still were.

At Monier's suggestion the next targets chosen were the Lavernède mine near Alais and the Comptoir Nationale d'Escompte near Nîmes. Their method at Lavernède would be the same as at rue Ordener: they would hold-up the bank clerk carrying the payroll and escape by car. 'Simentoff' would send a cryptic message by telegramme to Dieudonné's flat at 47 rue Nollet, the day before the robbery was to the take place. Bonnot and Garnier had also planned another job in the east of the country, presumably around Nancy.

Late at night on the 26th February, Bonnot, Garnier and Raymond-La-Science, all wearing bowler hats, travelled to the exclusive Parisian suburb of St Mandé, just west of the Bois de Vincennes, to steal another luxury car. As before, at Boulogne-sur-Seine, they crowbarred their way in, pushed the car into a neighbouring street, turned the starting-handle, and were away. Again it was a Delaunay-Belleville, although a different model, a pearl-grey, double-phaeton worth twenty thousand francs. The owner, a M. Buisson, had it all ready for the *Tour de France*; there were fifty-seven litres of petrol in the tank, while on the seats they found a fox-fur-lined cloak, an overcoat with astrakhan collar, gloves, stop watches and maps. They planned to travel south to Alais early in the morning, but before catching a few hours sleep, they painted on a false number-plate.

The Left Hand of Darkness

They took the usual route south, past Melun, but were held up by a puncture at Montereau. Changing the wheel was not a great problem, but a little further on the car began to develop more serious trouble, and Bonnot was forced to pull up at Pont-sur-Yonne and find a mechanic. The repairs took four hours, so that it was getting on for two in the afternoon before the car was roadworthy again. The three men had lunch at Villeneuve-sur-Yonne and continued to Sens, but having covered only forty miles, and with another fourteen hours motoring to go, they decided, after an argument, Bonnot judging the repair insufficient for a long trip, to head back to Paris; after all, they had not yet received Monier's telegramme, so the delay was not disastrous.

Returning via Fontainebleau (Octave Garnier's birthplace), they raced alongside the left bank of the river Seine, through Ivry, and into Paris without stopping at the customs barrier at Porte d'Italie. The car was doing seventy kilometres per hour as Bonnot sped up the Avenue des Gobelins, into rue Monge and straight across the Île de la Cité, right past the Palais de Justice and the Préfecture de Police, in the very heart of Paris. Their sense of invincibility must have been absolute. Turning left at speed into the fashionable rue de Rivoli, the car knocked down a market stall, but made no attempt to slow down. At seven that evening the Delaunay-Belleville was observed by detectives watching 47 rue Nollet, when it halted on the corner of that street and the rue des Dames. The occupants got out and replenished the tank with petrol taken from a few cans on the back seat; however they did not visit Dieudonné, despite being so close and still awaiting Monier's telegramme. Perhaps they sensed the address was being watched. Instead, they jumped back in and headed down the rue d'Amsterdam.

The downward slope increased the breakneck speed of Bonnot's driving, and as the car careered round the corner into the place du Havre he was forced to swerve to avoid colliding with a St Germain to Montmartre bus which was reversing out of one of the bays in front of Gare St Lazare. The car mounted the pavement, almost knocking over two people in the process, and came to a halt. A traffic policeman had seen the whole incident, and hurried over to demand the driver's papers. Garnier meanwhile jumped out of the back seat and ran round to restart the engine with the starting-handle; Bonnot resolutely ignored the cop, who was now brandishing his notebook, and, as the motor burst back into life, slammed the gearstick into reverse. Again he had to brake as a lorry came up behind him; as Garnier dived back into the rear seat and Bonnot thrust the gear lever forward, the traffic cop jumped onto the car's running-board and tried to grab the steering wheel. Garnier leant forward, his left hand gripping a 9mm Browning, and fired three bullets into the policeman's chest and stomach, causing him to reel backwards and collapse onto the road as the Delaunay-Belleville roared off down rue Tronchet.

Two 'honest citizens' attempted to give chase in their own automobile, with one man brandishing a gun, but they were mistaken for the 'bandits' by the crowd and surrounded. Despite this, they managed to speed off, only to run over a young woman. Their pursuit was abandoned, and they were severely questioned by the police. (The unfortunate woman was badly injured but never received a sou in compensation from the State or the two men responsible, despite several months in hospital.) The policeman was quickly ferried to hospital, but died on arrival.[1] Leaving chaos in their wake, the gang, with Bonnot at the wheel, sped at full tilt down the rue Royale, careered round the place de la Concorde, and tore up the Champs-Elysées in fourth gear towards the Porte Maillot. The Delaunay-Belleville was last spotted leaving Paris in the direction of Pontoise.

After this devil-may-care madness Jules, Octave and Raymond lay low for twenty-four hours, their plans for the two jobs temporarily shelved. It would be virtually impossible to get all the way down to Alais in the Delaunay without being spotted, and in time to meet with Monier. But they did not wish to abandon the car without having made some good use of it.

Around midnight on 29th February Bonnot parked the limousine in front of the Pontoise town hall, opposite the house of a well-to-do lawyer. Raymond and Octave stealthily made their way over to the side door of the house and levered it open using a crowbar. It did not take them long to find the old freestanding safe in the study, as they had obviously done some 'homework' beforehand: perhaps Bonnot was still introducing himself to unsuspecting lawyers as a local businessman, as he had previously done around Lyon. Unfortunately, the two illegalists made some noise trying to move the heavy old safe, and disturbed the *bourgeoise* upstairs. (Despite their bravado, Raymond and Octave were still amateurs.) The wife roused her husband, who reluctantly went over to the window, and, seeing the baker passing by, called out to him to check that his doors were secure. He obliged, made his way up the path and tried the door handle. As he did so, Callemin and Garnier leapt out, fired into the air and raced for the car. Amazingly alert for that time of night, the lawyer grabbed his revolver and managed to loose off all six shots from the upstairs window before the pair had even reached the car. They both turned and sent several bullets flying through the window before diving into the car and roaring off towards Paris.

---

1 By a bizarre coincidence, not only was this policeman's surname 'Garnier' but the incident had taken place outside the 'Restaurant Garnier' as well.

Half an hour later they were approaching the northern outskirts of the capital, where they intended to abandon the car, as it was obviously too dangerous to try entering one of the gates into the city. In St Ouen, they found a suitably quiet location between a factory and a garage at the end of a new stretch of road. Garnier was determined that they should destroy their latest appropriated luxury item, and to this end began scrabbling around gathering straw and flammable material, which he stuffed inside the car. He hurriedly poured petrol over it, and then tossed in a match, causing the Delaunay to burst into flame. All three of them ran off south towards the Butte de Montmartre on which the bare outlines of the Sacré-Coeur could just be made out in the pre-dawn light.

Stalemate

The blatant murder of a policeman at one of the busiest crossroads in Paris had immediate repercussions: Guichard was summoned before Lépine, the Prefect of Police, to explain why these *auto-bandits* had not been arrested after three months; he had their names, he knew their milieu, surely he must be close to making some significant arrests? The police were being made to look like fools by a bunch of crazed anarchists, and the press was having a field-day; the Minister of the Interior was up in arms about it—there was already enough to cope with, with the taxi drivers' strike, which was still dragging on from the previous year, and which was getting more violent, what with bombs going off in scab taxis. Both he and the Minister wanted to see some results which would prove to the press and the public that they were on the case. Guichard promised to see to it immediately, and promptly got onto Jouin. The time for patient surveillance was over.

The premises of *L'Idée Libre* were still under constant surveillance since Garnier's lover, Marie, had been found there during the raid on 23rd January. Detectives disregarded the fact that the third issue of the magazine had subtitled itself, 'Neither for illegalism, nor for honesty'. The police had warrants out for both De Boe and Dieudonné, and they knew that the former had worked there as a typographer, and that Louise, the latter's wife, had been living with Lorulot until sometime around the previous Christmas. Besides, not only were Garnier and Carouy associates of Lorulot's from Romainville, but, since the start of February, Jeanne Belardi, Carouy's erstwhile lover, had moved in with Lorulot.

The police kept a constant watch on all people going in or out of the premises at passage de Clichy and on 25th February trailed one of the typographer's girlfriends, Madeleine Nourisson, to 47 rue Nollet. Two days later, on the very morning of the incident at the place du Havre, detectives had succeeded in renting a room from the widow Rollet right opposite the suspect's room. Having ascertained that the man 'Aubertin' was there with his wife and child, Jouin was sure that he now had Dieudonné, and that further patient surveillance would lead him to the principal perpetrators of the rue Ordener hold-up.

Another luxury Delaunay-Belleville, this one worth twenty thousand francs. The first murder of a policeman took place in this car. Garnier shot and killed his namesake at the place du Havre.

Not surprisingly then, Guichard's order immediately to arrest Dieudonné came as a bombshell to Jouin; he was almost on the verge of solving the case when this insane order came through telling him to abandon his best lead on the gang, simply in order to save face and pander to the press and Government ministers. Jouin could hardly contain his exasperation: this could set the case back weeks. Nevertheless, it was his duty to carry out the orders of his superior, so he calmly went and explained to the surveillance team what had happened at the place du Havre and what now had to be done here.

The detectives reported that 'Aubertin' had received a telegramme earlier reading: "Our mother in good health", upon receipt of which he went out and made a telephone call; besides that there was nothing to report except that the 'Aubertin' family now had a visitor, a dark-haired man in his early twenties. Given that the gang were classed as 'armed and extremely dangerous', Jouin decided not to carry out the arrests until the suspects were outside the apartment. He didn't want to go bursting in and provoke a shoot-out which might result in another police fatality. Jouin's approach was strictly 'softly, softly'.

Soon enough, the visitor left, making his way down the stairs and into the street. Unknown to him, he was followed by four detectives who waited until he was some distance away, and then pounced. Jean De Boe suddenly found himself with his face pressed against the cold stone of the *trottoir*, and his hands handcuffed behind his back. The police plucked a 9mm Browning from each pocket as well as twenty-three loose 9mm rounds.

Not long after, Eugène Dieudonné left the apartment, but he didn't even make it down the stairs; Jouin and three other officers seized him from behind, and disarmed him. They burst into the flat and arrested Louise, and then ransacked the place. More weapons were discovered, as well as maps upon which were marked points at which the Swiss and Italian borders could be crossed, so avoiding customs posts. They also found a ticket for the left-luggage office of the Gare du Nord, which tied in with information received that some of the stolen cheques and bonds from the rue Ordener hold-up were being kept in *consignes* in the main Paris railway stations: Guichard had already ordered that they all be put under surveillance.

Following these three arrests, the police pulled in the typographer, his girlfriend Madeleine, and Bouchet for questioning, while Victor was put under further pressure to cooperate by the re-arrest of Rirette. Jean De Boe's flat at 16 boulevard des Vignes, which he'd rented in the false name of Henri Migny, was thoroughly searched and the standard 'burglar's equipment' found, but Dieudonné's mother's house in Nancy was declared to be 'clean'. Other detectives hastened down to Alais to try and find out about the mysterious telegramme that had been sent from there to Dieudonné. They soon realized their suspect 'Simentoff' had flown, forewarned of trouble by the press reports of the 'outrage' at the place du Havre, which he obviously recognized as the work of his illegalist comrades.

Back at the Sûreté, Jean De Boe and Eugène Dieudonné were initially charged with carrying prohibited weapons, although other charges were likely to follow; the others, Bouchet, Madeleine Nourisson, Louise and Rirette, were all released on the 1st March, the same day as the funeral of policeman François Garnier. The Prefect of Police, Louis Lépine, gave a short graveside oration during which he bemoaned the fact that, "the criminals of Paris are numbered in their thousands".

But the problem for the police was that they weren't just 'ordinary criminals', they were 'illegalists', who had strong ideological motivations behind their actions, and whose non-acceptance of the hierarchical ordering of society could lead them to carry out much more daring, if desperate, acts. They were not like the five-man burglary gang arrested in Clichy, who were 'straight' criminals without an ideological justification for their acts—acquiring money and commodities in order to be able to live a bit more like the bourgeois; the high spot of their year being to take a holiday in the fashionable resort of Deauville, on the Normandy coast; their 'self-realization' acted out on capitalist terms, without giving any thought to transcending capitalist relations.

But although the police clearly saw the illegalists as a special case, not everyone agreed with them. The socialists made a blanket condemnation not just of illegalism, but also of criminality (and of course, anarchism) which they declared was quite simply 'capitalist' activity. For the anarchists, however, the problem was closer to home, and many activists were worried about the repression that might fall on the rest of the movement, as well as the sullying of the anarchist ideal'. As the Italian anarchist Luigi Galleani had written a few years earlier, there were those, "especially in the more respectable circles", who, "disturbed by problems of conscience, made uneasy about the threat of reaction, distressed by residual evangelism" rushed "to belittle, to shame the act of rebellion". Lorulot had already made his position against illegalism clear in the columns of *L'Idée Libre*, but now even *l'anarchie* was beginning to ask questions. Armand had taken over the editing of the paper in the second week of February, and was in Paris each Monday and Tuesday despite still living in Orleans. In the second edition, under his editorship, Hermann Sterne asked about the illegalists, "*Sont-ils des Notres?*" ("Are they Ours?"), but concluded that it was not the time to break solidarity with them. The illegalists knew that there were still some comrades in the milieu that could be counted on: they might yet make up for the arrests of Jean and Eugène.

There was the old Russian refugee, Gorodesky, a veteran of *l'anarchie* since its inception, who allowed the gang to use his flat in Montmartre; there was young André Poyer, an acquaintance of the now imprisoned Louis Rimbault, who could provide them with brand-new high quality weapons; David Belonie, Bonnot's old friend from Lyon could always be relied on; ginger-haired René Valet, withdrawn but intense, was already helping out his comrades by renting safe houses and casing banks with his companion, Anna; and Élie Monier, from Alais, would be a 'sleeper' in the southern suburbs of Paris.

But, besides these particular individuals, from whom Bonnot, Garnier and Callemin might expect direct support, there was, perhaps more importantly, the general anarchist sense of 'duty' to provide shelter for all those trying to escape the authorities—and of course that meant no questions asked. Despite its nominal 'individualism', this anarchist network was not only quite widespread but also possessed a keen sense of practical solidarity towards other comrades from the milieu; they also had none of the moral qualms that certain other anarchists exhibited in aiding and abetting crime. Even comrades such as Lorulot, who disagreed with the illegalists, would never help the police.

It had taken the Sûreté three months to track down Eugène Dieudonné, their first major lead, and now, with his arrest, they were virtually back to square one. Paris was swamped with detectives and police, watching, listening, awaiting that indiscretion, that hint of something suspicious that might put them back on the scent again.

9. Calm before the Storm

*Whether you have lived enough depends not on the number
of years but on your will.*
—Michel de Montaigne (1533–92)

'Simentoff'

ÉLIE MONIER WAS in Paris by late evening on 1st March. Rather than
skip the country or move to another part of France, he had chosen to
come straight to the lion's den, to the capital city which was once again
to be the focus of a French social drama. For, although Paris housed the
headquarters of the Sûreté and the Government, it also served as the
operational base of the illegalists. As a thriving cosmopolitan city with
well over a million inhabitants, it was a natural habitat for those trying to hide from the authorities, especially given the revolutionary and
'criminal' character of sections of the Parisian working class. It should
be easy enough for Monier, alias 'Simentoff', to hide out in Paris without
attracting any undue attention.

He spent his first night with René Valet and Anna Dondon at their
rented apartment in rue Ordener, but this was only a temporary measure, as he wished to stay with someone outside the gang's immediate circle: the person he had in mind was Antoine Gauzy, the brother of a friend
of his, Louis Gauzy, a supervisor with the 'Compagnie d'Eaux' in Nîmes.

The next day Monier met up with Pierre Collin, a friend of Lorulot's
and one of the defence witnesses at the 1910 affray trial, who lived in
Maisons-Alfort, and they went together to Gauzy's shop in Ivry-sur-
Seine. It stood just outside the fortifications, only a few hundred metres from the Porte d'Ivry, at 63 rue de Paris; a sky-blue secondhand
clothes shop bearing the sign, *'Les Halles Populaires D'Ivry'*. Antoine was
a middle-aged anarchist who lived above the shop with his wife and two
young children, the younger of whom they had named 'Germinal' after
Émile Zola's novel of the same name.

Gauzy remembered the young man from when they'd first met three years ago in Nîmes; he was very glad to see a fellow southerner, and agreed to put him up if he could help out in the shop. He introduced him to a close friend, Pierre Cardi, a thirty-six year-old Corsican who ran a similar shop across the river in Alfortville. Painted in the same sky-blue, this drapery-cum-fancy-goods shop bore the legend '*Au Soldeur Populaire*' over the door, and was mainly run by two women, Cardi's lover, Marie (who was Pierre Collin's sister) and her seventeen year-old friend Marie Besse. It was the latter (who the press later described as "petite, brown-haired, well-dressed and coiffured, but with the hands of a domestic servant") who soon fell to the charms of the dark-skinned, handsome, moustachioed anarchist from the Midi.

Monier had therefore experienced little difficulty in getting a place to stay, some regular work, and a young lover; he even dined out in Montmartre with Lorulot and Jeanne Belardi, despite the risks. If the gang needed him, they knew where he was, but for the time being he was a 'sleeper' who would 'awaken' when they called him. The daily papers informed him of the arrest, in Alais, of Paul Sazy and his girlfriend on 5th March, but admitted that the police had no leads on the whereabouts of the sender of the telegramme; the Sûreté had not paid much attention to a letter from a certain Madame Y, dated 30th January, who said that her husband had been asked to hide the bandits, who were two secondhand clothes dealers named Cardi and Gauzy.

Of Human Bondage

At the same time as Lépine was sermonizing over the grave of the dead policeman, and Monier was sitting in a third-class railway carriage rolling north towards Paris, Bonnot was secretly meeting his two old associates-in-crime from Lyon in the Bois de Boulogne.

Neither Bonnot nor Garnier had been too happy about leaving the bonds with Vandenbergh in Amsterdam, especially as he couldn't seem to sell them; there were fifty thousand francs' worth of Turkish, Nord-Sud, and Ville de Paris transferable securities—they were hot property, sure, but even a ten per cent return would give them almost as much as they'd seized in cash from the rue Ordener robbery. And they needed the money now, not later.

Bonnot and Garnier arranged a series of meetings in the Bois de Vincennes during February with David Belonie and Alphonse Rodriguez, to discuss the retrieval of the bonds and placing them with a reliable receiver in Paris. As it turned out, Bonnot contacted none other than Pierre Cardi from Alfortville, and took the opportunity to speak to Monier and Gauzy. Cardi knew several 'fences' in this line of business— it was he who had introduced Édouard Carouy to the two young men, Pancrazi and Crozat de Fleury, who were currently engaged in negotiating cheques stolen from the burglary at Thiais. For a large amount such as this, Cardi suggested Georges Taquard, alias *Le Juif*, aka *L'Algérien*, aka *l'Usurier*, who had enough funds to speculate on the *Bourse* (the Stock Exchange). Unfortunately for the gang, *Le Juif* said that he could not possibly give them more than five per cent of the total value, given the extreme riskiness of trying to negotiate them. Jules, Octave and Raymond were rather sulkily forced to accept, as there were no better offers on the horizon.

So it was that Bonnot met up with Belonie and Rodriguez in the Bois de Boulogne on Friday 1st March, and informed them that they should go to Amsterdam to get the bonds and meet back in Paris at seven the following Thursday evening at the 'Nation' Metro station. David Belonie went back to an insalubrious little hotel he'd just moved into in rue Jouye-Rouve, Belleville, where he was staying under the name of 'Monsieur Breuil'; during February he'd been living in Sotteville, just outside Rouen. Alphonse was going back to Lille for the weekend, where he had rented a place since the previous July with his lover, Anna Lecoq, a fancy leather-goods worker. Before that he'd been serving a prison sentence for forgery in HMP Dartmoor; on his release he'd returned to France, settled in Lille, been expelled from Belgium and taken up his old 'profession' as a pedlar-cum-forger of ten-franc pieces. It is not known when the gang contacted him in Lille before his arrival in Paris on 18th January, when Belonie had checked him into a grotty 'hôtel' in the rue Belhomme, near Barbès, in the name of 'Monsieur Lecoq'.

On Tuesday 5th March Belonie and Rodriguez took a train to Amsterdam and retrieved the bonds from Vandenbergh; returning the next day, they deposited the package containing the goods in the left-luggage office of the Gare du Nord, and went to their respective hotels. The next evening they met Bonnot as planned at the Nation Metro station, and went together to Gorodesky's flat at 6 rue Cortot, just behind the Sacré-Coeur, where Garnier and Callemin were waiting. They discussed the arrangements for meeting Taquard in the Café Marcel the following Sunday. Taquard was expecting to meet only with Belonie and Rodriguez, but in fact Bonnot, Garnier, Callemin and René Valet were all to be there at nearby tables to keep an eye on things. If they'd been betrayed to the police then *Le Juif* would certainly not escape with his life.

The police were not entirely wrong when they said they were looking for "a gang who plotted their *coups* on the boulevard de Clichy", for Café Marcel, at 54 on the boulevard Rochechouart stood on a street that was simply the continuation of the former. Taquard sat at a table with the two go-betweens, apparently unaware that his every action was being watched by other members of the gang. He explained to Belonie that he'd had a very poor day at the *Bourse* the day before and hadn't been in a position to sell shares sufficient to raise the agreed two thousand five hundred francs; however he did have five hundred francs and he could get the balance the following day.

Belonie was not particularly impressed with the explanation but said he would take the five hundred francs in exchange for one fifth of the bonds, and meet him the following day to finalize the transaction. Belonie and Rodriguez then left first, followed a few minutes later by Taquard, and then the rest of the gang. Belonie and Rodriguez strolled down to the Gare du Nord and left the package in the consigne, then walked back through Montmartre, up the steep slope of La Butte to rue Cortot. After sharing out the proceeds, Belonie and Rodriguez made their way back to their respective hotels.

Around ten o'clock the next morning, David Belonie left his room in Belleville and went to retrieve the package from the left-luggage office, but no sooner did he have the package in his hands than he was seized by several detectives. Under questioning, he refused to give his name and said that the package had been left in his safekeeping by 'Charles' whom he'd met in a café on the boulevard Clichy; he knew his companion only as 'Roger'. He did admit knowing Bonnot from Lyon, but that was not in itself a crime.

Belonie knew that if the others had not heard from him by the end of the day, they would surely realize something was wrong. As it was, the police were being incredibly inefficient, for not only did they not raid rue Cortot, but they even let Rodriguez slip out of his hotel unnoticed. All they found of any interest were some false collars of Dutch make, exactly the same as worn by Dieudonné and De Boe. They had more luck, however, searching Belonie's hotel room in the rue Jouye-Rouve, where they discovered some letters that had, rather stupidly, not been destroyed: they were from Rodriguez, and gave his address in Lille.

As Anna and Alphonse were sleeping peacefully in their room in the rue du Barbier-Maes that night, the street outside was already alive with the movement of police from the *Brigade Mobile* disguised as stone-masons. An inspector from the Sûreté had arrived at midnight with a warrant for Rodriguez' arrest, and proceeded to direct operations. One detective was dressed as a painter and pretended to be cleaning the fa-cade, while another four were sent to occupy the owner's dining room, after he had awoken.

Rodriguez slept late that morning, but finally clambered down the stairs at eleven o'clock. The police burst from the dining-room and a violent struggle ensued, but Rodriguez was no match for the four burly detectives, although he did try and make a break for it in the street. He protested his innocence and gave the name 'Ferdinand Delgado', thirty-three years old, born in Buenos Aires. Upstairs in his room they found Anna, who of course was arrested, but, more significantly, they discovered letters whose contents directly implicated Rodriguez in the affairs of the *auto-bandits*—gang members and their meeting places were mentioned. And, as if this were not enough, the police also took away a strong suitcase containing pliers, files, burglar's tools, instru-ments for forging coins, as well as lead, antimony, ammonia and imita-tion ten-franc pieces ready to be gilded.

On the Wednesday morning, the national press gave details of both arrests, such that when Rodriguez arrived at the Gare du Nord on the Thursday, a large crowd gathered chanting: "*A Mort! A Mort!*" ("Death! Death!"). The police put out the story that they'd first spotted Belonie and Rodriguez in the Gare du Nord on the Saturday, their suspicions being aroused because they observed that neither had a ticket for travelling when they'd left the package in the *consigne*. On inspection, detectives were said to have found it contained the bonds stolen in the rue Ordener robbery. To further substantiate their story, the police said they had had a tip-off from their Dutch counterparts to watch the left-luggage offices of the main railway stations. But if this was all true, why was there no raid on rue Cortot? Why were Belonie and Rodriguez not arrested on the Sunday evening? What happened to Taquard? How was Rodriguez allowed to escape from his hotel in the rue Belhomme? In fact, this whole operation was riddled with un-answered questions.

Taquard was not an anarchist, though he was a well-known fence in the Montmartre underworld; for him and other criminals the activities of these anarcho-bandits was a hinderance to their usual criminal activities, given that Paris was now swarming with police on the lookout for anything suspicious. It is quite likely that he informed on Belonie and Rodriguez to the police, either on the Sunday evening or before. If the police were only told on Sunday evening, then this would explain why Belonie was only arrested on Monday morning as he tried to retrieve the package at the Gare du Nord; it would further explain why Rodriguez slipped out of rue Belhomme unobserved, and why rue Cortot was not raided—because the police had not spotted Belonie and Rodriguez on the Saturday and had consequently not tailed anybody to rue Cortot. Taquard, of course, was completely unaware of its existence as Bonnot and Garnier's current hideout.

The only other puzzling thing is the conspicuous absence of Jouin, the Vice-Chief of the Sûreté, in this operation. He had personally supervised the surveillance of Dieudonné in February, but he had not gone to Alais in search of 'Simentoff', nor had he been present at the arrests of Belonie and Rodriguez. In fact, Louis Jouin had disagreed so violently with Guichard over his order to arrest Dieudonné that the two men had hardly been speaking to each other since. Previously, the actual conduct of operations had been Jouin's responsibility, but now he'd virtually washed his hands of the entire investigation and left his inspectors in charge. He was sure that only patient, unobtrusive surveillance could lead them to the 'ringleaders' of the gang—while premature arrests could jeopardize the whole operation. And indeed, he was right, for the police were even closer this time (though they did not know it) than they had been when watching rue Nollet. The result was that Bonnot, Garnier and Callemin escaped for a second time.

Guichard, however, was still smarting from the dressing-down he'd received at the hands of Lépine, the Prefect of Police, and while the incident at the place du Havre was still fresh in public memory he was determined to continue the policy of making immediate arrests. In this way he could maintain his self-esteem in front of his superiors, and stave off criticism from the press. His only problem was that the gun-toting, moustachioed attacker of the rue Ordener was not yet behind bars . . . Or was he?

Dieudonné in the Hot-Seat

Whereas David Belonie had said very little under interrogation by detectives and the examining magistrate, Monsieur Gilbert, Rodriguez
made a full confession. It was not difficult for Guichard to put pressure
on him: he had ten previous convictions, and this time he was facing
probable transportation to Devil's Island if found guilty. At his time of
life this could quite easily be a death sentence. Rodriguez was not stupid,
he realized that even a full confession could not add much to what the
police already knew, so he went further in cooperating with them and
told the police what they wanted to hear: he'd heard from Bonnot that
Dieudonné was involved in the rue Ordener hold-up.

Eugène Dieudonné already had a few awkward questions to answer.
For a start, he'd been found in a flat previously occupied by Belonie and
Bonnot, in which they had found those Dutch-made collars and cuffs,
which were exactly the same as found in Belonie's hotel room. There
was also the left-luggage ticket found on him which produced the pig-
skin medical briefcase stolen from Ghent in January. Then there was the
matter of the two telegrams, one saying, "We anxiously await you. Come
at once. Raymond", sent two days before the rue Ordener hold-up; the
other reading: "Our mother in good health", sent from Alais the same
day as the policeman was killed in the place du Havre. Lastly, there was
the matter of the automatic pistol found in his possession. All in all,
enough circumstantial evidence to suggest a continuous involvement
with the gang, but not enough to prove that he had played any part in
the actual robberies or burglaries themselves. Eugène was aware of the
tricky position he was in, but as a good comrade preferred not to say
anything that might implicate his friends. Even threats against Louise
left him unmoved.

Guichard now played his trump card, and wheeled on his star witness, the bank messenger, Monsieur Caby. Rather than an identity pa-
rade, Guichard arranged for a 'confrontation' in which the witness was
shown into an interview room in which the handcuffed defendant was
already seated. Dieudonné could hardly believe his ears when Caby began shouting that he, Eugène, was the man who had shot him in rue
Ordener. Caby had already 'identified' Carouy, and then Garnier, as his
attacker (from photographs) but now declared that he'd been mistaken
and swore that this was the man responsible. Dieudonné hardly knew
what to say except that Caby had made a terrible error, why, he had

not even been in Paris at the time, he even had witnesses who could vouch for the fact that they had been with him in Nancy that very day. Guichard ignored Dieudonné's alibi—doubtless all his 'witnesses' were anarchists, who would say anything to save a comrade. Guichard had what he wanted, a palliative to serve up to the press, the public and his superiors: within two weeks of the outrage at place du Havre he had effected four important arrests, including that of the principal robber of rue Ordener. So long as Bonnot and Garnier lay low until their eventual arrest (not far off now, surely), then he and the Sûreté as a whole might be saved further embarrassment.

To counter Rodriguez' assertion, David Belonie straight away declared that Garnier had told him that Dieudonné had played no part in the rue Ordener robbery, but his words did not carry much weight in the face of Caby's 'identification'. Louise was extremely shocked by this unexpected development, and immediately raced over to Nancy to try and find witnesses who could support her husband's alibi. But she was increasingly worried that Eugène would go to prison for a long time simply out of solidarity with the others: she announced publicly that she was considering talking to the police. To avoid this possibility, Dieudonné was left with no choice but to say that he himself would talk in the hope that the comrades on the outside would do something to attest his innocence. On the Tuesday, the next day, the dailies all carried the same headline: "Dieudonné will talk in 48 hours".

Garnier's Challenge

The gang had been somewhat in the doldrums since the arrests of Belonie and Rodriguez. They'd only got a few hundred francs from the sale of the bonds, which was perhaps only to be expected: they should never have trusted Taquard anyway—he was not a comrade, nor even an anarchist. But then again, there were plenty of comrades even in their milieu who could not be relied upon, given the vitriol that had been flung at them in a recent article in *l'anarchie*. The author of the piece, who had signed himself 'LA', had ridiculed them as, "feeble, narrow-minded simpletons" who wanted to be "strong men", "lazy, non-working thieves" whose theories were a load of twaddle. Their lives would be short, but in the meantime it was necessary for the rest of the milieu to part company with them. Of course there had been a spirited reply the following week by Victor Méric, which concluded by appealing for more money for the new prisoners. And the previous month, three hundred people had attended a *Causerie Populaire* in support of *Les Anars contre la Loi*. Nevertheless, overall they were more and more isolated and shunned by their comrades.

The gang had abandoned rue Cortot, and were now staying with René Valet and Anna Dondon in the flat in rue Ordener, of all places; Gorodesky had given up his job as a typographer at the Hotel de Ville (City Hall!) and disappeared. The gang hadn't really had any success since their first trip to Ghent in January; their second had been a fiasco, the Alais job had been aborted, and they'd almost got shot at Pontoise; and now Garnier had killed a cop, which, while it no doubt gave him satisfaction, meant they were definitely Public Enemy Number One. But to top it all, that miserable little bank clerk had identified Dieudonné— doubtless another of Guichard's tricks. Bonnot and Garnier had been collecting newspaper cuttings about their opponents, in case they one day soon came face to face. Eugène's and Louise's declarations that they would soon talk, meant that something had to be done, and, for Garnier, that meant something spectacular. He would write a letter to the press exonerating Dieudonné and ridiculing the police, and emphasize that they were still in business, by making an even more daring attack on Society. The papers said that Dieudonné would talk in forty-eight hours; that meant the letter had to be posted that day. He composed it that afternoon, then hurried down to the rue du Louvre, right in the heart of the capital, to post it.

Le Matin received it the next morning and published it in full on the front page the day after that. It read as follows:

> *Paris. 19th March 1912 4:25 pm*
> Monsieur the Editor,
> Would you please insert the following:
> *To Messrs. Gilbert, Guichard and Co.*
> From the time that the press has (through your intervention) put my modest personage into the limelight, you have, to the great joy of all the *concierges* in the Capital, been announcing my capture as imminent; but, believe me, all this noise won't stop me from tasting all the joys of life in peace.
>
> As you have definitely admitted at different times, it's not due to your intelligence that you were able to pick up my trail again, but thanks to a grass who got in amongst us. Be

convinced of one thing: me and my friends will know how to give him (and a few over-talkative witnesses) their just desserts.

And your ten-thousand-franc bounty, offered to my companion to betray me, what a trifling sum for you who are so lavish with the State's money; multiply the sum by ten, messieurs, and I will surrender myself to your mercy, bound hand and foot, lock, stock and barrel.

I swear, your inability for the noble office you exercise is so obvious that a few days ago I had a mind to present myself at your offices in order to give you some fuller information and correct a few of your errors, whether intentional or not.

I declare Dieudonné to be innocent of the crime that you know full well I committed. I refute Rodriguez' allegations; I alone am guilty.

And don't think I'm going to run away from your police; on my word, I believe they're the ones who are afraid.

I know there will be an end to this struggle which has begun between me and the formidable arsenal at Society's disposal. I know that I will be beaten; I am the weakest.

But I sincerely hope to make you pay dearly for your victory.

Awaiting the pleasure of meeting you,

Garnier

Another sheet of paper bore Garnier's finger and right-hand prints, and, scrawled below, "Bertillon, you nutter, bung on your glasses and watch out".[1] Another letter sent to Guichard in person suggested a rendezvous outside a cinema in the rue des Pyrénées. The police hastened down there, but Garnier failed to turn up.

Bonnot, however, was not to be outdone in this display of bravado: he walked brazenly into the offices of the *Le Petit Parisien*, another popular daily, in broad daylight and complained to a journalist, Charles Sauerwein, about one of the stories they'd run. Bonnot placed his Browning 9mm semiautomatic on the table as the journalist noted down his challenge, which was published in the next day's edition:

---

1 Bertillon was the Sûreté's forensic expert who had developed his own anthropomorphic system of identification known as 'Bertillonage'.

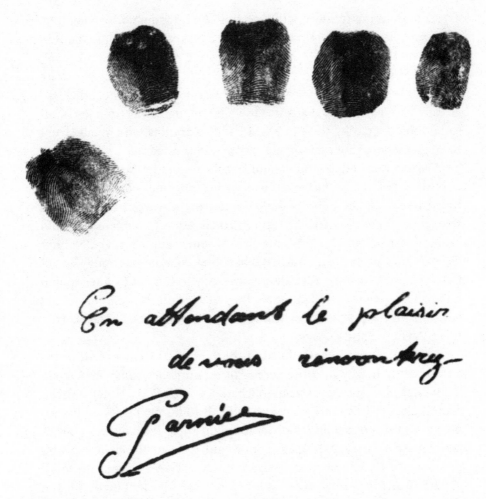

Octave Garnier's letter to *Le Matin,* in which he declared Dieudonné innocent and told the police they would pay dearly for their inevitable victory, was accompanied by this paper with his fingerprints for Bertillon to identify.

"We'll burn off our last round against the cops, and if they don't care to come, we'll certainly know how to find them". Bonnot then picked up his gun and left; of course it would have been against journalistic ethics to have called the police. Partly out of respect for the pair's audacity, and partly out of a political-cum-general hostility to the police, certain sections of the press began to call them "the tragic bandits", while *Le Petit Parisien* stuck with "the Bonnot Gang".

Back at 96 rue Ordener the gang were preparing their next *coup.* As usual, Garnier was the motivating force, determined to carry out an even more daring robbery, although not without some prior planning. For a start he was determined to use more powerful weapons, and he'd bought no less than four Winchester repeating rifles from André Poyer; this would give them even more of an edge over the police, who were armed only with heavy old cavalry revolvers. René Valet and Anna had already 'cased' a suitable bank in a town far enough away from Paris not to be too affected by the hysterical bandit paranoia which had swept through the local bourgeoisie like a contagious disease.

Garnier decided that they should steal a car on the day his letter was published, and attack the bank the following morning, a Friday. And this time there would be more of them: René Valet was eager to join in the struggle, and had also asked, at André's own request, that Soudy should be allowed to come along; Monier would join them from Ivry. Neither Garnier nor Bonnot were satisfied that young, tuberculous Soudy was of the right mettle to enter their desperate struggle, but René's intercession made them give way, and, after all, they needed all the help they could get. Still, for the purposes of stealing the car it would just be the old trio: Jules, Raymond and Octave.

While Raymond kept a lookout, Bonnot and Garnier went to try and force their way into the garage of a bourgeois house in Avenue d'Epremesnil, in the quiet village of Chatou, west of Paris. What with the 'bandit alert' it was more risky and difficult to burgle places now, with people on the lookout and doors double and triple-locked. A dog began barking as they were at the garage doors, and woke up the chauffeur who immediately seized a pistol and began shooting. Garnier shone the torch in his face and fired off a few rounds before he and Bonnot made off. The three of them got back to Paris safely, but it was another setback; maybe there was an easier way of stealing a car?

The incident was reported the next day, but bandit-scare stories took second place to the continuing saga of the taxi drivers' strike, now in its seventeenth week. Since the bomb attacks by strikers' hit-squads on scab taxis, the scabs, many of whom were specially imported Corsicans with scant knowledge of the Paris streets, had begun organizing attacks on union officials, doubtless with the blessing of the company and the police, who generally turned a blind eye to such righteous-to-work anger. However, things got out of hand on the Saturday evening, when a striker named Bedhomme was shot down by a scab after leaving a meeting. The police signally failed to apprehend the culprit. When it came to murder, the State was nothing if not discriminatory.

The next day, a Sunday, the gang learned that Rirette had been re-arrested (for the last time), charged with receiving stolen weapons, and sent to the women's prison of St Lazare.[2] Paul Sazy had been brought to Paris for further questioning, and Rodriguez, now seen by all as an informer, had tried to hang himself in his cell. In the streets, taxi drivers began flyposting posters proclaiming: "Lépine: Chief of the Murderers", and handed out leaflets calling for a mass demonstration, demanding that Bedhomme be avenged. For the illegalists it was time to set to work.

---

2 André was particularly distressed at the arrest and charge of Rirette, who was his only real friend and comrade now that Victor was in prison. This may have been a prime motivation for him to throw his lot in with the gang.

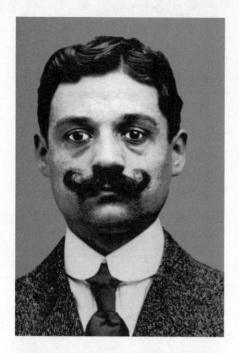

Eugene Dieudonné (top left), falsely accused but sent to Devil's Island nevertheless. Élie Monier (top right), anarchist at sixteen, draft-dodger at eighteen. A subscriber to *l'anarchie* from Alais, he came to Paris to join the Chantilly raid. André Soudy (bottom left), the tuberculous grocer who knew he was to die young and became briefly notorious as the man with the rifle at Chantilly. Rirette Maîtrejean (bottom right), who nominally took over the editorship of *l'anarchie* and became the lover of the handsome young Victor Kibalchich.

10. Kings of the Road (Part Two)

Arise, revolt, attack, expropriate, strike! Strike without pity,
for there comes a point where revenge takes on the necessity
and the awesomeness of justice and hastens its triumph.
—Luigi Galleani

Attack

AFTER THEIR FAILURE to steal a car in Chatou, the gang decided on a change of tactics. As the bourgeoisie, and car-owners in particular, were now even more security conscious, the illegalists planned to hijack a car on the open road and then proceed immediately to rob the bank that they had targeted. Afterwards, they would dump the car in a suburb and simply walk back into Paris, hopefully before the police even knew that the bank had been robbed. It was to be an almost guerilla-style hit-and-run operation.

In the rue Ordener flat the gang armed up; everyone had a 9mm automatic Browning, and André Soudy was given charge of a Winchester repeating rifle, which he concealed under his outsized greatcoat. They split into two groups and took a suburban train out past Bercy and Charenton to Maisons-Alfort, where they reunited and strolled down the road towards Villeneuve-St Georges, scene of the massacre of demonstrators in 1908, and long a syndicalist stronghold.

Bonnot knew this route well; they were on the main road to Lyon, Route Nationale 5, which, in a few kilometres passed through the thick forest of Sénart, and which was where Bonnot was intending to stage the ambush the next morning. The previous November he had been walking through the very same forest, although in the opposite direction, on a path that had led him towards a notoriety he had not sought, as France's Most Wanted Man. He had arrived in Paris desperately seeking allies and had been fortunate enough to find some comrades to whom he was indispensable, but it was a dependence he did not like. If, tomorrow, they were at last successful, then he would go his own way.

As they neared Villeneuve, they stopped for a rest on a small bridge spanning a brook that ran down to the Seine. It was a pleasant spring evening, and in the distance a group of drunken workers could be heard singing *L'Internationale*. Raymond and René went into a local grocer's to buy sweets and biscuits to curb that late-evening appetite. Half an hour later they had entered the forest. Dusk had fallen.

While Soudy, Valet and Monier bedded down for the night in a road-side hut, Raymond tried to make himself comfortable on a heap of sand and pebbles; Bonnot and Garnier nestled under their overcoats on the grass nearby. It was rather different from the country visits they used to go on from Romainville, only nine months earlier. The days of those care-free Sunday outings with Louise, Édouard and Rirette had gone for ever.

They were awoken early by the cock-crow, but did not get up until the birds had started singing in earnest; it was an average spring morning, with a trace of fog in parts; the sun was having difficulty trying to break through the cloud. The gang were near the twenty-five kilometre stone, only a few hundred metres from the crossroads where the notorious attack on the Courrier de Lyon had taken place in 1796. A gang of five had killed the two drivers, dumping their bodies by the roadside, and made off with all the money destined for Napoleon's army in Italy. One hundred and sixteen years later a gang of six stood ready to carry out their own ambush.

At seven o'clock that Monday morning, a spanking new eighteen-horsepower luxury limousine left the De Dion Bouton showroom on the Champs-Elysées, driven by one of the Marquis de Dion's chauffeurs. A young secretary beside the driver had been charged with making the eighteen thousand-franc purchase for the Comte de Rougé, the Colonel of dragoons who had ordered the charge at Villeneuve-St Georges four years previously.[1] He was now sunning himself at Cap Ferrat on the Cote d'Azur, which was the vehicle's destination. To get there, the chauffeur intended to take the usual route, the N5, which ran through the forest of Sénart.

Hiding amongst the trees, Bonnot, Garnier and Callemin watched the road, while the others stayed in the little cabin. A few workers, a

---

1   The Comte de Rougé had an impeccable aristocratic lineage going back a thousand years, members of the family serving in the oldest regiments of the French army for the past three hundred years.

An artist's reconstruction of the seizure of the Comte de Rougé's luxury De Dion Bouton limousine at Montgeron. The first time that Bonnot fired first, in self-defence. He regretted the death.

cyclist, then a motor car passed by, the latter at some speed. They had to make sure the first car that they tried to stop did so, otherwise the police would be alerted. Fortunately, two horse-and-carts were coming down the road, so the three of them ran out and ordered the carters to block the road and not do anything foolish. Almost at the same instant the noise of an approaching car became audible, and sure enough a blue and yellow De Dion-Bouton came into view. The chauffeur had seen the signs warning of resurfacing work, so perhaps he thought that the man in the road before him waving his handkerchief meant to tell him that the road was up.

As the car came to a halt, Garnier lowered his arm and walked forward, flanked by Bonnot and Callemin; each of them had a Browning in their hand, and Raymond shouted out, "It's the car we want!" Then Matthilet, the driver, made a fatal error—he pulled out his own gun, but Bonnot was too quick for him and shot him once through the heart. Simultaneously, Garnier fired at the other man, hitting him four times in the hands, which he'd raised to try and protect himself. Valet, Monier and Soudy ran out from under the trees, while Garnier and Callemin dragged the bodies to the side of the road, and Bonnot turned the car round. As soon as the last of them had scrambled in, Bonnot put his foot down and the limousine accelerated away towards Paris.

As they sped along, the chauffeur's *accoutrements*, a travelling bag, baskets and clothes, were flung out of the window, while the curtains, drawn down, flapped madly about in the wind. Bonnot burst into song, and the others joined in rousing renditions of *Le Temps des Cerises*[2] and the antimiliatrist *Gloire aux soldats du 17e*. They were enjoying a freedom of the road that few other workers could enjoy at that time. Normally, *l'automobilisme* (which warranted its own column in the conservative daily, *Le Figaro*) was an aesthetic pleasure reserved for the rich, even if anarchist sympathizers like Octave Mirbeau highly praised the feeling of individual freedom that it imparted.

The gang skirted around Paris through the eastern suburbs as far as St Denis, and then picked up the main road, the N16, which led north to the sleepy, unsuspecting little provincial town of Chantilly, where they intended to attack the 'Société Générale'—the bank, that is, but also, by so doing, 'Society' in general.

---

2   A poignant popular song from the Paris Commune, which implied that the heady pleasures of revolution were as short lived as the blossoming of the cherry tree.

It took Bonnot almost two hours to cover the seventy kilometres separating Sénart from Chantilly. He cruised through the town and drew up right outside the bank in the main square. While he stayed at the wheel, Garnier led the assault on the bank followed by Callemin, Valet and Monier; Soudy remained on the pavement with the Winchester raised menacingly at his shoulder. The bank clerks jumped up in surprise as the gang stormed in, with Callemin shouting "*Messieurs*, not a word!" Noticing that Callemin was having difficulty drawing his pistol, one of the clerks dived to the floor, which prompted Garnier to shout: "Fire!" He pumped six bullets into the eldest cashier, while Callemin shot a seventeen year-old clerk four times, and Valet hit a sixteen year-old in the shoulder; a fourth man escaped by scrabbling out the back door, with bullets zipping past his head; Monier stayed by the entrance. Garnier leapt over the counter and barked: "Take the money first". He didn't want them to end up with a pile of worthless bonds again. Finding a bunch of keys they began rifling the safe.

Outside, the noise of the shooting had attracted the attention of the locals, including the absent bank manager, who began to walk back across the square. Aiming his rifle, Soudy shouted: "Hold it! Hold it, or I'll pick you off!" and then loosed off four rounds over the man's head, which convinced him to beat a hasty retreat. Soudy continued to fire over the head of every person who ventured into the square or showed themselves at a window, effectively keeping the local citizenry at bay.

The others now ran out of the bank, guns blazing to cover their retreat, and threw themselves into the waiting car. André Soudy fired off a parting shot, then sprinted after the already-moving car, passing the rifle in through the window, but slipping as he jumped onto the running-board. The others managed to haul him inside, only to discover that he'd fainted in all the excitement. Callemin had cut himself on the broken glass of the back window and was bandaging his hand with a handkerchief, while Garnier was still firing at a courageous, if foolhardy, pursuer, who soon fell, wounded in the foot. Another shot in the leg of a horse prevented a cart blocking their getaway. Within minutes they were clear of the town and racing south back towards Paris at an even more breakneck pace.

At Luzarches, two policemen alerted by a telephone call from Chantilly, frantically attempted to pursue—one on a bicycle, the other on horseback—but they were easily outpaced by the eighteen horse-powered limousine. At eleven o'clock the car was sighted at

Épinay-sur-Seine, and twenty minutes later two police cyclists began to give chase in Asnières, but quickly lost the car from view. Not far from the station the gang abandoned their getaway vehicle, clambered over a fence and made off over some waste ground alongside the railway line. They left bowler hats and overcoats in the car so as not to hinder their movement, and threw the rather conspicuous Winchester, wrapped inside a coat, into a hedge some distance further on.

Inside the stolen limousine the two policemen found, besides the hats and overcoats, a couple of blood-stained handkerchiefs, assorted 9mm and Winchester bullets, wallets and safe-keys from the bank, and a few odds and ends belonging to the dead chauffeur—some tins of sardines, maps and a pair of gloves. Seeing a slow-moving train heading for Paris, the police assumed that the gang had jumped aboard and dashed off to the local station, where the Station Master spent a frustrating thirty-five minutes trying to get a connection to the Sûreté. In fact, the gang had split into two groups of three and simply strolled across the bridge into Levallois-Perret, which just happened to be crawling with police and soldiers due to the fact that this municipality housed the 'Consortium's' main garage as well as the striking taxi drivers' headquarters. The 'Bonnot Gang' walked right through the largest concentration of police in the whole of Paris and got clean away with almost fifty thousand francs in cash.

State of Siege

Bourgeois society, and the press in particular, now went hysterical over 'the drama of Chantilly'. The police guards on the city gates and all the main railway stations of Paris were heavily reinforced and even traffic police on point-duty were issued revolvers which they wore conspicuously strapped outside their tunics. Police and Customs officers were put on high alert all along the French frontier with all the main routes in and out of the country closely monitored, especially to Belgium. A special watch was placed over all the main banks. France was effectively in a state of siege.

Prime Minister Poincaré convened a special cabinet meeting to discuss ways of strengthening police powers, and was then summoned to the Elysée Palace by President Fallières. It was agreed that the Prefect of Police, Louis Lépine, should be given *carte blanche* to take whatever measures he deemed necessary. Jouin, Assistant Chief of the Sûreté, was ordered to remain at his post, despite having requested a transfer due to his differences in method and character with Guichard. In the Chamber of Deputies, in reply to a question from M. Franklin-Bouillon, Deputy for Seine-et-Oise, the Minister of the Interior announced that a special police motorized unit was to be set up and armed with rifles if necessary.[3] The Deputies were concerned that the police had been made to look foolish, equipped only with bicycles and old-fashioned cavalry revolvers, while the bandits had access to the fastest cars and the best weapons. There was an almost unanimous vote of an eight-thousand-franc supplementary credit to the Sûreté; the only votes against were cast by three Socialist Deputies, Vaillant, Colly and Déjant, who had perhaps not forgotten that the police shooting down of teenage union members during strikes had not evoked such outrage, let alone punishment.

Lépine announced that two hundred extra men were to be drafted into the Sûreté over the next month, while the strength of the Parisian Police force was to be increased by six hundred a year, up to a total of seven thousand. More importantly, a *Brigade Criminelle* was to be created, similar to Scotland Yard's 'Flying Squad', with eight motor cars at its disposal, and armed with automatic magazine-style pistols and repeating rifles.

The same night as the Chantilly robbery, over one hundred detectives went into action, raiding known anarchist addresses throughout the capital and the suburbs; searches continued the next day and concentrated especially on the working class areas in the north and east, the XVIIth, XVIIIth, XIXth and XXth *arrondissements. L'anarchie* was raided for the third time.

The Société Générale declared that in future its bodyguards would be armed, and upped the reward to a staggering one hundred thousand francs for anybody who gave information that led to the arrest of the robbers.[4] Lastly, the Government belatedly announced that the appar-

---

3 In 1907, following the outrage over the activities of bandits in the Nord and the Drome, Georges Clemenceau, the Radical Party Prime Minister, set up twelve well-armed and vehicle equipped "Brigades Mobiles" (commonly known as the 'Brigades du Tigre' after Clemenceau's nickname) in some of the main provincial cities. Paris was excluded. The new Parisian 'Brigade Criminelle', armed with Browning 9mm pistols and also equipped with the latest De Dion Bouton automobiles had no impact on the Bonnot Gang as they were not functional until 1913.

4 The bank could well afford to be generous, given that its total assets, announced that very day after Chantilly, exceeded two thousand million francs.

Guns blazing, the Bonnot Gang storm over the counter of the bank at Chantilly to seize fifty thousand francs. Garnier justified the killing of "vile slaves" and by his actions definitively parted ways with anarchism.

ent precariousness of telephonic communication between Paris and the outlying suburban towns was to be investigated.

None of these measures, however, managed to stem the tide of hysteria that gripped Paris and spread across the Nord and into Belgium. The sinister figure of the unidentified rifleman taking pot-shots at honest citizens was particularly disturbing—if this was the use workers made of the compulsory two years in the army, then heaven help the Republic! As it was, the number of draft-dodgers had doubled over the last decade, and there were increasing discipline problems within the army such that in the preceding year, over two thousand soldiers had been sent to the punishment battalions in Africa (mainly in Algeria and Tunisia) for antimilitarism, insubordination or other such offences, a fifty per cent increase on the 1910 total. The new Three Year Law might provoke mutiny amongst the conscripts.

To counter the threat of armed working class bandits, many bourgeois began to arm themselves; from dawn to dusk they queued up to buy guns and learn how to use them, while car-owners, feeling particularly threatened, offered their vehicles to the police until such time as the bandits were caught. Cars were not yet widespread, and the idea that workers could not only have access to them, but make this particular use of them was very worrying.

The hysteria did not let up. Virtually every break-in or murder was greeted by the hushed declaration, "*C'est encore un coup de la bande à Bonnot*". The very night of the Chantilly raid, shots were reportedly fired at a car on a country road near Beauvais, and in the days following, the gang were 'spotted' in such diverse places as Chartres, Rennes, Arras, Calais, Brussels, Charleroi, Béziers and Marseilles. Every day, hundreds of letters poured into the Sûreté disclosing the gang's latest supposed hiding place, but the police said they were only following up twenty leads. The press continued to report any incident which might possibly purport to show the mysterious movements of 'the Bonnot Gang'; on the Thursday, three of the gang were thought to have hailed a (scab?) taxi in the rue de Rivoli to take them to St Germain-en-Laye, but when the driver stopped to telephone his wife, his passengers jumped out and transferred into a car containing two men and a woman, which had drawn up alongside, and which proceeded to speed off. The fact that this sort of trivial and meaningless incident was reported at all shows both how great was the general hysteria, and also how determined were the press to sell papers using the gang's spectacular image.

In another incident, a Belgian Station Master fired on innocent travellers, thinking that they were the bandits, while in Paris one 'Jules Bonnot' surrendered himself to the police, and was put in a mental hospital. All in all, such a panic amongst the bourgeoisie had not been witnessed since the 'anarchist terror' of the 1890s.

But in the working class neighbourhoods, the young kids were cheerfully running around playing 'Bonnot Gang' rather than 'hopscotch' or other such traditional games.

11. The Sûreté Fights Back

Around the hero, everything turns into tragedy.
—Friedrich Nietzsche

To Catch an Anarchist

AFTER CHANTILLY, THE gang split up but continued to stay in the Paris area, except for the tuberculous André Soudy who sought refuge at Berck, a well-known seaside health resort. It was not foreseen that he would join up again with the gang. Élie Monier went back to Ivry and his little room above Gauzy's shop, while the others booked into various hotels for a few nights, until they had found suitable safe houses. As for Garnier, the challenge contained in his letter suggested that he, at least, wished to carry on his 'intense living' until death at the hands of the police.

The gang had stopped using rue Cortot[1] after Belonie and Rodriguez' arrests, yet Gorodesky apparently still stayed there until the 28th, after which he disappeared never to be heard of again. There were rumours that he was hiding out amongst the highly cosmopolitan immigrant community in the Marais, which was full of revolutionary refugees, especially Russians, who would not betray a fellow rebel to the police. The sixth floor garret in rue Ordener had also been abandoned; two days before Chantilly, René and Anna had informed the *concierge* that they were going to the country for a few days, but they had not returned. In the meantime, Garnier had contacted another comrade, Millet, a friend of his syndicalist stepfather, with a view to organizing a safe house for himself, René Valet, Anna Dondon, and his lover Marie, who was staying with his mother and was undoubtedly under strict surveillance. At the end of the week Raymond-La-Science found shelter again with the

---

1   Number 6 rue Cortot was a suspect address known to the Brigade des Anarchistes since January 1910; the gang were lucky not to have been caught there.

anarchist Pierre Jourdan and his girlfriend in lower Montmartre, while Bonnot moved elusively every night from hotel to hotel.

The illegalists' problem from the security point of view was that they still had to rely on comrades who were not known to the police as associates of the gang, and were therefore not necessarily one hundred per cent reliable. The huge reward on offer must have been tempting: it meant never having to work again for the rest of one's life. The gang had to hope that anarchist principles would triumph over the possibility of massive individual gain. Indeed, this was why Guichard had ordered such widespread, almost random, raids on anarchists throughout Paris and its environs. The Sûreté was driving home the message that the activities of the illegalists had made all anarchists suspect, and, if they knew what was best for them, they should inform on these 'bandits' who, to quote Louis Jouin, were "discrediting a great ideal". It was a classic 'stick and carrot', 'hard cop/soft cop' method, and finally it proved successful.

Isolated amid the sand dunes on the beach at Berck stood chalet 'Suzanne', the home of Bartholémy Baraille, an old railway worker. He had been sacked in the great strike of 1910 by the Compagnie du Nord, and now worked on the local tramway between Berck and Berck-Plage, the chalet being close to the terminus. He had long subscribed to *l'anarchie* and was known locally as an anarchist, which meant he was also on the list of the *Brigade des Anarchistes*. It was here that André Soudy had come after the Chantilly job, although he intended to go and stay with another anarchist, Inger, in Amiens on Sunday. In the meantime, the sea air would be good for his health.

One Saturday evening, Jouin, Inspector Colmar, three detectives and a special Commissioner left the Sûreté for an unknown destination, acting on 'information received'. By sunrise, chalet 'Suzanne' was staked out by detectives. At two in the afternoon they positively identified André Soudy as he emerged from the chalet wearing an overcoat and sporting a jockey's cap, and walked towards Berck station. He was jumped by the five detectives just after purchasing a ticket to Amiens, and handcuffed without resistance. On his person they found the, now standard, loaded Browning, six bullets, a thousand francs in cash and a phial of potassium cyanide. On the train to Paris, he consumptively smoked the few cigarettes they offered him, and doubtless reflected that he always had been unlucky: the last to join the gang and the first to get caught. After lengthy questioning, but little in the way of reply, André was taken to the prison of La Santé. An anonymous informer reportedly got twenty thousand francs reward.

Édouard Carouy was perhaps the most elusive of all the illegalists; his whereabouts during the three months from 3rd January have never been discovered. Pierre Cardi and Arthur Mallet probably helped him at some point, but the latter had been denounced to the police and arrested. Carouy was about to discover just who that informer was. He cycled down to Lozère (which coincidently was near where his sister was working as a waitress) to meet with a bookbinder, Victor Granghaut, who had been involved on the fringes of *L'Idée Libre*, and who had promised him shelter. Unknown to Carouy, this 'comrade' disapproved strongly of illegalism.

At six o'clock on the fine spring evening of 3rd April, Carouy walked to Lozère station, at Granghaut's behest, but hardly had he got through the door than half-a-dozen plainclothes cops took him by surprise and wrestled him to the floor. From each pocket they pulled a loaded 9mm Browning semiautomatic, while in his jacket they found a hundred and fifty francs in cash and a military service card in the name of 'Nicolas Passac'. The score of travellers who were in the waiting room quickly realized that they were face to face with a 'bandit' and began to attack him, but merely succeeded in striking the police instead. Jouin and Colmar forced a way through the mob and eventually Carouy was bundled into a car and taken to the Sûreté. On the way he talked about his fear of prison, which he saw as a living death, and said he would rather die than end his days there. He seemed cooperative during questioning, and Jouin realized that Carouy had had nothing to do with the crimes of the 'Bonnot Gang', save interceding with Dettweiler so that the Delaunay-Belleville might be stored in his garage at Bobigny. Taken to cell number one in the Conciergerie prison, the warders allowed his request that his handcuffs be taken off, only to see him make a sudden movement with his right hand. Before they could do anything, Carouy had stuffed some pills into his mouth, taken from a hidden pocket, made from the finger of a glove, that he'd sewn into his trousers. But his attempt at suicide did not result in the kind of release he'd expected. The chemist had sold him ferro-cyanide, an emetic, instead of the lethal potassium cyanide, with the result that he was violently sick and suffered from terrible stomach cramps; it was a cruel irony of fate for the one illegalist who was serious about taking his own life rather than face prison. Transferred to La Santé, warders were detailed to spend twenty-four hours a day at his side in order to prevent any further suicide attempts.

The day after the Chantilly raid was Raymond's twenty-second birthday; but he was hardly able to celebrate, despite the seven thousand francs in his pocket, which was his share of the loot. Still, by the end of the week he'd found refuge with Pierre Jourdan and his lover at number 48 in the rue de la Tour d'Auvergne in the IXth *arrondissement*. Pierre was a twenty-five year-old anarchist draft-dodger and pedlar, a native of Foix who also went under the name of Rossini, Cambronne and in this case, 'Clément', the maiden name of his lover, a married woman called Louise-Marceline. It was a woman who now, apparently, betrayed Raymond to the police. By the end of the first week in April the house was under observation by plain-clothed detectives disguised as workers. Pierre and Louise went out and did the shopping (which included a racing bike and a second 9mm Browning) while Raymond stayed indoors, paying for everything and planning his next move.

At seven o'clock one morning Pierre came to the door and looked up and down the street; he saw only a couple of tramps and a worker. Then Raymond emerged, dressed as a cyclist, with a brand new bicycle which he pushed down to the rue des Martyrs. As he disappeared round the corner, Pierre shut the door, unable to see what happened next. For just after Raymond had turned that corner the police ran up, punched him to the ground and handcuffed him, despite the vigour with which he struggled—almost managing to seize one policeman's revolver. A shopkeeper, witnessing the scene, dashed over, grabbed Raymond by the hair and hit him in the face before he was restrained, then the 'bandit' was dragged to the local police station. Hidden in the lining of his cyclist's breeches they discovered four-thousand-franc and sixteen-hundred-franc bills; in his pockets, two loaded Brownings and fifteen loose bullets; and in the saddlebag of his bike, a further ninety-five bullets.

Guichard now personally supervized the raid on 48 rue de la Tour d'Auvergne, ordering his men to drag Louise out of bed without any attempt at observing normal bourgeois proprieties; she screamed as they did so. By the time Pierre and Louise were pushed out into the street a crowd had gathered, rabidly shouting "*A Mort! A Mort!*", but the police received most of the violent blows that were destined for Pierre. They were bundled into a waiting car and taken away to the police HQ at the Quai des Orfèvres. In the apartment, the police found two automatic pistols, thirty false keys, a diamond glass-cutter, a hacksaw, metal piercer, pincers, a flashlight, a lead-filled cosh, and three hundred francs in cash—enough to suggest that he was a professional burglar.

Questioned, Jourdan simply said that he couldn't refuse a comrade shelter, although he was unaware that he'd been involved in the bank hold-up at Chantilly. Callemin at first boasted to his captors: "My head's worth a hundred thousand francs, and yours just seven centimes—the price of a bullet", then he quietened down, except to make the periodic reply: *"Je m'en fous!"*—"I don't give a fuck!"

Hide and Seek

The police continued to decimate the anarchist-individualist milieu. They now had most of the old Romainville colony behind bars, and most police 'trawling operations' brought a few draft-dodgers, deserters or thieves to the surface. Most of these anarchists had something in their possession which could lay the basis for charges against them: André De Blasius had just been done for a typewriter stolen from a factory in St Ouen. The Sûreté had a dozen places under continuous observation, including 6 rue Cortot and 96 rue Ordener. The raid on rue Cortot came much too late, Gorodesky having swept it clean of all possible clues. Knowing that the flat in rue Ordener was rented until the 8th April, the police hung around for four days, then raided it on the 9th. Inside there were three Winchester rifles and two Brownings (stolen from Smith and Wesson on 9th January) and a quantity of correspondence. The thing that worried the police was the whereabouts of the other five Winchesters.

Millet, aka Couvin, aka Carré, aka Mathurin, was a longstanding comrade in the movement, an associate of Libertad's and known to Garnier's stepfather, Lescure. Octave now contacted him to arrange a safe house, which he did through Millet's lover, Florence Trinquet, who rented an apartment in the Avenue de St Ouen, on the western edge of the XVIIIth *arrondissement*. Garnier seemed determined to stay in this area, which was the old stomping-ground of the *Causeries Populaires*, and site of the working class insurrection of 1871; the rue du Chevalier de la Barre, rue Cortot, rue Ordener and the Avenue de St Ouen were all within twenty-five minutes walking distance of each other.

The police were in no doubt as to who they were after now—Bonnot, Garnier, Monier, and lastly Valet. Of all the gang, the press were mostly sympathetic to René Valet because he was from a 'good home' (his father being a small manufacturer from the boulevard de Port-Royal) and he was seen as an intelligent, hard-working young man without a criminal record, who had fallen in with a 'bad crowd'. The press were always more indulgent towards those from bourgeois or petit-bourgeois backgrounds, while the bourgeoisie viewed even minor acts of resistance by the working class as more serious than greater crimes, in value terms, by members of their own class. On the other hand, the socialist supposition that *all* crime was reactionary, because it proceeded from a capitalist mentality, ignored the class question by opposing 'workers' to 'criminals'.

The police, however, were none too happy with all the coverage being given to 'the bandits'. After chatting to detectives about the affair, the Paris correspondent for the London *Times* sent in a report saying, "It is suggested that the present epidemic of crimes with violence may, perhaps, be in part due to the psychological effects of the wide publicity, which in an age of popular newspapers is inevitably given to the picturesque but dastardly exploits of desperate bandits". The problem was that despite the press portraying the bandits in a 'spectacular' way, somewhat divorced from reality, it might still inspire other desperate souls into copycat action. The police continued to be a little wary in their relations with the press.

In the Avenue de St Ouen, René and Octave scratched their newly sprouted beards and pored over the papers, taking cuttings of any stories about the gang or, more importantly, photographs of the opposition—Guichard, Gilbert and Jouin. Octave, however, was missing female company; René always had Anna, but Octave had not seen Marie since January when she'd been temporarily arrested. He had toyed before with the idea of going to fetch her from his mother's house in the rue des Laitières, but had decided it was too risky. He picked up a recent edition of *l'anarchie* headlined: 'The Bourgeoisie have got the wind up!', and noted down the sentences which covered the front page in bold type:

"Capital is nothing other than the proof of the stupidity and resignation of workers. If only they would reflect on it"; "The workers are the sheep. The cops are the sheepdogs. The bourgeoisie are the shepherds"; "If the people made use of their arms against those whom they had armed, war would be dead"; "The person who goes and votes so as to obtain good laws is similar to a child who goes to the wood to cut good canes to be spanked with"; "The elector resembles a peasant who gives a leg-up to a thief, so that the latter may eat the fruit from his pear tree"; "Voters ask for the moon from the candidate who impresses them most with his promises of it, but when he is elected he can only keep his promise by showing them his arse"; "Whether one prostitutes one's brains, one's hands or one's womb, it is always prostitution and slavery"; "The value of money is fictitious and illusory, work is the most valuable; let us take our place"; "Develop your life in all directions, opposing to the fictitious riches of the capitalists, the real riches of the individual possessed of intelligence, energy and strength".

Then Garnier added a few lines of his own:

"If I became an anarchist, it's because I hated work, which is only a form of exploitation.

"Why kill workers?—They are vile slaves, without whom there wouldn't be the bourgeois and the rich.

"It's in killing such contemptible slaves that slavery will be destroyed".

The theory of the Nietzschean Superman seemed to have triumphed in his mind over any vestige of class solidarity or even classical anarchism.

It was obvious to Garnier that the climax of the struggle between himself and Society was rapidly approaching. He resolved to take the risk and go and fetch Marie.

Meanwhile, down in Ivry, Bonnot had changed places with Élie Monier, who was now staying in a different hotel every night in his efforts to escape the attentions of the police. Bonnot was lodged in a little back room above Gauzy's secondhand clothes' shop. By coincidence it seems that Bonnot had also recently read through the 4th April edition of *l'anarchie* in which, in an article by Lionel, were also the lines: "if you apply your wicked laws, then too bad for you; social violence legitimates the most bloody reprisals, and following on from the muffled voice of Brownings you will hear another, more powerful voice: that of dynamite!" So when Bonnot, like Garnier, was fired into writing a few last words, they too were reminiscent of lines from *l'anarchie*—still, it appears, their ideological mentor. But his thoughts also turned to Judith (now in prison in Lyon) due, in some measure, to recent newspaper reports of the divorce obtained there by his first wife, Sophie, in which she had painted him in a very bad light. He began to write:

"I am a famous man. My name has been trumpeted to the four corners of the globe. All those people who go through so much trouble to get others to talk about them, yet don't succeed, must be very jealous about the publicity that the press has given my humble self.

"I am not appreciated in this society. I have the right to live, and while your imbecilic criminal society tries to stop me, well too bad for it, too bad for you!"

Then his thoughts turned to Judith:

"I didn't ask for much. I walked with her by the light of the moon in the cemetery in Lyon. It was there that I found the happiness I'd dreamed about all my life, the happiness I'd always run after and which was stolen from me each time.

"I am determined to take a lover.

"I believe it useful to submit these few lines. For the six months that Petitdemange and M. and Mme. Thollon have been detained, what is there against them? Nothing serious. Petitdemange was my business partner in the Route de Vienne, nothing more. All my burglaries took place before his appearance in Lyon. The workshop's tools were transported without his assistance.

"At Montgeron I didn't intend to kill the driver, Mathillet, but merely to take his car. Unfortunately when we signalled him to stop, Mathillet pointed a gun at us and that finished him. I regretted Mathillet's death because he was a prole like us, a slave of bourgeois society. It was his gesture that was fatal.

"Should I regret what I've done? Yes, perhaps, but I will carry on".

Signing the bottom, "Jules Bonnot", he folded up the four pieces of paper and slipped them into his pocket. Now it was only a question of time.

Exit Jouin

Although Élie Monier wasn't spending more than two nights in the same hotel, he was taking an incredible risk meeting Lorulot and Jeanne Belardi for dinner. They met in the place du Châtelet and dined in a restaurant in the boulevard Delessert—under the eagle eyes of detectives detailed to follow Lorulot everywhere.

At dawn on the morning of the 24th April, Jouin, Detective Inspector Colmar and five other detectives were ready and waiting outside the Hôtel de la Lozère on the boulevard de Ménilmontant. This time, rather than wait for their suspect to come out, they decided to shoulder the door and take him by surprise. They were fortunate in that, despite his desperate struggle, Monier was unable to reach two loaded Brownings on the table next to the bed. In his jacket there were a couple of 9mm magazines, a military service card in the name of 'Doats', an electoral card in the name of 'Brivet', and just one hundred-franc note. More importantly, though, there was some correspondence mentioning addresses in Ivry and Alfortville.

Back at the Sûreté, Jouin called in Detective Sergeant Robert, who was assigned to trying to trace the remaining stolen goods in the Thiais case. They knew that Monier knew Carouy, and that both men knew Gauzy and Cardi; the police suspected that the two secondhand shops might be fronts for receiving stolen goods. They decided to search both places right away, leaving their revolvers in their desks, as carrying weapons was only authorized when effecting an arrest. By ten o'clock Jouin, Colmar, Robert and a detective constable were at Pierre Cardi's shop in Alfortville, only to be informed by Marie Collin that the proprietor was out visiting a friend. They got back in the car and crossed over the Seine to Ivry.

Antoine Gauzy was somewhat relieved that Bonnot was leaving; as a precaution, he'd packed his wife and kids off to his brother-in-law in Nîmes for a week. Now he was able to pop out and telegraph his wife: "Am alone. Come soon. Antoine". He expected her back the following day. When he got back to the shop he found Pierre Cardi waiting for him; inside, they drew up a couple of chairs and began to chat.

Upstairs, Gauzy had two rooms above the shop facing the street, while another tenant, a Madame Winel, occupied the two small rooms at the end of the corridor overlooking the back yard. Gauzy's bedroom was a rather sombre affair with the shutters closed, and simply furnished with two iron beds, a mirrored wardrobe and a table; the floor he had covered with red tiles, reminiscent of his southern origins. Through a door at the back was the children's room with a cot and a bed, a chest of drawers and a chair. On the mantlepiece stood three sepia-tinted photographs and some scattered *Temps Nouveaux* pamphlets; a dusty shelf nearby was furnished with some rather tasteless knick-knacks. The shutters were drawn here as well, but in the gloom could be seen a seated figure reading a recent edition of *l'anarchie*, his yellow leather travelling case by his feet, and his grey overcoat thrown across the bed. Bonnot had not yet left.

Gauzy's surprise at seeing four bowler-hatted gentlemen walk in through the back entrance to the shop was only countered by his immediate realization that they were police officers. Jouin introduced himself and his colleagues, said that he had a warrant to search the premises

An inaccurate portrayal of the death of Jouin. In the struggle, Bonnot felled the Deputy Chief of the Sûreté with three bullets from the Bayard pocket pistol he carried as backup to the trusty Browning 9mm.

for stolen goods, and asked a few questions about 'Simentoff'. Gauzy tried his best to field the questions and appear cooperative. Was there anybody else here? No, said Gauzy, he was alone, except of course for Monsieur Cardi, and he was expecting his wife back tomorrow. Telling the detective constable to remain with Cardi, Jouin turned to Gauzy: "Let's go upstairs then".

The Vice-Chief of the Sûreté, soon to become the operational commander of the *Brigade Criminelle*, tried the handle of the bedroom door without success. Gauzy fumbled with the key and unlocked it, deferentially standing back for Jouin and Colmar to enter. Detective Sergeant Robert remained with him on the landing. Having been out in the daylight, the detectives' eyes were not used to this sudden darkness, but a cursory glance did not reveal anything of particular interest—except another door.

Bonnot jumped up in surprise as the door was flung open, and thrust his right hand in his pocket, in desperate search of the small calibre 'Bayard' he knew to be there. But immediately Jouin was on him, wrestling him to the ground in a life-or-death struggle. Bonnot's finger closed on the trigger and pulled three times, sending bullets pumping into Jouin's body; the third, in his neck, killed him outright; a fourth shot felled Inspector Colmar. Robert now rushed in to find three motionless bodies lying in a heap in the middle of the floor, the only sound being the groans of the wounded Colmar. He picked up his colleague and dragged him through the rooms and downstairs, intending to summon assistance.

Despite the shock of what had just happened, Bonnot knew that there was no time to lose. He pushed himself out from under Jouin's corpse and staggered to his feet, gun in hand, blood flowing from his forearm where a bullet had grazed him. Running out into the corridor he came face to face with Madame Winel whose attention had been drawn by the noise of gunfire. "Shut up or I'll burn you", growled Bonnot as he pushed her inside and ran into the bedroom.

"Give me a curtain".

"Honest, I haven't got any", replied the terrified Madame Winel. He opened the bedroom window, looked out, then leapt onto the shed roof, slid down the side into a neighbouring courtyard, then over the fence into the back alley. As he ran off, a trail of blood followed after him.

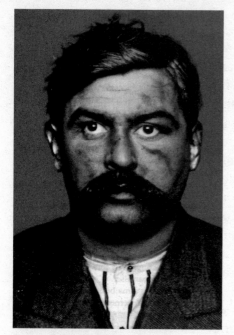

Antoine Gauzy (top left), was beaten by detectives and enraged bourgeois as he was led to the to the police car following Jouin's death. Deputy Chief of the Sûreté, Louis Jouin (top right), the intelligent detective whose patient methods could have netted the gang much sooner had not his boss intervened. Xavier Guichard (bottom, left), Chief of the Sûreté, ex-officer of Marines, he conducted relentless mass raids on anarchists all across Paris. Louis Lépine, on his left, Prefect of the Paris Police. Victor and René were amongst anarchists who took a pot-shot at him at the Ferrer demonstration in 1909. Lépine was also lucky to miss a bullet at the siege of Bonnot's hide-out three years later.

12. Twilight of the Idols

Find an exalted and noble raison d'être in life; seek out
destruction for its own sake! I know of no better purpose
in life than to be destroyed by that which is great and
impossible!
—Friedrich Nietzsche

The Wrath of Guichard

THE POLICE WERE incensed by Jouin's death, especially since Bonnot had vanished without trace, and vented their fury on the unfortunate Gauzy, who was accused of leading the unarmed Jouin to his death like a lamb to the slaughter. When the police discovered a little spy-hole in the floor of Gauzy's bedroom, their rage mounted—it had been a deliberate plan to assassinate the Vice-Chief of the Sûreté.

Gauzy vigorously protested his innocence, citing his telegram message as proof that he had no idea that the room was still occupied. He had only hidden the fellow because his former employee, Monier, had introduced him as 'Alexandre', a Russian revolutionary who needed shelter, and how could he refuse such a man in the wake of the terrible news of the Lena massacre.[1] Detective Sergeant Robert's response was to lay into Gauzy like a punch-bag until Guichard arrived. As head of the Sûreté, Guichard treated the loss of another of his officers as a personal insult. He detested those vile anarchists and intended to take his revenge. He too began to hit Gauzy around the face and told him of the good beating that he'd soon get at the hands of the hostile crowd that

---

1 Lena Goldfields was an Anglo-Russian company, with its own shops and barracks, where the workers were forced to do a fifteen-hour day, six days a week; on 17th April a hundred and sixty-three striking miners were shot dead and two hundred were wounded by Czarist troops called in by the company. One of the principal shareholders was the Czar's mother. After the massacre nine thousand workers and their families simply left the goldfields and production ceased.

had by now gathered outside. "Your shop will be sold. You'll starve—your wife and kids as well". Then he began going through the merchandise, shouting, "That's stolen! That's stolen! That's stolen!" Pushed outside, and with minimal police protection, Gauzy and Cardi were forced to run the gauntlet of the enraged local citizenry.

Upstairs in the bedroom the police went through Bonnot's few belongings—an overcoat with ten gold Louis in the pockets, and a case, inside which they found some flasks of hair dye, some 9mm bullets, and a novel by Anatole France, Bonnot's favourite author.

Back at the Sûreté, Guichard faced further bad news: the very same morning not just Bonnot but Garnier too had given them the slip. He had obviously grown suspicious that they were being watched, and had made the women leave the day before. Valet and Garnier had abandoned the flat that morning and split up, but although he was followed, Garnier gave the detectives the slip by running into a Metro station and leaping onto a train that was just pulling out.

The Prefect of Police, Lépine, organized a conference to bolster morale in the force, and ordered that henceforth all detectives on the case would be armed at all times. Legrand was named as Jouin's successor, doubtless hoping that he would not be the third Vice-Chief to fall prey to anarchist desperadoes. Prime Minister Poincaré visited the wounded Inspector Colmar in hospital and promised him a medal, while arrangements were made for Jouin's corpse to be laid out in Ivry for mourners to pay their respects. Meanwhile, Le Gaulois prepared its editorial with the heading 'Messieurs, Shoot First!' and even the London Standard saw fit to call for greater police powers and urge the authorities to resolve the problem of the anarchists, "one way or another" (doubtless having in mind the way the Latvian revolutionaries were wiped out at Sidney Street two years before). It was clear that from now on "shoot-to-kill" was the order of the day and the police had licence to carry out extra-judicial executions of the remaining bandits still at large.

Guichard could now confidently fall back on his favourite policy—that of terrorizing all those anarchists who might possibly give aid to the remaining fugitives, Bonnot, Garnier and Valet. He decided to round up all those not yet in prison who'd had anything to do with the gang. Guichard, Legrand and a dozen armed detectives made their first early morning call on Lorulot in La Villette, who was dragged out of bed and arrested for making collections for the 'bandits'. After his flat had been turned over, they went to the premises of L'Idée Libre on the boulevard de la Villette and arrested Bouchet, the assistant editor, and another comrade. Then it was south to Alfortville where Marie Collin and Marie Besse, the female companions of Cardi and Monier respectively, were brought in for questioning. Madame Gauzy and her two children, fresh off the train from Nîmes, were also taken directly to police headquarters where Guichard, whose ire had still not been assuaged, made a series of threats and insults: her children could starve for all he cared, though he supposed she was still young enough to earn her living on her back; but her husband and all the rest were going to the guillotine; any defence witnesses would be put straight on the 'Carnet B'[2] list as subversives; still, he might consider lighter sentences for those who gave evidence for the Prosecution.

Nevertheless, despite the hard time they'd received, all those arrested were released on bail the following morning. Meanwhile, down in Ivry and the XIIIth *arrondissement*, the manhunt for Bonnot continued. Only one potentially relevant piece of information had come their way—a local chemist had treated a man the day before for a nasty wound on his left forearm. But as yet there was still no trace of him.

On the Friday, the searches continued. First came the Friedlander brothers, Russian refugees and acquaintances of 'Simentoff' who ran a secondhand shop in the rue Domrémy: nothing was found. Next, an anarchist-run garage in the now strike-free area of Levallois, the taxi drivers' stronghold.[3] Again nothing. Then they went to the home of twenty-three year-old Marie Vassant, another of Pierre Cardi's shop assistants-cum-lovers, in the rue des Cloys. Here they found several stolen cheque books, bankers' drafts, and assorted forged papers, and from intensive questioning of Marie they learned in more detail of the Cardi-Carouy circle.

Around eight on the Saturday morning, an elegantly dressed gentleman left a bar on the corner of the boulevard des Batignolles and the rue de Lévis, on his way to meet a friend, but he had scarcely gone a few paces before he was punched to the ground by three bowler-hatted assailants. Roughly searched, he was thrown into a waiting taxi and then formally arrested; the taxi swung round and crossed to the south side of the boulevard, where the detectives sat waiting and watching. A quarter of an hour later another well-dressed man emerged from a house in the

---

2 A special list of all those considered a danger to the State to be arrested in times of emergency.

3 They'd voted to return to work after a hundred and forty-four days on strike, with none of their demands met, and one man dead. Union leaders spoke of 'victory' in the sense that nobody had believed they'd be able to stick out that long.

nearby rue Pelouze and headed towards the 'Villiers' Metro station. The taxi drew level with him, and then the police went into action, leaping out and seizing him before he had time to defend himself with the Browning he'd tried to pull from his pocket.

These two men, Crozat de Fleury and Pancrazi, despite being 'of excellent family' made their living by passing 'rubber cheques' stolen in the course of burglaries, or by disposing of antiques. Being acquainted with Cardi, Carouy and Metge, it was they who had received some of the stolen goods, for instance the Japanese ivory statuettes, and all the bonds and securities from the Thiais burglary. They had successfully negotiated thousands of francs' worth of the latter in the Banque Suisse-Française in the rue Lafayette, and in various Parisian *bureaux de change*. It just showed that there could be as much money to be made in fraud and burglary as there was in armed robbery, but—*chacun à son goût.*

With the Thiais burglary and double murder more or less cleared up from the police point of view, all attention was now fixed on the hunt for Bonnot, who had stolen the limelight from Garnier since the drama at Ivry that Wednesday. The press now almost exclusively referred to the gang as *La Bande à Bonnot* (the Bonnot Gang), which was to be the name by which they were to go down in history.

The questioning of Gauzy had not let up; the police were determined to extract any detail that could be of use to them in their efforts to track down Jules Bonnot. Gauzy had mentioned to his captors that he'd set up shop three years earlier with the help of the fifty year-old philanthropist Pierre Alfred Fromentin, the 'anarchist millionaire' who had put his fortune at the service of the libertarian movement. His riches had been acquired through marriage to a Marie Ogereau, daughter of the well-known photographer Charles Ogereau, a woman from whom he was now separated. Police however suspected Fromentin's fortune was more the result of insurance fraud after his seaside villa on the Atlantic coast burnt down in 1905 netting him one hundred and sixty thousand francs. Another villa had been similarily destroyed by fire in 1901 with a payout of over a hundred thousand francs.

Fromentin was something of a sentimentalist with ideas more akin to the Tolstoyan pacifist wing of the anarchist movement, and who believed that social transformation would come about through (libertarian) education. He had befriended the radical Catalan educationalist Francisco Ferrer, founder of the *Escuela Moderna*, during a visit to Spain in 1903, and had written a pamphlet subsequent to his execution in 1909 on *The Truth of the Work of Francisco Ferrer*. His other written work consisted mainly of 'social drama' type plays that were performed in what might now be called 'fringe' theatres across the country.

Fromentin was not guilty of sectarianism in his philanthropy, being prepared to help the various schools of anarchism, from syndicalists to anarcho-individualists.[4] Thus, in 1906 he had been roped into a (police) conspiracy alongside the syndicalist leaders Victor Griffuelhes and Pierre Monatte, while four years later he consented to appear as a defence witness at the *l'anarchie* affray trial along with Arthur Mallet, Pierre Collin and Jean Dubois. This last fact increased police interest in Fromentin, for through Mallet he was connected to Carouy and through Collin to Cardi and Gauzy.

Jean Dubois was of course already known to the Sûreté and the *Brigade des Anarchistes* as an anarchist suspected of involvement with stolen cars: his place had been searched twice already in the last six months. It was Fromentin who had given Dubois the lease of the place in 1909, and who had recently transferred ownership to him. The business was running smoothly and Dubois got on well with Fromentin's two young daughters, who would play with his Alsatian dog and show Jean their homework. Dubois' rickety two-storey shack with its lean-to garage was in fact part of a whole libertarian community which Fromentin had set up in Choisy-Le-Roi,[5] south-east of Paris on the right bank of the Seine, and which was known locally as *Le Nid Rouge*—The Red Nest. Several dainty little bungalows, named after famous anarchists such as Elisée Reclus, Louise Michel and Kropotkin, were put at the service of comrades, while Fromentin himself had a small villa not too far away. Dubois' place was isolated from the rest, standing on a patch of waste ground between the Avenue de la République and the rue Jules-Vallès.

Yet the substance, if not the detail, of this information must have already been placed at the disposal of the Sûreté so that the link between Gauzy, Fromentin and Dubois was not necessarily relevant to the whereabouts of Bonnot. It seems that the Sûreté was aware that Bonnot and Dubois were already acquainted, and that Guichard's decision to search the place on Sunday morning, 28th April, was based on the information that a man had been spotted arriving there the previous evening and that the dog had not barked, which presumed that he was a friend. And the man was still there.

---

4   He was on good terms with Libertad and Paraf-Javal and ran his own journal *Le Balai Social* from 1904–1906. He died in 1917 at the age of fifty-nine.
5   Once a favoured retreat of Louis XV.

Shoot-out at 'The Red Nest'

Bonnot had spent three nights in the open, not knowing where to go, and not daring to venture back into Paris which was heavily guarded; finally, tired, hungry and exhausted, he had come to this garage in Choisy-Le-Roi, his last possible refuge. Jean had taken him in, no questions asked, in the almost certain knowledge that the police would soon be following after—why, even last December it had been too risky to keep the Delaunay-Belleville here, at the very outset of these adventures. From the garage Jean led him up the wooden stairs, which ran up the outside of the building, to his two small rooms above, where he fed him and gave him his bed for the night.

Dubois rose early the next morning, seeing as it was bright and sunny, and, leaving Bonnot in bed, went down to do some work on one of the small 'Terrot' motorcycles he had in the garage.

At about seven-fifteen, sixteen armed detectives, led by Legrand and Xavier Guichard, arrived by car at Choisy-Le-Roi and disembarked. Guichard ordered most of them to fan out around the garage that was their target, but to keep back while he led a handpicked party up to the doors. At seven-thirty, Guichard's posse hurriedly advanced across the bare terrain, revolvers in hand, and pushed their way into the garage. Dubois jumped up from the motorbike as one detective barked out "Police!" and immediately began to shout a warning to Bonnot, drawing his pistol as he did so. The detective facing him had already aimed and pulled the trigger, but had forgotten to release the safety catch; Dubois shot him in the wrist, but this drew a flurry of bullets from the other detectives which sent him diving for cover behind the car, wounded in the shoulder and wrist. "Murderers! Murderers!" he screamed and fired two further shots at his attackers. Guichard ordered his men to cease fire and called out to Dubois, the ex-Foreign Legionary, to surrender: "Come out with your hands up. You won't be harmed". It was now or never. Seizing his chance, Dubois tried to push his way through a large gap in the back door only to be felled by a well-aimed shot that hit him in the back of the neck, killing him instantly.

Bonnot, awoken by the din of the fusillade below, grabbed a gun and strode out onto the balcony to find a bunch of detectives just about to climb the stairs below him. His first two shots hit the leading detective twice in the stomach, but the rest missed as he was forced to step back to avoid the bullets that came flying his way. Still, Garnier's premonition had been correct, it was the cops who were running away, carrying their wounded colleagues with them, and trying to cover their retreat with wild shots at the house behind them. Bonnot ran in to replenish his magazine, then stepped back out to take pot-shots at his adversaries who were now hiding behind the trees or lying on the ground. It was Bonnot's last chance to try and escape, but this time the odds were against him; he snapped another magazine into his ever-faithful Browning and prepared for the final battle.

Guichard packed off his wounded and telephoned Lépine, requesting reinforcements from Paris. As a stopgap he sent a man off to the local Mayor telling him to bring all the help he could. Soon enough the Mayor arrived leading a bunch of locals armed with pitchforks and shotguns, giving them the appearance of a lynch-mob. A Fire Brigade Sergeant turned up with eight Lebel rifles and two hundred cartridges from a couple of local 'Military Appreciation Societies', which Guichard ordered to be distributed to some soldiers home on leave. More arrivals followed: police motorcyclists, detectives, special constables, *gendarmes* and sightseers, all trying to hide behind the trees or the grassy bank towards the river. From time to time they were treated to the spectacle of Bonnot coolly stepping out onto the balcony and taking deliberate, aimed shots at anybody who showed themselves, seemingly oblivious of the bullets that must have been whistling about his ears. More than once the police tried to advance behind the shelter of commandeered mattresses, but the precision of Bonnot's shooting, using his favoured nickel-plated bullets, forced them to retreat. He succeeded in wounding two further detectives before he was forced inside for good, due to the more accurate fire from the rifles. He had three Brownings and the little 'Bayard' to choose from, and over four hundred rounds that he'd hurriedly scattered across the floor; he overturned the iron bedstead in order to use the mattress as a shield and barricaded the door with the desk and a few chairs, then took up position by the window, firing alternately with guns in both hands.

By the time one company of Republican Guards,[6] and one reserve company of the Gardiens de La Paix,[7] arrived, the house was well and truly surrounded. The thin walls, made only of wood, plaster and

6   Formed after the 1848 revolution to provide security in the Paris area, including protection of the President and Prime Minister. A military body formed from ex-soldiers at the disposal of the civil authorities.
7   The National Police, not under the control of the Paris Préfecture.

vitrified slag, were holed in hundreds of places and the house began to look like a pepper-pot, with a gun occasionally protruding from some of the enlarged holes and flashing at the besiegers.

Some time after ten, Lépine himself turned up in the company of other bigwigs, including Guichard's brother Paul, the Special Police Superintendent for the central market of Les Halles, Gilbert, the investigating magistrate, and the Public Prosecutor Lescouvé. Soon after taking charge Lépine narrowly missed being hit by a bullet fired either by Bonnot or by one of the many trigger-happy idiots who had already succeeded in slightly injuring the odd spectator. Sightseers were now arriving in droves, keen to see the final hours of France's most redoubtable bandit; some, holding onto picnic hampers, were even going to make a meal of it, and for those who couldn't be in at the kill, it was all being recorded on celluloid as some of the earliest *cinéma-vérité*. By now, Lépine was using most of the forces at his disposal simply to hold back the crowds. When a second company of Republican Guards was ferried to the front in a fleet of taxis, the mass of spectators greeted them with cries of, "*Vive La Garde! Vive L'Armée!*" in a scene reminiscent of some Napoleonic battle. Meanwhile the fusillade continued like some ritualistic ceremony designed to purge society of its enemies, its necessary scapegoats, in order to maintain its own fictitious unity. By midday it was quite evident that all this shooting was getting them nowhere, so Lépine ordered a cease-fire to be announced by a fireman's bugle, it would also give him some peace and quiet in which to consult with his colleagues about what to do next. They were still awaiting the arrival of the artillery from the fort at Vincennes, but Churchill hadn't made use of it at Sidney Street, and it was thought better to try something else in the meantime. Some army sappers had already brought a case of dynamite, and it was agreed to act on Lieutenant Fontan's readiness to go forward and blow the house up. By coincidence Fontan was from a regiment based in Lyon, and had only been in the Republican Guards two weeks; he was one of the few to gain combat experience on French soil before August 1914.

In the acrid-smelling upstairs room, now shredded by hundreds of bullets, Bonnot sat crouched behind the mattress nursing his many wounds. A bullet had just hit his large nickel pocket-watch, stopping the hands at two minutes to twelve—for Bonnot time had run out. Here he was, the Individual standing alone against Society, in that role so well thought, talked and written about by Stirner, Nietzsche, Ibsen and others. He plucked his own writings from his pocket and found those last few paragraphs that he'd written in the eye of the hurricane, and which would now be left for posterity. With an old pencil he just managed to add a last few words: "Mme. Thollon is innocent. Gauzy is innocent. And Dieudonné. And Petitdemange. And M. Thollon . . . I die". He peered out of the window and saw a strange contraption coming towards him.

It was a large hay wagon, reversing slowly with (unseen by Bonnot) the horse still attached, and the carter alongside. Mattresses had been piled on top to act as a shield for the Lieutenant who carried a satchel full of dynamite, but as it got halfway across the waste ground, the mattresses fell out, and Fontan and the wagon were forced to retreat. A quarter of an hour later the cart was back again, this time filled with hay. The Lieutenant and his cart were almost up to the house when Dubois' Alsatian dog ran out and attacked him, causing Fontan to draw his revolver and shoot it dead. Bonnot fired off a magazine at his attacker, but without success—the dynamite had been placed against the wall and the fuse lit. While the Lieutenant retired double-quick behind the cart, Bonnot dragged the mattress and himself into the little back room in anticipation of the explosion. But nothing happened, the Bickford fuse having gone out. Fontan was forced to return and light another fuse, this time successfully, but the resulting explosion did not have the desired impact. He retired again with the wagon to seek further orders. This time there were no half measures. The Lieutenant was ordered once more into the breach, with all the remaining dynamite; it was third time lucky: a tremendous explosion blew in half the front of the house and set it on fire.

As the dust settled, the mass of spectators, their collective consciousness whipped into a frenzy by the noise of battle, began their habitual chant, "*A Mort! A Mort! A Mort! A Mort!*" and tried to surge forward to attack the object of their hatred. Only with difficulty did the police and Republican Guards manage to restrain them. Lépine ordered his men to wait and see if there was any sign of life, and to let the fire take a better hold. After ten minutes they plucked up the courage to advance, the cart rolling forward once more, sheltering Lépine, Fontan, the Guichard brothers and more than a dozen detectives. They dragged Dubois' corpse from the smouldering garage and laid it out on the grass, then began the slow advance up the outside stairs protected by mattresses. Finding the first room empty, the Lieutenant fired four shots at random into the back room, and received a half-hearted shot in reply from a barely conscious Bonnot lying underneath a mattress. He had just enough strength to shout out, "Bunch of bastards", before a hail of lead struck him in the head and arms, and the last thing he felt was the Browning being plucked from his hand. Guichard strode in, pointed his gun at Bonnot's head and delivered the coup de grâce.[8]

As the blood-spattered body was being carried down the stairs, the crowd broke through police lines and ran towards the house, shouting and cheering. The detectives dissuaded them from lynching the unconscious Bonnot, still alive despite his eleven wounds, and so having given his body several good thumps the crowd turned their attention to Dubois, trampling his lifeless corpse as though they were pressing grapes. The detectives bundled Bonnot into a car and sent it off to the Hôtel-Dieu, the old Paris city hospital. Upstairs they just had time to gather up a few bits and pieces before the fire took a proper hold: three Brownings, two small calibre pistols, boxes of 9mm rounds, copies of *l'anarchie*, newspaper accounts of his crimes, and cuttings from the small ads which suggested that the gang had used such columns for communicating with each other.

The crowd gathered around the burning house as though they hoped to see a final mystery unravelled from this funeral pyre of anarchism. After it was reduced to a smouldering heap, people began sifting through the wreckage for souvenirs, only to discover neatly composed photographs of the Fromentin family and loose pages from the young daughters' schoolbooks, implying, perhaps, that the bandits weren't quite as terrible as they'd been made out.

As the car carrying Bonnot to the hospital sped towards Paris, the police went through his pockets and found a plethora of stolen papers: a driving licence in the name of Gillecroze of Levallois, a birth certificate in the name of Comtesse, his brother-in-law, a certificate in the name of Fernandez, a *livret militaire* in the name of Talzerny and another in the name of Comtesse, his father-in-law. There was also a receipt for the car stolen from St Mandé, and Monsieur Buisson's driving licence, with the name scratched out, as well as a road map of France, a watch on a chain, a false black moustache, a notebook, newspaper photos of Guichard, Gilbert, Jouin and Colmar, and *petit correspondence* cuttings.

---

8   This was a summary execution, illegal in both the domestic and international law of the time. Not a word of complaint was ever raised about it.

A specially made trouser pocket contained a sachet of potassium cyanide powder. Lastly, there was what was effectively Bonnot's last will and testament, which Guichard refused to release to the press as it was "a justification for criminal acts", of which the law forbade publication. The car arrived at the Hôtel-Dieu at 12.35 pm, but Bonnot was pronounced dead at a quarter past one, and his body taken to the morgue an hour later, to lie next to that of Dubois.

Two days later, around noon, the bodies were taken to Bagneux, the big cemetery on the southern outskirts of Paris outside the city walls, and dumped into hastily dug graves in the pauper's part of the cemetery. As the grave diggers were shovelling the earth on top, one stepped back and mopping his brow asked, "Where are the crosses?" The detectives exchanged embarrassed glances, but made no reply.

Obituaries

A full state funeral was held for Louis Jouin in the cathedral of Nôtre Dame on the day after Bonnot and Dubois were killed. The politicians made self-satisfied speeches now that police honour had been avenged, and laid wreath upon wreath of carefully chosen flowers as the organ played 'Nearer, My God, to Thee', the same mournful but uplifting hymn that the musicians aboard the *Titanic* had played as she went down only two weeks before. Special security measures were taken just in case the remaining bandits tried to disrupt proceedings, and to keep the anarchists on their toes, hundreds of known houses and meeting places were raided, particularly in the southern suburbs where the police fancied they might stumble across Garnier and Valet.

Thousands of people were still journeying to Choisy to see at first hand the last hiding place of the man who had kept France in a state of panic for the previous month, but they were not indulgent to those who expressed their solidarity with him: one nineteen year-old was arrested by sightseers for daring to say that it was a pity that he hadn't shot more cops, and others were being sent to prison for eight days or even a month for shouting, "*Vive Bonnot!*" The press and the politicians licked their lips at the sight of working class blood, and reassured themselves about the new mood of realism that was appearing; the *Journal des Débats* recorded, "There has certainly been, in recent years, a good deal of false humanitarianism in France, but there are now signs of change". Gold medals were struck specially and awarded to Lieutenant Fontan,

Xavier and Paul Guichard, and the two policemen wounded at the very start of the siege.

But was the working class solidly behind the bourgeoisie on the issue of the bandits? There are indications that this was not quite the case: in a popular Parisian cinema, thousands turned out to see a newsreel which featured actual footage of the shoot-out at Choisy, Bonnot's celluloid obituary. But the director of the cinema felt it only proper that public morality be upheld by preceding it with a rather tedious, didactic homily to *Les Braves Gens* ('Honest' or 'Upright' Men). After only a few minutes, public irritation began to manifest itself in derisive whistling and clapping, followed by an increasingly loud stamping of feet. One young man finally jumped up from his seat and shouted up to the projection room, amid much applause, "We're fed up with 'honest men', it's Bonnot we want to see!"

Two days later it was May Day, the workers' holiday, but the lacklustre demonstration reflected how far the French working class had been cowed by the series of defeats over the previous three years, which of course made the spectacle of Bonnot's revolt all the more appealing. Bonnot's immediate legacy was announced that day with the formal coming into existence of the *Brigade Criminelle*, two hundred detectives provided with automobiles and automatic weapons. The Attorney-General urged all public prosecutors to crack down hard on criminals, and generous bourgeois, conscious of a good investment, offered to supply the police with steel shields to protect themselves from the bandits' bullets.

Amongst some of the anarchists, however, it was not all gloom and despondency, despite being at the sharp end of current police operations. As the illegalists were from their circle, the anarchist-individualists were more or less obliged to make some positive propaganda from the whole affair, if only to avoid a wholesale anarchist capitulation to the socialist and syndicalist position that illegalism stemmed from a 'bourgeois mentality'. Lorulot, the erstwhile opponent of illegalism, organized a series of meetings across Paris with 'The Bandits' as the theme. A May Day gathering in the Perot Rooms in rue Ordener (of all places) drew twice as many people as expected, and a hundred francs was collected for the prisoners from a sympathetic audience who refused to condemn them. Another meeting was announced for the following Wednesday in the Faubourg St Antoine. Yet strangely, Bonnot's death was given no prominence at all in *l'anarchie*, which printed a rather meagre column simply stating that for the police it was a squalid victory won without honour. Even Jean Grave ran a front-page editorial in *Temps Nouveaux* where he appreciated Bonnot's hastily scribbled note trying to clear the others, but in which he deprecated the illegalists whose acts, far from 'living their lives', were only a mad race towards death. Some comrades were certainly unhappy with the way that Bonnot's death had been passed over, and one subscriber, Émile Renaud, regretted that Victor Kibalchich wasn't still in charge, as Armand wasn't 'combative' enough. On the same day the trial began in Lyon of Petitdemange and the Thollon couple (in which Bonnot appeared on the indictment). 'Lionel' tried to rectify the position in an article entitled *'Des Hommes'*. It was very much a eulogy of Bonnot and Dubois written in a style and tone similar to Victor's article *'Deux Hommes'*, about the Sidney Street siege the previous year. The last paragraphs were addressed to those revolutionaries who, preaching the theory of the collective revolt, could not bring themselves to accept the practical acts of individual rebels: "Don't you understand that if there were a hundred Bonnots, a thousand Bonnots, the bourgeois world would be no more than a chapter in history?"

To the Nogent Station

Since the twin dramas of Jouin's assassination and the siege at Choisy, Bonnot had, posthumously, stolen the limelight from Octave Garnier, with the result that these illegalists went down in history as 'The Bonnot Gang', despite the police themselves readily agreeing that the gang had no leader. But of course this acknowledgement was a central part of the prosecution case, which intended to prove that the gang's outrages were an organized conspiracy on the part of two dozen anarchists all consciously acting in its furtherance. On the other hand, the police believed that Bonnot and Garnier were the prime motivators, and did not intend to relieve the pressure while Garnier and Valet were still at large.

Octave was still regarded as a threat, and justifiably so. For a start, he was determined to get even with some of the informers who he rightly regarded as being responsible for the gang's downfall. Soudy, Raymond, Édouard, at least, had all been 'grassed up', and probably by erstwhile 'comrades'; Taquard was almost certainly in the pay of the police, but had disappeared; and it was surely more than simple coincidence that Carouy, whose previous contact had been the irreproachable Millet, was arrested after arranging to stay with Victor Granghaut. Garnier had met him the previous year hanging around *L'Idée Libre* and had had disagreements with him on the subject of illegalism. He decided to give this 'grass' his 'just desserts' as he'd said he would do in his letter to *Le Matin*. This would show both that he was capable of carrying out his threats, and serve as a warning to others who were rather too talkative in front of the police.

Two days after he'd given the police the slip at the Metro station, Garnier snapped a fresh magazine into both his Brownings and caught one of the suburban trains out to Lozère.

It seemed a pleasant enough Friday evening as Victor Granghaut and his father strolled home from work along the dusty lane which led from the station, but it suddenly turned sour when Garnier sprang out from behind a hedge brandishing a gun in each hand. The old man tried desperately to defend his son with his umbrella, but could not prevent Garnier shooting him twice in the legs. "That'll teach you to grass up Carouy", he cried as he ran off down a path through the trees, then skipped over the railway line and vanished from sight. Leaving his son bleeding in the road, the distraught father rushed to the nearest house to get help, shouting, "Garnier's just shot my son". The next day, fearful of further reprisals, the Granghaut family left their house for an unknown destination.

Just over a week later, a comrade decided to follow Garnier's example, after all Dieudonné's witnesses, the Reinart couple and the Bill brothers were all arrested on suspicion of having harboured the gang in February. On 4th May, two days after his arrest and release on the same day, Charles Bill shot and killed his former employer, the joiner Blanchet, in Nancy, for informing on Reinart. Despite a massive police manhunt, he successfully evaded his pursuers and made it across the border into Germany. He was never caught.

But these desperate rearguard actions were too late to stem the relentless advance of the police, now that a score of close friends and comrades were behind bars, and given that most of those still outside were either too afraid or unreliable to be of any use. Guichard really was scraping the bottom of the barrel by arresting Dettweiler's mother, but he wasn't prepared to let up. In the rue Ducouédic two days later he arrested Marius Metge's erstwhile lover, Barbe Le Clech, not withstanding the resistance put up by her new companion, Édouard Forget, who was armed with a Browning. She had nine hundred francs hidden in her bodice, while his pockets were full of forged ten-franc pieces: yet another anarchist illegalist, with twelve convictions for burglary, theft and assaulting police.

On Sunday 12th May Guichard and twenty detectives kicked in the door of *l'anarchie*'s new premises in rue Grenier-sur-l'Eau: the sixth raid on *l'anarchie* in as many months. Lionel and the resident editor Gillet were arrested for the publication of the *Des Hommes* article, and a draft-dodger, Weber, was taken in for good measure. To try and impede publication and distribution the police seized any documents, registers, brochures and other material that they could lay their hands on. The next day Guichard planned to raid *Le Libertaire* for its publication of an article on Bonnot by Mauricius. Most of the syndicalist papers were already being prosecuted for one reason or another in what was a general crackdown by the authorities on the libertarian press.

On the same day as the police were turning over *l'anarchie*, Monsieur Girard, charged with the administration of the estate of Dubois, organized the sale of whatever had been salvaged from his garage, namely a bed, a motor, a lathe, two bench vices and the Terrot motorbike. The Dubois family, however, refused the one thousand four hundred and twenty-three francs that were the total of the proceeds.

Garnier and Valet read about these events, in the apparent security of their new safe house, as they cropped up sporadically in the daily newspapers. Since abandoning the flat in the Avenue de St Ouen, as well as their lovers, Octave and René had spent two weeks scouring the suburbs for a safe house, and this time they decided not to use any intermediaries. On 4th May, Garnier, clean-shaven and his hair dyed blond, put on an accent and enquired about the lease of a summer house in Nogent-sur-Marne. It stood in rue du Viaduc, the last in a line of seven detached houses, two streets away from the station, and a hundred and fifty metres from the river. Overshadowing it stood the imposing railway viaduct over which frequent trains chugged to and from Paris. An annual rent of four hundred francs was agreed and the lease signed in the name of 'Monsieur Rochette'. René and Octave ordered furniture from one of the big stores on the Faubourg St Antoine, where Dieudonné used to work, and installed themselves in their new home on 8th May. Due to ill health, Anna had remained in Paris for the time being, but Octave was determined once more to take a huge risk and go and fetch Marie from his mother's house on rue Jeanne-Hachette. Again his luck held and she agreed to come with him to Nogent, despite the strong possibility that they too might end up like Bonnot and Dubois. But she was necessary for appearance's sake at least: two men without a woman might be considered odd by the neighbours. Marie was obliged to cut her hair and dye it dark brown before she was allowed to venture out to do the shopping. The three of them lived an outwardly relaxed, but internally tense few days, behaving 'normally' to try and allay suspicion. They sang, worked and played in the pretty garden bordered with flowers and trees, or did gymnastic exercises on the trapeze that they'd set up there. On Monday evening they dressed up and went to a local fête, and even dined in a restaurant alongside the river Marne. It must have brought memories flooding back of the previous summer, when Marie and Octave, in the company of Raymond, Édouard, Louise and Rirette had cycled from Romainville to Nogent, hired a boat or two and drifted along the river almost without a care in the world.

On Monday morning the police received the following letter, dated the previous Saturday:

> Excuse me for not writing sooner, but the day before yesterday, on my way back from the Summary Jurisdiction Court in Paris, about a quarter to midnight, I was passing through the Bois de Vincennes. In the middle of the Bois, on the Nogent tramway, two individuals got on and sat down opposite me on the top deck, and above the driver. Straight away I thought I recognized Garnier, but as he was quite settled, although his face and features were haggard, befitting a hunted man, I thought I was mistaken. But on arriving home I carefully examined his photograph and recognized Garnier, despite his make-up. Here is the person such as I saw: wearing a cap of milk-chocolate colour, he must have a false blond wig, or have dyed his hair rather badly, I believe he was accompanied by a young, dark-haired man, as this young man did not leave him and they got off together at the second stop after the Nogent station bridge.

By Tuesday morning the police had both Millet and Anna Dondon in custody; Guichard's men were now very close to Octave and René, Millet being the only comrade on whom Garnier was prepared to rely. Whatever happened that morning, whether they forced some admissions out of Anna, found an address on a scrap of paper in Millet's pocket, or got information from another source, the Sûreté suddenly became a hive of activity. Certainly it seems unlikely that they relied on the letter alone, although the suggestion of a rendezvous in the Bois de Vincennes added credibility to its contents. In the late afternoon of Tuesday 14th May, fifty armed detectives, with Guichard and Lépine at their head, left the Quai des Orfèvres in a convoy of vehicles. Their destination: Nogent.

The Last Battle

René was standing in the garden taking some air, while the smell of cooking wafted out from the kitchen. Marie had put the macaroni in the oven on a low heat, while Octave was preparing the leeks and potatoes, for a simple vegetarian meal. It was about six o'clock on this warm, mid-May evening, when a bearded, moustachioed and bowler-hatted man wearing a bright red, white and blue sash appeared at the garden gate and shouted, "Surrender in the name of the Law!" René Valet was not caught totally unawares, for he managed to fire off a couple of shots at Guichard as he ran into the house under a hail of bullets. A full-scale gun-battle commenced, between Garnier and Valet firing from various windows, and the detectives who, crowding behind their ballistic shields, now surrounded the house. In the shoot-out three police were wounded, one seriously, and Lépine, reportedly, narrowly avoided being hit, as at Choisy-Le-Roi.

Lépine called a cease-fire in order to give the occupants a chance to surrender, shouting at them that they should come out with their hands up seeing as they were totally surrounded and outnumbered: their situation was hopeless. By way of reply, Marie ran out of the house and down the path to the police, and was taken into custody; she had not even had time to partake of the last supper with the man she loved. The two men, fighting on an empty stomach, gulped down some water to quench their thirst and (forgetting their strict diet) some coffee to keep them alert. At their disposal they had seven 9mm Browning semiautomatics, two long-barrelled Mausers, twelve magazines and a thousand rounds of ammunition, but they had no cartridges for the Winchesters. Garnier and Valet stripped to the waist and prepared to do battle. Knowing that there was to be no escape, they piled all their loot onto the floor and set fire to it, watching ten thousand francs go up in smoke. The eight hundred and fifty francs' worth of coins would have to be left to the victors.

Lépine summoned reinforcements, while Marie was interrogated, and they waited to see if Garnier and Valet would surrender. A further enquiry from the police was answered with a flurry of bullets, so the battle recommenced, this time to the finish.

All the time the besieging forces were increasing: two hundred and fifty police arrived from the capital, some with dogs, then came members of the *Gendarmerie* and scores of Republican Guards bringing a vast crowd of civilians in their wake. The Military were ordered to come to the aid of the civilian power, from the nearby forts of Nogent,

A contemporary illustration of the May 1912 siege at Nogent at which René Valet and Octave Garnier met their deaths.

Vincennes and Rosny. A batallion of four hundred bearded Zouaves dressed in red bloomers, embroidered blue jackets and fezes arrived at the double from the fort at Nogent, and took up positions on the railway viaduct overlooking the house, and began to set up their machine-guns. Many had arrived without arms and so were used as stewards to keep the ever-growing crowd at bay. A company of the 23rd Dragoons[9] came from Vincennes, but without any dynamite, which had to be brought from Rosny. The odds were now five hundred to one and going out further every minute, and the crowd of punters, over twenty thousand strong, stretched right down to the casino and ballroom on the riverside. As night fell, they were treated to a real *son-et-lumière* experience: firemen illuminated the house with a searchlight set up on the viaduct and stuck acetylene flares in the grass all around, while detectives lined up their automobiles and switched on all the headlights.[10]

The withering fire from the Zouaves' machine-guns had forced Valet and Garnier to retreat into the cellar as the rest of the house had become completely untenable, but two dynamite explosions failed to flush them out of their new hiding place. Nevertheless, Guichard and Lépine launched an assault, with detectives advancing like Roman legionaries behind long sheet-metal shields. But some highly accurate shooting by the two anarchists in the cellar, no doubt from the Mausers, wounded two policemen, who consequently failed to press home their attack. René and Octave could congratulate themselves, for what it was worth, that they'd held out for six hours, two hours longer than Bonnot had done at Choisy. Not only were the two men facing the most lethal weapon that was to dominate the tactical direction of the coming world war, the machine-gun, they were also now confronted with the most recent of French military developments: melinite. Twenty-five petards of the nitric-acid-based high explosive were brought by sappers from the depot at Vincennes, where it was kept instead of dynamite.

At midnight, with the rain now falling, the sappers managed to insert one and a half kilos of melanite into the breach made by one of the earlier dynamite explosions. The force of the melanite blast was so powerful that the windows of the cars and nearby houses were shattered, and the house torn apart. Under the cover of machine-gun fire, the Zouaves

---

9 The same regiment who cut down the strikers at Villeneuve-St Georges in 1908.

10 Still, in all the confusion, smoke and din of battle, this lighting did not prevent a gendarme from accidentally shooting a Zouave in the hand, and several Gardiens de la Paix being hit by police bullets.

led the advance at bayonet point, followed by the police, with Guichard at their head, and with the cry, "*A Mort! A Mort!*" echoing behind
them. A Zouave sergeant and a detective, the first to enter, found the
walls splattered with blood, and saw Garnier and Valet lying semicon-
scious behind mattresses. Around them were scattered no less than six
hundred spent cartridges. As other detectives ran in, abandoning their
shields and pushing the Zouaves out of the way, the coup de grâce was
delivered, both men being shot twice in the head from close range. Valet
had already been hit twice in the face and once in the right shoulder. The
crowd tried to lynch the corpses as they were carried out and dumped
on the back seats of two of the *Brigade Criminelle*'s new automobiles.
Enthusiastic cheering greeted Lépine, the 'lionhearted' Guichard and
the Zouaves. In the course of plundering the house for souvenirs, three
brand new police shields were stolen, and handkerchiefs were dipped in
the dead men's blood.

The bodies were whisked off to the city morgue for autopsy, and
the causes of death were given as two bullets in the head in each case;
both Garnier and Valet had one bullet in the head from a police issue
revolver, while Garnier alone had a 9mm bullet in the right temple, and
Valet's other mortal wound had passed clean through, so in each case
there was a possibility of suicide. Garnier, who was left-handed, would
perhaps be unlikely to shoot himself in the right temple, and some detectives had just gained access to Brownings, but on the other hand it
might be thought strange that the police should shoot him in both sides
of the head like that. Nevertheless, as potassium cyanide capsules were
found intact on both men, suicide perhaps seems unlikely. The Zouave sergeant (trading on the fact that the dead Jouin had once been the
same) and the detective, who had been the first to enter the room, wrote
a series of letters to the Prefect of Police, full of contradictory accounts,
anxiously hoping to be awarded medals for killing the bandits, but to no
avail. Perhaps it was because Lépine knew that it was Guichard who had
in fact carried out the coup de grâce.

The Valet family, despite their respectability, were forbidden to
see the body of their son, either due to malice or the shocking state
that the body must have been in. In any event they refused to allow
Monsieur and Madame Valet to give René a proper funeral, saying that
the bodies of both bandits were state property and theirs to do with
as they pleased. The bewildered and humiliated parents were reduced
to beseeching the President of the Republic to help them, but by the

A photograph of the house as it appeared after the siege.

following morning it was too late. At nine o'clock the bodies were transported to Bagneux cemetery guarded by dragoons who rode with sabre in hand. One detective acted as witness as Garnier and Valet were laid to rest in unmarked graves in the forty-second division, at the start of the nineteenth line, not far from Bonnot and Dubois at the end of the twenty-first.[11]

In the days following this last drama and societal catharsis, no less than a hundred thousand people visited Nogent to survey the scene of Garnier and Valet's last stand. Some anarchists were also drawn to the scene, and one Italian-based group announced a special outing for the following Sunday afternoon. Throughout Paris, shops sold special souvenir postcards of the bandits, causing considerable annoyance to the police, who viewed such behaviour as pro-bandit. Nobody bothered to print pictures of Jouin, Guichard or Lépine.

In Garnier's clothing the police found a notebook full of aphorisms taken from *l'anarchie* and other sources, and twenty-four loose sheets of paper entitled 'My Memoirs' in which he had explained:

---

11 It is possible to go to the location today but of the four men there is no trace, their bones are presumably still under the earth nearby.

FIN D'UNE TERREUR — LA TRAGEDIE DE CHOISY-LE-ROI
Gardes Municipaux et habitants tirant sur la maison

Three views of the April 1912 siege of Bonnot's hide-out at Dubois' garage. The explosion wrecked the premises, which caught fire. Hundreds of police, troops and armed bourgeois joined in the fusillade. At bottom Bonnot's last scribbled words retained in the Paris police archives.

Madame Thollon est
innocente. Gauzy aussi
Dieudonné aussi.
Petit Demange aussi.
M. Thollon aussi

Jules Bonnot

Why I stole. Why I killed.

Everything coming into the world has the right to life, that's indisputable because it's a law of nature. Accordingly, I ask myself why on earth are there people who expect to have all the rights to themselves. They argue that they're the ones with the money, but if you ask them where they got it from, what will they say? I say as follows: 'I allow nobody the right to impose their will on me, no matter what the pretext; I don't see why I shouldn't have the right to eat some grapes or apples just because they're the property of Mr X. . . . What has he done that I haven't that makes him the sole beneficiary? I say, nothing, and therefore I have the right to satisfy my needs, and if he wants to stop me by force, I will revolt and oppose my strength to his, as, being attacked, I will defend myself by whatever means possible.

That's why, to those who tell me that because they've got the money, I should obey them, I say: where does the money come from: from the earth, money being a part of the earth transformed into a metal that has been designated money, and one part of society has monopolized this money, and has, by force, and through utilizing this metal, compelled the rest of the world to obey it. To this end they have invented all sorts of systems of torture, such as prisons etc.

Why is this minority of possessors stronger that the majority of dispossessed? Because the majority of people are ignorant and devoid of spirit; they support all the whims of the possessors on bended knee. These people are too cowardly to revolt.

It's for all these reasons that I rebelled, it's because I didn't want to live this life of present-day society, because I didn't want to wait and maybe die before I'd lived, that I defended myself against the oppressors with all the means at my disposal.

Garnier's manuscript broke off in mid-sentence and, as with Bonnot's last words, Guichard refused to release the text of Garnier's last message to posterity.

13. In the Belly of the Beast

Living is just the problem.
—Raymond Callemin (1890–1913)

Limbo

OVER THE NEXT few months, the examining magistrate, Monsieur Gilbert, interviewed all the accused and sifted through the mass of evidence in order to test the strength of the prosecution case. None of the defendants made any admissions of guilt, but several declined to give alibis because, so they said, this would implicate others in matters for which they could be charged. Any stolen goods found in their possession had been left in their safekeeping by other comrades who, obviously, they could not name. Most of the prosecution's evidence was circumstantial, the nature of events surrounding the most serious crimes remained obscure, and even the identities of the participants could not be established with any certainty.

Two warrants were still outstanding, one for the veteran Russian anarchist Gorodesky for letting the gang use his flat in rue Cortot, and the other for André Poyer for supplying stolen weapons to the gang earlier in the year. Gorodesky was never heard of again, but detectives caught up with Poyer on the 20th June and found him in possession of no less than three revolvers and a capsule of potassium cyanide. A search of his room revealed a 'complete burglar's kit', two flasks of chloroform and a formula for the manufacture of explosives. Six months to the day after the rue Ordener robbery, the Sûreté had at last solved the case and tied up all the loose ends. On 12th September 1912 all twenty-one defendants were formally charged, to appear before the Assize Court of the Seine in December. There were twenty-six separate counts on the indictment covering eight charges of murder or attempted murder and eighteen thefts over the period from January 1911 to May 1912, amongst the separate charges were murder, attempted murder, wounding, assault, armed robbery, robbery with violence, burglary, unlawful possession of firearms, theft and receiving stolen goods. A general charge of 'criminal conspiracy' was laid against the defendants under the provisions of the second of the three infamous 'Wicked Laws' passed in response to Vaillant's bombing of the Chamber of Deputies in December 1893.

The prosecution sought to establish that there had been a criminal association centred on the premises (both theoretical and material) of *l'anarchie*, first at Romainville and then at rue Fessart. As the gang's ideological mentors, Victor and Rirette were made the pivot of the conspiracy, despite the fact that they'd played no active role in any of the gang's crimes, but, the prosecution argued, *l'anarchie* had shared in the proceeds of these robberies and burglaries, which had helped sustain the weekly paper as well as the needs of comrades. In turn, members of the gang could find shelter there and get hold of guns and false papers.

As the activities of the 'Bonnot Gang' had become almost legendary, a few individuals attempted 'copy-cat' crimes, something that the police and the London *Times* correspondent had feared might happen following their spectacular treatment in the press. Attacks were made on passing automobiles in the Clamart woods and the forests of Sénart and Senlis. The attempted ambushes in the forests of Sénart actually took place in the same spot that the illegalists had hijacked the De Dion Bouton, but this time the drivers escaped unharmed with their vehicles; in the other incidents, the men responsible were promptly arrested. Two young criminals arrested in Beauvais in June avowed complicity in all the affairs of the gang, saying that they had assisted Garnier and Valet set up some gymnastic apparatus in Nogent, where they themselves had subsequently rented their own houses. Their stories were disbelieved: confessions did not come from the guilty in this affair according to the police.

Meanwhile, the accused languished in prison; the eighteen men in La Santé and the three women, Rirette, Marie and Barbe in St Lazare. Rirette later complained about the hard regime that was imposed upon them all: their laces, ribbons and pins were removed, making it hard to dress and they were searched every morning and evening; every ten minutes a warder looked in, making it even harder to sleep in the white-washed cell which was permanently illuminated by an electric light. Still, she tried to make the best of it by teaching Barbe to read during the periods of association; Marie, however, seemed lost in a world of her own.

The regime was equally hard for the men: Louis Rimbault had already attacked a warder, then began to exhibit signs of mental instability, warranting his transfer to a mental hospital. Monsieur Boucheron, the leading defence lawyer who had defended the individualist anarchists previously, was approached by a psychologist, Émile Michon, who asked if he might do a study of some of the leading 'bandits'. It was accepted that he could regularly visit Raymond-La-Science, André Soudy, Élie Monier, Édouard Carouy, Eugène Dieudonné and Jean De Boe, in order that he might delve into their souls and hopefully light upon something that explained their abnormal and antisocial behaviour. He was rather surprised by his findings. He found these young anarchists to be intelligent, surprisingly calm and good-humoured, and always desirous of good conversation or argument. They were very fond of writing poetry and of reading philosophical, literary and scientific works, and engaging in discussion about such subjects. Raymond, in particular, he saw as "the brains of the gang" and talked to him of life, love and of course, science; they even exchanged letters, in which Michon discovered how, behind all the talk of science and reason governing life, Raymond was at heart a true romantic. All the illegalists tried to stay relatively fit and healthy by doing their Swedish exercises and keeping to a vegetarian diet. Michon felt that it was this keen interest in keeping a healthy mind and body that kept them going, and stopped them from being quite so 'crushed' as some other prisoners.

As 1912 drew to a close, with the trial now postponed to February, the accused concentrated on their defences with the aid of the fifteen attorneys instructed to defend them. They all decided to declare their total innocence on all counts, and to leave the question of their anarchism to each individual. On this last point, Raymond was having doubts; on Christmas Eve he wrote to Arthur Mallet, "I don't know if I am an anarchist, many are in this case. I am convinced that the individuals of the rue Ordener were good people wanting to live, that's all".

Victor and Rirette, accused of being the theoreticians behind the gang's actions, were anxious to put forward a more 'high-profile' defence which would separate them from the other defendants. They took their cue from the famous anarchist 'Trial of the Thirty' in 1894, in which nineteen leading theoreticians found themselves in the dock beside eleven professional expropriators. The first group were acquitted, after the prosecution had failed to establish any material link between them and the burglars, who were all convicted. Victor and Rirette hoped to present themselves to the jury as simple journalists-cum-propagandists who had absolutely nothing to do with the heinous crimes of the 'Bonnot Gang', but were only being arraigned because the state was intent on criminalizing the anarchist movement, as it had tried to do in the 1890s. Unfortunately, this type of defence put Victor and Rirette in rather an awkward position regarding the others, who were afraid that such a presentation might suggest to the jury that the others were indeed members of the gang. Victor was obliged to try and explain himself in a tortuous letter to Armand, the most recent editor of *l'anarchie*. He wrote as follows:

> How many comrades, including yourself, are mistaken about our views! Certainly we have the desire soon to 'live again', a passionate desire to see an end, whatever it may be, to this stupid unwarranted nightmare. But if I am associated—by the prosecution—with acts which repulse me (I write the correct term), I will have to explain myself. In this case I will do it, be sure, in terms clear enough so that my words cannot be used against our co-defendants. Besides, do I need to tell you that if the prosecution tried to make use of an (always possible) slip of the tongue I would rectify it? It's not self-interest that makes me not want a forced solidarity at any price. If it was only a question of my interests the defence could get round the difficulty. But no. It is that I am—we are—disgusted, deeply aggrieved, to see that comrades—comrades that I have had affection for since their first and purest passions— could commit things as deplorable as the butchery of Thiais. I am heartbroken to see that the others, all the others, have madly wasted and lost their lives in a pointless struggle, so tragic that, beneath the facade of such desperate courage, they cannot even defend themselves with self-respect.
>
> I will try to find a way in court either to avoid or to make M. Le B[reton] avoid tackling the question of illegalism—to which these sad events seem to me to have given the all-too-evident conclusion, if I can't achieve that, I won't mention it even then. I will restrict myself to proving that never have I advocated, nor have I ever been a partisan of that theory. I will add nevertheless that I have defended the rebels every time that it was necessary to do so.

If I am soon free, it goes without saying that I will explain the above more straightforwardly. I believe it necessary, after these experiences, to bring things to a conclusion. I am sorry for not having done so long ago. Perhaps if I had been more steadfast, Valet would be alive and poor Soudy free. Only I lacked the will to fight it out.

However, you wrote to me: 'One can still object to you, after your articles in *l'anarchie*, by bringing up certain details from your past life . . .

No, one cannot. If I allowed myself to approve in front of the jury of acts of comrades who are no longer theoretical adversaries but really 'crushed people', using Méric's terminology, then surely many objections could be raised against me.

But if I say that I have never been partisan to a disastrous system of action, whether I say it later as I mean to, or whether I am forced to say it to the jury, one cannot raise any objections against me, for it is true. My articles in *l'anarchie*? Have I done nothing other than defend the illegalists, or have I made use of situations to promote our way of thinking—and the legitimacy of all revolts (which doesn't mean to say that I advocate all of them)? Didn't I write in the most militant amongst them ('The Bandits') that, 'the bandits are the effects of causes situated above them'?

At Libre-Recherche, at the Causeries Populaires (rue de Clignancourt), at Romainville, in many a discussion, I said how much I dreaded illegalism. Obviously I wasn't able to push this, given that it may have been necessary to support my arguments with documents out of place in public meetings. I contradicted Lorulot on this subject one evening which Paris comrades must remember. (And I had, at the time, three opponents: our excellent Fallières—five years, Valet—dead, Pierre Jacob—remanded in custody in Mantes.) Don't you remember that, from your first visit to Romainville we spoke of illegalism and that I told you I had numerous reasons which decided me against it? Shortly before taking up the editorship of the paper I had, moreover, made myself refuse a very fair, too fair, article on this same subject. And a few days before my arrest, I spoke to Liénard (of La Vie

Anarchiste) of why, in our paper, I didn't wish to publish my feelings on illegalism. He even offered, with Butaud, to insert the copy that I had shown him!

You see one can neither 'bring up my articles' nor our past life. That, besides, constitutes a chapter which I will not allow to be brought up for discussion. Without being a supporter of waged work, I could be waged. Without being a supporter of theft, I may be forced to make use of it. That is my concern alone. That people discuss my ideas, I desire. That people discuss my actions, which only concern myself, I will not allow. In other words, I may let people talk and slander me, but I won't consent to a debate about it.

What I've recounted above is only to show you that you needn't see a 'change in attitude'—as you've written—in our conduct.

Moreover, if there was a change of attitude it would be understandable. The experiences which are drawing to an end are well constituted to abolish illusions and correct 'theories', alas!

Give me the pleasure of making this letter known to the comrades with whom you've conversed about our defence.

As I conclude, I've just got word from Rirette who rightly expresses the opinion that we must enter into explanations of this nature only if we are forced to.

I will address your letter for publication after the trial, in the case that I am found guilty. I give myself sixty chances in a hundred of acquittal. Not one more.

Wishing you well,

Le Rétif

Armand and the other comrades may be forgiven for thinking that Victor had done an about-face on the question of illegalism and armed struggle; of all the anarchist-individualist propagandists, he had been the most 'combative', the one who sang the praises of Sokolov and the Sidney Street revolutionaries, and even the 'bandits' with whom he was allegedly incarcerated. It was true that he had said that the bandits had arisen in a situation not of their own making, but that was a truism akin to Marx's dictum, "People make history, but not in circumstances of their own choosing". The overall impression created by his articles was extremely favourable to illegalism. Besides this, the major obstacle to his 'simple propagandist' defence was his possession of two stolen Brownings, which provided a direct material link to tie him in with the rest of the gang. He was being rather generous to bourgeois justice in giving himself a sixty per cent chance of acquittal.

Meanwhile, some of the comrades, in neighbouring cells, were thinking less of defence and more of attack, in the form of an attempted breakout. One prisoner called Eckerlen was not connected with the gang and was not being as closely watched, and managed to smash a way through the cell's skylight and crawl through into the warder's room next door. Once inside, he donned a spare uniform and armed himself with a revolver, then studied the piece of paper that had been supplied to him, indicating the way out and the numbers of some cells to open— those of Callemin, Carouy, and other members of the gang.

Unfortunately, the gang's hopes of escape were dashed when a passing warder noticed Eckerlen's absence. Trapped inside the warder's cell, he was captured and disarmed. From now on, all the prisoners in that section were carefully watched, and it was announced that special security precautions would be taken for the trial, to be held at the Palais de Justice on the Île de la Cité.

Judgement

In Paris, the anarchist-individualists continued to step up their propaganda drive in anticipation of the forthcoming trial, while certain sections of the bourgeois press were preparing to put anarchism itself on trial, much to the chagrin of the anarcho-syndicalists, who were equally determined to show that the defendants had nothing to do with 'true' anarchism. Armand had given up the nominal editorship of *l'anarchie* in September to Delmyre, a week after complaining that he was fed up with all the 'parasites' who were hanging around their new premises in rue des Amandiers without contributing anything. Meanwhile, musical and artistic *matinées* and *soirées* were held as benefits for the prisoners, and meetings were organized.

In December the singer, Lanoff, was arrested and prosecuted for his article 'From Rue Ordener to Aubrais', but this did not discourage Fourcade, who had taken over the editorship in the new year, from publishing a series of pertinent pamphlets, namely, *A Justification of Crime*, *The Criminals before the Courts* and *The Real Bandits*. But he rather overreached himself with the front-page article sporting the banner headline 'Aux Douze Fantoches'—'To the twelve puppets'—which contained a series of implied threats to the serving jurors, if they were so rash as to return the wrong verdict.[1] Interestingly though, it gave a breakdown of the status of the forty-strong jury panel which was made up of nine small businessmen, four rentiers, three landlords, four tradesmen, one stockbroker, two legal clerks, one retired senior officer, and sixteen others including doctors, engineers and bank employees. L'anarchie then gave the names and, provocatively, the addresses of all those chosen to serve, and listed their professions: doctor, civil engineer, rentier, car manufacturer, stockbroker, legal clerk, landlord, small businessman, tradesman, engineer, a retired man, and an employee from Noisy. The stand-bys were a landlord and a rentier. In other words, it was a petit-bourgeois jury par excellence, and the outcome was, surely, almost a foregone conclusion. For the implied threats to these braves gens, Fourcade was hauled off to jail, and René Hemme (Mauricius) took over.

The trial opened on Monday 3rd February 1913, and all around the Palais de Justice special security measures were in force. Not only were the general public completely barred from entering the building, but no crowds were allowed to gather outside the court, groups being dispersed and forced to stand across the road in the place Dauphine. Troops guarded the so-called 'public entrance', while, inside, the building was continuously patrolled by armed police and Republican Guards, some of the latter being placed as sentries at the entrances to the courtroom. The public gallery was packed with police and a few carefully selected invitees, while journalists were vetted and only allowed in on production of a pass signed by the President of the Court. Despite this stringency, the dock itself had been altered to exclude any possibility of communication between the accused and the 'public'. Each prisoner was guarded by a warder and the six more 'desperate characters' were in the custody of the Republican Guards. Sitting in three rows behind the fifteen defence counsel, most of the men looked like workers in their 'Sunday best', some looking anxious, others affecting an air of indifference. Victor Kibalchich was distinguished by his Russian peasant-style blouse, while Rirette, wearing a black blouse and her dark hair cut in a bob, appeared very young, and attracted the sympathy of the press who compared her to the naive 'Claudine', heroine of Colette's famous series of novels. Arranged

---

1 Maison-Hachette, the major French newspaper distributors, refused to touch it.

on the tables between the attorneys and the judge's dais there were approximately seven hundred exhibits, including a notably impressive collection of firearms. The jury had to hear the evidence of between two and three hundred witnesses, and decide on three hundred and eighty-three matters; in case the newly installed electric lighting failed, a gas supply was laid on and the court was supplied with oil lamps and candles, so that there would be no interruptions to the administration of justice. A film crew was refused permission to capture the proceedings on celluloid. All in all, it had all the features of a 'show trial'.

Before proceedings commenced, the judge directed that this was not a 'political' trial, and announced his intention to prevent the importation of any political element into the trial. He then asked Lescouvé, the public prosecutor, to open the case. In his opening he outlined the salient features of the prosecution case and the intention to prove a general conspiracy among all the defendants, whom he classed in five categories: first there were the six principal offenders, Callemin, Soudy, Monier, Dieudonné, Carouy and Metge; then five 'intermediaries', De Boe, Belonie, Rodriguez, Dettweiler and Crozat de Fleury; five 'harbourers', Gauzy, Jourdan, Reinart, Kibalchich and the absent Gorodesky; two

A photograph of the courtroom, defendants clearly outnumbered by police.

providers of firearms, Bénard and Poyer (Rimbault being in a mental hospital); and lastly the three women, Henriette Maîtrejean, Marie Vuillemin and Barbe Le Clech, graciously defined by Lescouvé according to their sex rather than by their alleged criminal role.

The case proceeded at a remarkably quick pace, so that all the prosecution and defence evidence had been heard after two weeks. Dieudonné's alibi, that he was in Nancy in the week leading up to Christmas 1911, was supported by several witnesses, but the bank messenger, Caby, insisted that he was his attacker in rue Ordener. He did indeed have some similarities to Garnier with his thick black moustache and hair, but unlike the latter, he was right-handed; Caby said that his assailant was left-handed (like Octave).

Callemin treated the proceedings with the lofty indifference characteristic of the young romantic faced with the scaffold. Sometimes he refused to answer questions put to him, and on occasion argued mildly with the judge over the ethics of anarchism. His defence, like that of the others, was that he was honest and industrious, an anarchist, yes, but that didn't make him a criminal; the stolen property found in his possession had been left in his care by friends, but he would rather assume the responsibility than betray comrades.

Carouy and Metge admitted that they had done some minor burglaries, being driven to it by poverty; the property stolen from Thiais had been given to them by Valet. Under cross-examination, the detective in charge of the case admitted that no less than ten different people had been arrested for the murders and burglary of Thiais, so Lescouvé was forced to call his 'expert' forensic witness, Monsieur Bertillon. He had previously developed a system of human identification based upon the proposition that a fully developed adult's bones varied in dimension from person to person, but the success of his system ("Bertillonage") depended too much on the technical skill of the measurer. Even as late as 1910, France was the only country still not using fingerprints as the primary method of identification, yet Bertillon was now called to give evidence as an expert in the science of fingerprinting! In the face of Metge's denials, the judge intervened: "He said that the fingerprints found could only be made by the fingers of a cook, and you are a cook". Confronted with such inexorable logic, Metge was lost for a reply.[2]

---

2 Around this time, Bertillonage was quietly abandoned as a 'scientific' method of identification in favour of fingerprinting.

Antoine Gauzy denied being an anarchist and said that he was first introduced to Monier as a friend of his relatives in Nîmes, a few days after the Chantilly robbery; as for Bonnot, he honestly thought he was a Russian revolutionary. Similarly weak 'defences' were put up by the rest of the accused, and seemed unlikely to bring about their acquittal, so defence counsel were forced to discredit the prosecution evidence, much of which was clearly contradictory. Better still, evidence was adduced to show that Guichard and other detectives had beaten up defendants, concocted depositions and pressed witnesses into making dubious identifications, as well as offering a deal for anybody who would give evidence for the prosecution. The next day in the Chamber of Deputies, the Socialist Deputy for the Var demanded Guichard's resignation for the inexcusable way he had treated Gauzy. Needless to say, his call went unheeded.

It was left to Victor Kibalchich and Rirette Maîtrejean to play the old-established tactic of trying to separate the criminal illegalists from the 'honest intellectuals'. If this had worked at the Trial of the Thirty, twenty years later circumstances were rather different. In 1894, no material links could be established between the Ortiz gang and the propagandists of the word, including Jean Grave and Sébastien Faure, who outnumbered the former by nineteen to eleven. In the present trial, Victor and Rirette were in a minority of two, besides being intimately known to the principal defendants with whom they lived as comrades. Most serious of all, the two pistols found at their address established a direct material link between them and the 'Bonnot Gang'. Kibalchich called two men from the editorial board of *Le Libertaire* to explain the distinction between anarchists and 'bandits', and then, seeking to prove that he was one of the former, put Lorulot in the witness-box, and argued that both he and Lorulot were propagandists who should be in the same boat. But why had Lorulot not been charged? After all, he had been editor of *l'anarchie* and had known the bandits equally well. Unfortunately, Victor's attempt to draw a parallel between himself and Lorulot did not convince the jury, not least because of the question of the two guns found in his flat. More importantly, though, his line of defence was suggesting that the others in the dock were indeed bandits, whereas he was simply an honest anarchist.[3]

The trial was now reaching its climax in an atmosphere of tension which had been increased by the news of the hunt for the anarchist

---

3   For further light on Victor's conduct at the trial see the Appendix.

LES CAMARADES
adresseront
TOUT CE QUI CONCERNE
l'anarchie
(rédaction et administration)
à R. FOURCADE
30, Rue des Amandiers, 90
PARIS (20ᵉ)

l'anarchie

PARAISSANT TOUS LES JEUDIS

ABONNEMENTS

FRANCE

Trois Mois 1 50
Six Mois . . . . 3 »
Un an . . . . 6 »

ÉTRANGER

Trois Mois . . . . . . 2 »
Six Mois . . . . 4 »
Un An . . . . 8 »

HUITIÈME ANNÉE — 405 | DIX CENTIMES | JEUDI 16 JANVIER 1913

Les 'Bandits' devant les Juges

Le droit, c'est la force !

« Le droit c'est la force. »
Le mot ne fut pas créé par les anarchistes.

Depuis longtemps déjà, on sait que a raison du plus fort est toujours la meilleure...Une telle vérité a toujours prévalu, et il est possible de la retrouver à toutes les époques malgré le soin jaloux que les roublards ont apporté à respectable dont il faut se ménager l'amitié !

Les peuples balkaniques se sont coalisés contre la Turquie, choisissant le moment le plus opportun. Les Turcs étaient épuisés par une guerre prolongée avec l'Italie. Leur Trésor était vide, leurs troupes peu brillantes ; les alliés en profitent pour assaillir la Turquie

En effet, les gouvernants ne sont pas qualifiés pour s'élever contre la criminalité, contre le banditisme, ils n'ont pas d'arguments à donner à des individus qui n'ont fait que s'inspirer de leurs propres principes.

La Société m'écrase. Elle m'impose un sort qui me déplait, une vie qui me semble horrible. Tant pis pour moi, je suis faible, isolé, ignorant. Mais voilà que mon esprit, tendu vers la libération, m'indique la solution. « Sois fort. Ne comptes que sur toi. Ton droit est équivalent à celui de n'importe quel

Que chaque individu travaille à développer SA force, qu'il l'emploie ensuite au service de SON droit. Qu'il ne se laisse plus exploiter par personne ; qu'il lutte avec nous pour réaliser une vie meilleure et alors les situations seront précises, on saura à quoi s'en tenir.

Pour y parvenir, il faut d'abord faire table rase des préjugés, des morales et des blagues humanitaires et nous convaincre à notre tour de la valeur de la devise bourgeoise : « Le droit, c'est la force ! ! ! »

André LORULOT.

NUMÉRO SPÉCIAL

LES CAMARADES
adresseront
TOUT CE QUI CONCERNE
l'anarchie
(rédaction et administration)
à René HEMME
99, Rue des Amandiers, 90
PARIS (20ᵉ)

l'anarchie

PARAISSANT TOUS LES JEUDIS

ABONNEMENTS

FRANCE

Trois Mois 1 50
Six Mois . . . . 3 »
Un an . . . . 6 »

ÉTRANGER

Trois Mois . . . . . . 2 »
Six Mois . . . . 4 »
Un An . . . . 8 »

HUITIÈME ANNÉE — 409 | DIX CENTIMES

Le seul crime est de juger !

" Magistrature gangrenée "

Avant d'être touché par la grâce ministérielle, le sieur Barthou, politicien de son métier, émit un jour, en guise de boutade, la suivante vérité : « Il y a quelque chose de gangrené dans la magistrature ! »

Encore que cette girouette ait cru devoir, pour des raisons très spéciales, modifier son appréciation et désavouer de son mieux la parole d'autrefois, elle n'en garde pas moins toute sa valeur.

« La Magistrature est gangrenée ! »
Le parlementaire en question est fort bien placé pour le savoir.
C'est sa partie.
Il travaille là-dedans.
Son odorat aurait pu courir le risque de s'atrophier et perdre l'odeur de la perpétuelle corruption sa finesse de perception. S'il n'en a rien été, nous pou-

restation et pour le déférer aux tribunaux.

Il s'agit de suggestionner des témoins. Voici comment on opère:

Un homme de *la Sûreté* se rend dans la localité où le crime a été commis, muni de la photographie de l'inculpé. Cette photo il l'exhibe à toutes les personnes susceptibles d'avoir aperçu l'« assassin ». Selon les réponses reçues, il le livrera à une sélection.

Les hésitants, ceux qui feront une réponse ambiguë ou négative, seront laissés de côté. On ne retiendra que ceux qui *reconnaîtront* le criminel. N'ayant rien vu lors du drame, mais n'osant pas le contredire lorsqu'il affirme : « C'est bien lui, n'est-ce pas ? » ils se laissent conduire, instruments

Si nous n'avions pas tant à souffrir, on pourrait rire d'une comédie aussi burlesque.

Mais hélas ! chaque jour quelques-uns des nôtres tombent entre les griffes de la sinistre gouge. Demain, ce sera peut-être notre tour. Ne sommes-nous pas des ennemis de l'Autorité ? Il faut nous réduire par tous les moyens.

On emploiera contre nous les armes basses de la calomnie, on nous jettera du venin. Policiers et maîtres s'insinueront à nos côtés pour nous épier, pour nous diviser, pour nous vendre. La Société transportera sa pourriture jusqu'à nous. Méfions nous !

Soyons avares de notre camaraderie, soyons prudents, sélectionnons ceux qui nous entourent. Mais sans exagérer, car cela aboutirait à la négation de toute camaraderie. Quand nous avons offert notre amitié à des hommes, il faut que ce ne soit pas un vain mot, il faut que notre camaraderie soit réelle, et que rien ne puisse la ternir ; ni la violence légale, ni la bave des crapauds acharnés contre nous.

AUX COPAINS

Notre dernier numéro n'a pas été mis en vente en province, la Maison Hachette ayant refusé de l'expédier, à cause de l'article *Aux douze fantoches*, qui est poursuivi.

Nous tenons ce numéro à la disposition des copains qui nous le demanderont directement, contre l'envoi d'un timbre de 0.10.

Nous comptons sur eux pour nous aider dans ces circonstances et répandre malgré tout les idées que l'on cherche tout particulièrement à étouffer en ce moment par les moyens les plus malpropres.

Notre gérant et administrateur étant arrêté et poursuivi pour le dernier numéro, nous prions instamment les copains d'adresser dorénavant tout ce qui concerne *l'anarchie*, à

René HEMME,
99, Rue des Amandiers, 90
PARIS (XXᵉ)

On juge les "bandits..."

L'anarchie du jeudi 13 février 1913

Lorulot's editorial 'Les Bandits devant les Juges' from January 1913. And, below, a copy of the special edition printed on 13 February 1913 to coincide with the verdict.

Lacombe, nicknamed *Le Chien* (the dog). The previous weekend, scores of Parisian detectives had laid siege to no less than three different houses in the desperate hope of tracking down this double murderer, but to no avail. To the press and the police, it seemed as if there might be no end to this string of anarchist desperadoes. It was against this background that, with the hearing of evidence concluded, Lescouvé began his speech for the prosecution.

Despite the judicial direction to the contrary (which the judge himself had ignored on occasion) Lescouvé felt obliged to address himself to the question of politics. Most prisoners called themselves anarchists and sought to clothe their crimes with some vague system of social philosophy. If they'd killed and robbed, they would argue it was not because they were 'bandits' but because they were ardent and convinced partisans of certain doctrines, and because they dreamed of suppressing the present organization of society by violence, as it did not correspond with their aspirations. This, declared the public prosecutor, was their own argument, and they were even proud of it. Their search for a formula with which to cloak their crimes was the strongest feature of the trial. This criminal anarchism of the prisoners, manifesting itself in murder, theft and terrorism, which left sorrow and ruin in its wake, this criminal anarchy which shot people down without mercy, had, it was argued, been merely a practical expression of the theories propounded by the prisoners. Yet how little in accordance with previous ideas of anarchism were the gang's activities; in days gone by, anarchists had worked for ends very different from material gain. But the accused, under cover of anarchism, had formed a gang which had no other object than murder and robbery.

On 20th February, at minus five degrees the coldest day of the whole winter, Lescouvé demanded six heads. The guillotine for Callemin, Soudy, Monier, Dieudonné, Carouy and Metge, and forced labour for life (in slang, *la guillotine sèche*, or the 'dry' guillotine) for the rest. During his speech, which had in fact lasted more than a day, Lescouvé had allowed himself to express an apparent sympathy for the ideals of anarchism, even using a form of argument propounded by Jean Grave and other anarchists who despised the illegalists. He had welded together different pieces of each person's defence and certain admissions to form a general criminal-anarchist conspiracy from which none of the accused could escape.

The next few days were occupied with speeches from the fifteen defence counsel, each addressing themselves to facts at issue in each particular case, and stressing that almost all the prosecution evidence was circumstantial, laving considerable room for doubt. The so-called conspiracy was a police fabrication, without any real substance. The trial drew to a close on the 26th February, and the defendants were given an opportunity to say a few last words in their defence.

In a few confused sentences, Raymond complained of the portrait painted of him by the prosecution, saying that he was a philosopher, not a bandit, then he stopped short and asked his attorney Monsieur Bruno-Dubron to finish off, as he was unable to do so. André Soudy, with some difficulty, tried a little better: "I am innocent, but I do not know what tomorrow has in store for me. Whatever your verdict may be, I am an anarchist and I will remain an anarchist. But I am not a bandit, and there is no trace of blood on my hands. You will not condemn a guiltless man, and I hope that you will allow me to take my place once more at the banquet of life. If you do, I will live a life of solitude and regret for the errors of my past. I am not 'the man with the rifle'". Carouy admitted that he'd committed some crimes, but not Thiais, and the jury could do with him as they wished. Metge declared his innocence, and asked them to have pity on him for the sake of his ill child. Rodriguez said that he might be used to prison, but that was no reason to add an eleventh year to the ten he'd already done in the course of his life. Dieudonné said nothing. Gauzy emphatically swore that he was innocent. Rirette wept piteously when called upon to speak and pleaded for mercy for herself and her two young daughters. Victor, however, had prepared something lengthier, and the *Times* reported his speech as follows, under the sub-heading 'A Self-Righteous Prisoner'.

> Kibalchich defended himself at the expense of his fellow prisoners with whom he soon became involved in a heated argument. Kibalchich is a typical street-corner orator, and has throughout the proceedings striven to impart to this sordid criminal trial an atmosphere of political idealism. 'I am glad that the end of this nightmare has been reached', he said in a weak voice.
>
> 'There is an enormous difference between Madame Maîtrejean and myself, and these other fellows in the dock. You, gentlemen of the jury, you have surely said to yourselves, "These two are neither bandits nor thieves. They are propagandists". I have no desire to sacrifice people I have

known, but I do not pretend to defend them, and if I have suffered in prison, it was at the thought of the fine forces which were lost to anarchy in the sieges at Nogent and Choisy-Le-Roi. My fellow prisoners are also anarchists, and you may say that my theories have led them to theft and murder. However, that is not so, for a gulf separates philosophical anarchists from those who committed the crimes of Montgeron and Chantilly.'

The other prisoners had followed Kibalchich's speech with growing impatience, and at this point Raymond-La-Science exclaimed in furious tones, 'Don't you say that. You don't know whether the bandits were anarchists. You're trying to separate yourself from your comrades, and it's cowardly'. Kibalchich, having again sought to show the difference between himself and his fellow prisoners, Raymond-La-Science once more interrupted him with the exclamation, 'This is becoming idiotic, and you bore me. Don't go on calling us murderers. I am innocent'. From all the prisoners arose the same protest, and some time elapsed before Kibalchich was able to conclude his very personal defence.

The judge gave his final directions to the jury, then sent them out. It was three o'clock in the afternoon. Perhaps they were somewhat comforted to know that Fourcade, who'd been responsible for publishing their names in *l'anarchie*, had been sentenced the previous week to five years in jail, and fined a thousand francs. The twelve petit-bourgeois gentlemen prepared to execute their duty.

Execution

Just before dawn the next morning, the jury returned their verdicts. After a thirteen-hour deliberation,[4] Rodriguez and the three women, Rirette, Barbe and Marie, were unanimously found not guilty on all counts. But the rest of the defendants were found guilty as charged, except for Gauzy who was cleared of complicity in Jouin's murder but found guilty of harbouring a wanted criminal. They asked the judge to be lenient towards

---

4   This would presume they spent approximately two minutes to reach a decision on each count with regard to each defendant.

Carouy and Metge, who had not been shown to be seriously involved in the crimes of the 'Bonnot Gang'. At one point, as the foreman had returned a guilty verdict against Dieudonné, Raymond had jumped to his feet and shouted out that he was innocent—but it was too late: at 7.55 am the judge pronounced sentence. For Raymond Callemin—death; for André Soudy—death; for Élie Monier—death; for Eugène Dieudonné—death. Raymond received his sentence with a sardonic smile on his lips, while the others seemed rather stunned. The judge exercised his powers of clemency in the cases of Metge and Carouy—forced labour for life. For Jean De Boe—ten years forced labour and five years in exile; Bénard—six years in prison, five in exile; Poyer—five in prison, five in exile; Kibalchich the same; Crozat de Fleury—five years in prison; Dettweiler and Belonie—four years apiece; Gauzy and Jourdan—eighteen months, and Reinart a year. One month was allowed for appeals.

At 8.45 am all the men were led away to the Conciergerie prison, including the acquitted Rodriguez who was detained for the counterfeiting charge to be heard in Lille. In retrospect, both the verdicts and the sentences were more or less to be expected, and 'fair' given the harsh laws and social mores prevailing at the time. Typically, the women were acquitted in a display of gentlemanly grace, for despite the compromising circumstances of each woman's arrest, it was condescendingly assumed that each woman was no more than an unwilling appendage of her male partner. Rodriguez, the only man acquitted, was of course the only one to have made full and frank admissions to the police. The sentences were not excessively savage given the generally savage nature of the French State, although three of those sentenced to death had neither shot nor killed anybody. The four condemned men were transferred to the La Santé prison.

In a cell at the Conciergerie, Édouard Carouy, *Le Rouquin*, whose motto was *'la vie libre où la mort'* (freedom or death!), had decided that, "rather than end up in a convict prison, I'd prefer to die straight away". He had been secretly passed a sachet of potassium cyanide during the trial, and as soon as the cell door boomed shut he swallowed the lot. This time, his third attempt at suicide, he was successful. He left a short epitaph for posterity written while awaiting the jury's verdict:

"I have lived through my wretched short life again tonight. I have had but little joy or happiness, and I confess that I may have made mistakes. All my dreams of happiness always collapsed just when I thought I was about to realize them. Not having known the joys of existence, I

A view of La Santé prison, about which Victor Kibalchich later wrote *Men in Prison*.

At La Rochelle, Dieudonné and De Boe in convict dress wait to depart for Cayenne. After many years both managed to escape.

shall leave this realm of atoms without regret. When I feel my muscles, when I feel my strength, it's hard to imagine that all this can disappear for ever on the strength of one statement of my guilt. I cannot believe that Monsieur Bertillon can, in cold blood, really dare to send me to my death, because he is obstinate and doesn't wish to admit that he's wrong. Science is playing me a dirty trick".

Was the thirty year-old Édouard, the man who liked to hear sentimental old love-songs and set caged birds free, really not guilty? Victor Kibalchich later wrote that Metge "paid for another's crime", and in his subsequent book he suggested that, "the gloved murderer is free", and 'The Cook' (ie Metge) was simply the lookout. But in a more unguarded moment in his private letter to Armand before the trial he had declared how 'disgusted' and 'deeply aggrieved' he was that, "*comrades*—comrades for whom I've had affection since their earliest and purest passions—could commit such things as deplorable as the butchery of Thiais". Édouard was, remember, an old friend from Victor's teenage days, when they'd lived together in the libertarian colony in Boitsfort; it seems probable that both Carouy and Metge were indeed guilty.

Victor himself was, not unnaturally, upset at his lengthy sentence, especially since Rirette admitted that it was she who had obtained the two Brownings that were found in rue Fessart. Nevertheless, Victor wrote her a heartfelt farewell letter, finishing, "I must ask a favour of you my love—never, never go back into that milieu". She took his advice and six months later sold, for an unknown sum, her *Souvenirs d'Anarchie* to the liberal daily, *Le Matin*, which tended to treat her erstwhile comrades as pathetic, tragic or comic figures.

On 3rd April 1913, the Supreme Court rejected all the appeals, while simultaneously in La Santé, prison warders made a thorough search of the condemned men's cells where they discovered some knives and a quantity of poison, the latter presumably ready for use in anticipation that their appeals would be rejected. The next day the cells were emptied of everything except the palliasses and the four men were forced into wearing straightjackets. Immediately they went on hunger strike in protest. The issue was only resolved two weeks later, due to an incident involving another prisoner, the anarchist Lacombe, now in custody.

Typically, Lacombe had only turned to thieving after finding it extremely difficult to find work due to bosses' reluctance to employ a known anarchist. The previous September in Aubrais he had shot and killed a pursuing ticket collector, and two months later he had done the same to a postmaster in Bezons. He took refuge with Ducret, aka Erlebach, who ran a libertarian bookshop in Passage de Clichy, but after a police raid in which he escaped unseen out the back, he returned, interrogated Ducret, and then shot him as an informer. It was in February during the mass trial of the illegalists that hundreds of detectives acting on false tip-offs laid siege to three houses in the suburbs of Paris where they supposed him to be hiding. In fact, Lacombe's end did not come in a 'Bonnot Gang' style siege; on 11th March he was spotted gazing at a booth in a local fair in La Villette, and quickly overpowered by three detectives. In his pockets they found two Browning semiautomatics and some sticks of dynamite.

On 16th April Lacombe tried a daring escape from La Santé by getting onto the roof during morning exercise. Unfortunately he could find no way off. He spent two hours up there hurling slates at the warders and officials, ignoring his lawyer Boucheron's request for him to come down, while the prisoners, their faces pressed against the iron bars of the windows shouted, "*Vive Lacombe! Vive l'anarchie!*" Finally he careered along the roof and hurled himself into space, avoiding the mattresses that had been placed below by the warders. His brief testament was published in *Le Libertaire* under the headline 'Death of a Rebel': "I would have liked to eat black bread with black hands, but I was forced to eat white bread with red hands. . . . Fate bears the responsibility for all this. It was the whole set of circumstances which arose, and with which I was faced that made me kill people of my own class, exploited like me, but ignorant and too zealous in defending the interests of their masters. I consider them as guilty as myself. I regret having killed workers, but aren't they made to kill each other patriotically on the battlefield or during strikes?"

After his death, the regime at La Santé was reviewed and the straightjackets were removed from the condemned men, Callemin, Soudy, Monier and Dieudonné. The executions were now set for 22nd April, at dawn.

Their only hope now lay in making a plea for mercy to the newly incumbent President of the Republic, Poincaré, Fallières' successor. Alone of the four, Raymond refused to sign the plea. Soudy's mother wrote her own appeal for clemency on behalf of her son who was barely out of his teens. Victor Kibalchich also made an appeal and was supported by, amongst others, the socialist Deputy, Jean Longuet, with a favourable appraisal by the Governor of Melun prison, where he had been moved.[5]

Meanwhile, in their cells at the Conciergerie, the four condemned men endeavoured to complete the writing of their reminiscences, memoirs, wills and letters. Dieudonné wrote short sketches of the four major participants—Bonnot, Garnier, Callemin and Carouy—in which he said that Raymond was the most 'cultured' and morally superior. Bonnot he saw as a professional, like Carouy, who would only kill in the last resort, as opposed to Garnier who was the one to kill first, without feeling, determined to leave no witnesses—it was on this point that he argued with Bonnot. Yet Dieudonné felt that Garnier, who loved children and helped old people, was superior in his relations with his peers than Bonnot, who only had friends of occasion, always anarchists. All the same, Garnier tended to discount people who did not share his opinions; he talked little, but sensibly, and liked to discuss ideas with Carouy and Bonnot with whom he felt an affinity. He was the only one of the four who did not like reading, except for newspapers. They were all vegetarians and water-only drinkers, and fond of sport, although Bonnot had more of a penchant for music halls, dances, cafés and casinos than the others; nevertheless, they all loved the theatre. It was clear from these observations that Dieudonné had spent a fair bit of time in the company of the

---

5   Victor's plea was rejected by the Minister of Justice.

gang in the months of January and February 1912, with the unfortunate consequence that he too was roped into the conspiracy, and was now awaiting execution.

Raymond wrote his own story of the gang's activities, which was later scrutinized in the Parisian paper *Le Journal*. Despite his assertion that, "I am not one of those who think it's necessary to 'dress up' the truth" (written in a covering note asking his lawyer to arrange publication), the account almost certainly exaggerated the importance of his own role, although several parts rang true. He was completely unrepentant, and boasted, "We were more brutal and less hypocritical, that's all". Raymond spent his last few hours reading the *Revue des Deux Mondes*.

Élie Monier drew up his will: the collected works of the enlightenment philosopher, Jean-Jacques Rousseau, went to his sister for the education of her son, while the rest of his books, including Darwin's *The Origin of Species* and a complete edition of Rabelais, went to the Paris Municipal Library. Lastly, he wrote:

"I leave to society my ardent desire that one day, not far off, a maximum of comfort and independence will prevail in the provision of social needs, so that in one's leisure time an individual may be better able to devote himself to whatever makes life more beautiful, to education, and all manner of science.

"I leave my revolver, seized in the room at the time of my arrest, to a Paris museum, in memory of an innocent victim of an affair which threw the country into a state of terror; and, if the present will is executed, I desire that on the pistol-grip be clearly inscribed the words of a great martyr—'Thou shalt not kill'".

André Soudy, having completed his short autobiography, pencilled an even more ironic will:

I, Soudy, condemned to death by the representatives of social vengeance, otherwise known as justice, acknowledging that it is my expected duty, and having finalized the details of my last wishes, do hereby make it known to all sentient persons:

1. I bequeath to Monsieur Etienne, Minister of War, my jemmys, my marmosets and my skeleton keys, to help him open the way to social militarism through the 'Three-year law';

2. My cerebral hemispheres to the Dean of the Faculty of Medicine;

3. To the Anthropological Museum, my skull, for which I order an exhibition to take place, with profits going to the *soupes communistes*;

4. My hair to the Union of Barbers and workers conscious or inebriated; hair which will be put up for public sale and for the benefit of the cause . . . and out of solidarity;

5. Finally, I bequeath to the paper *l'anarchie* my autograph, so that the priests and apostles of the philosophy may make use of it to the profit of their cynical individuality.

In the margin he scrawled a poem, entitled *La Vie?*

Paradis éphémère
Que voile la sombre chimère
Et que couvre un réalisme trompeur
Faire de souffrance et de douleur.[6]

On the afternoon of 20th April the bolts were thrown back and the door to cell number thirteen was pulled open. Dieudonné had been reprieved. For him, as for Metge, it was to be *la guillotine sèche*, meaning transportation to French Guiana, and in all probability Devil's Island: a life, if not a death, sentence. The time set for the execution of the other three men was brought forward twenty-four hours, to the following morning at dawn.

An incessant drizzle was falling over Paris as the first of the spectators began to gather around midnight. All streets around the prison were blocked by a triple barrier, while numerous detectives were sent to infiltrate the crowd in case of trouble; the time of the executions had been brought forward precisely to avoid such a possibility. But this time there were to be no masses of outraged workers furiously battling with the police as had happened at the execution of Liabeuf three and a half years before. Extra police from the Xth *arrondissement*, four brigades of reserves and a squadron of Republican Guards were drafted in to maintain order. At 2.30 am the guillotine (of a new type—with a silencer)

---

6 This doesn't translate well but means something along the lines of: 'Life? / Ephemeral paradise / Hiding the dark chimera / And concealing a deceptive reality / Made up of suffering and sorrow'.

was erected on the pavement of the tree-lined boulevard Arago, and the public executioner, Deibler, tested its working. Just before midnight the Préfecture de Police issued a special invitation card to two hundred selected guests, which entitled them to watch the executions at close hand, among them being, of course, Guichard, Gilbert, Lescouvé, Robert and Colmar.

As dawn broke, there was a sudden flurry of activity inside the prison. At 4.10 am the doors to cells seven, eleven and twelve were unlocked and a warder growled, "Get up, let's go", followed by a deputy of the public prosecutor's office who monotoned to Soudy and Monier, "Your plea is rejected".

André Soudy asked for a cup of coffee and two croissants, and enquired whether his comrades had been pardoned. Following a reply in the negative, he soliloquized, "I haven't got the taking of any human life on my conscience. Things have come to a sorry end, but I'll have courage to the last. My poor mother!" He was shivering as he dressed himself, but explained, "like Mayor Bailly,[7] it's due to the cold". Lastly, before leaving the cell he added, "It's the best thing, it's better than the forced labour camp".

Raymond was asked by the Deputy Public Prosecutor if he had any revelations to make, but declared that he had nothing further to say. He scribbled a few lines on a piece of paper that he handed to his lawyer, Boucheron. Exiting the cell, he said aloud, "It's a day without a tomorrow", and then, "It's a fine thing, eh? The final agony of a man".

Monier declared that he too would have courage to the end, then shook hands with some of the detectives from the Sûreté who were there. As he walked along the corridor, he mused, "I suspected yesterday that it would be this morning. . . . I had a wonderful dream that I was making love". He addressed his lawyer; "Embrace Marie Besse for me".

As the prisoners washed, Raymond asked for a glass of water, while Monier turned down the offer of a glass of rum, saying jocularly, "I don't want to get drunk". The three men were chained hand and foot then led out to the tumbril traditionally used to convey the condemned to the guillotine. They arrived in the boulevard Arago at 4.35 am. André Soudy, still shivering, was the first to mount the scaffold. He turned and said, "It's so cold . . . goodbye". Élie Monier replied, "So long".

---

7   Bailly was the Mayor of Paris executed during the Jacobin 'Terror' of 1793.

Soudy was told to lie flat, and then secured in place. The blade fell, and his severed head tumbled into the basket. It was Raymond's turn next. He gave one of his habitual sardonic smiles and, addressing the few men gathered around the guillotine, repeated "It's nice, eh? A man's final agony". Then he too was decapitated. Lastly came Élie Monier, who said in a loud voice, "Goodbye to you all *Messieurs* and to Society as well". The blade fell for the third time.

Callemin's body was taken to the Faculty of Medicine as he had wished, to be used in the furtherance of scientific research; Monier was buried in the cemetery of Ivry-Parisien, and Soudy's body was claimed by his mother for burial in Beaugency, his birthplace.

14. The End of Anarchism?

*Too often, especially in the more responsible circles, we rush
to belittle the act of rebellion . . . we become disturbed by
problems of conscience, made uneasy about the threat of
reaction, distressed by residual evangelism, tormented by
the burning need, if not of confusing ourselves in the limbo of
common morality, certainly of lessening the contrasts.*
—Luigi Galleani

IN THE WAKE of the mass trial of the 'Bonnot Gang' came the theoretical autopsy of the corpse of illegalism. The bourgeois press had
used the 'outrages' of the illegalists as a stick to beat anarchism as a
whole. It was argued that the trial of these particular anarchists had
put anarchism in the dock, and that modern anarchism tended towards just such a conclusion as the practice of *Les Bandits Tragiques*.
Some papers said that revolutionaries as a whole were to blame for
being against property and law in the first place, and it was only to be
expected that *Humanité*, the daily paper of the Socialist Party *arriv-
istes*, had shown itself, "more vile, more police-like than the bourgeois
rags".

Until the advent of the Bonnot Gang, the anarchist-individualists
had been largely ignored or ridiculed as inconsequential by the wider anarchist movement, but now they were forced to devote time and
space to demonstrating that illegalism and anarchism had nothing in
common. Jean Grave's rather staid weekly, *Temps Nouveaux*, was in the
vanguard of the anti-illegalist backlash, and printed the most virulent
article, by Marmande, in April 1913:

"For many years, shielded by a most surprising impunity, the chiefs,
pontiffs and orators of the milieu have encouraged a hatred of work, a
disdain for love, and trickery and cheap jibes at the expense of friendship. They celebrate the beauties and joys of forging money, crafty thefts
and nocturnal burglaries.

"They are no longer anarchists—Alas! They never were! Their lives, full of errors, blunders and wild gestures, followed by obsessions, humiliations, desperate escapes, spluttering lies, mental torments and physical discomfort, I pity, having at first hated them".

Jean Grave modified the position that they were never anarchists, by declaring that, "at the moment when they committed this act [robbery] they ceased to be anarchists. Such actions have nothing anarchist about them, they are actions which are purely and simply bourgeois". In the words of André Girard, another regular columnist for *Temps Nouveaux*, they were, "the ideal of worthy sons of that bourgeoisie for whom the ideal pleasure and luxury was once formulated by Guizot: Enrich yourselves!" The same line was pursued by syndicalists such as Alfred Rosmer (*Vie Ouvrière*) and Gustave Hervé (*Guerre Sociale*) who agreed that "their actions proceeded from the capitalist mentality, which has as its end the amassing of money and leading a parasitic life". The illegalists were "pseudo-anarchists who dishonour the fine anarchist ideal", and as killers of those, "poor buggers working for a hundred and fifty francs a month", wrote Hervé, "they disgust me. Frankly, I prefer Jouin".

Whatever the 'chiefs and pontiffs' of the movement thought, the illegalists, as far as they themselves were concerned, thought and acted as anarchists.

As for saying that "their actions proceeded from a capitalist mentality"; surely, if anything, their actions proceeded from the social reality of the unfortunate situation in which they found themselves, their concrete experiences of the bourgeois world. Bonnot might have been wryly referred to by his friends as *Le Bourgeois*, but the whole history of his life and death, and that of the other illegalists, showed that they were proletarians forced to struggle for survival in a hostile world dominated by a ruling class noted for its brutality.

To equate working class criminals, born into a class which owned nothing but its labour power, with unscrupulous bourgeois, born into a class which owned everything, was arguably a clumsy sleight-of-hand that conveniently ignored the class question, and blotted out the harsh truth of social reality. If the bandits aimed to become bourgeois, surely the same could be said of honest employees working regularly for a wage, most of whom must have dreamt of escaping from a life of relative poverty. But, of course, not all workers became bandits, despite similar experiences of these harsh social realities, for the subjective element was still needed. The anarchist-individualist milieu, within which the theoretical bases of illegalism had been articulated, was perhaps forced into much more soul-searching and reflection than the other anarchists who had come up with the glib 'all crime is bourgeois' theory.

Most of the so-called 'theoreticians of illegalism' in fact denied that they had ever been such, or claimed to have been grossly misinterpreted. The journal *l'anarchie* had, "never wanted to say that it was advantageous to be a burglar . . . the illegalist theories have been badly understood, and above all badly carried out". Armand had attempted to clarify his position in 1912: "I wish to assert most strongly that unrestrained illegalism is not the fatal or unavoidable outcome of individualist anarchism put into practice on the economic terrain, the individualist-anarchist philosophy can lead as a last resort to illegalism (which is itself only one of the forms of a-legalism) . . . but the 'illegalism' which I expounded did not have as its final end the appropriation of hard cash for the use of the illegalist alone". Mauricius reflected that although "illegalism is explainable and justifiable perhaps in theory, in practice isn't it just suicide?" Lorulot, the first editor of *l'anarchie* to break publicly with the illegalists, wrote the front-page farewell article in the week of execution:

"I wonder if we haven't some unintentional, indirect responsibility in these hecatombs. Not in preaching illegalism, something which few of us did (may it please our detractors) but in calling to the struggle, to revolt, to life, characters who were morbid or impatient, simplistic or unbalanced. But no, it is the fate of the human word to be sown on varied soils and for there to arise the most different of fruits".

In other words, the argument seemed to be that most individualist-anarchists didn't preach illegalism, but if they did (and only as a theoretical justification) the apparent consequences were due to personality disorders, misunderstood theories, unforeseen consequences and bad practice. Yet even the liberal sociologist, Émile Michon, found that the young illegalists, rather than being 'unbalanced', were intelligent, thoughtful and articulate. If they had misunderstood the theory or badly practiced it, this really begged the question, what was the correct theory and the correct practice? Naturally, 'unforeseen consequences' was the problem with all theories, and Lorulot's rather philosophical conclusion that it was the "fate of the human word to be sown on varied soils" meant that it was always possible to abnegate all responsibility if one's theories didn't turn out as one wished.

Victor Kibalchich was the one who suffered most for his propaganda, but was he no more than an unwilling victim forced to succumb to peer-group pressure and eulogize the bandits because he knew them to be his old comrades? Given that he had already sung the praises of Sokolov and the Sidney Street revolutionaries, it seems more likely that he simply wanted to make a name for himself as the most 'combative' writer in the milieu. He had got away with some quite outrageous statements in *Révolté*, but the French authorities were not as lenient as the Belgians: he, Lionel, Lanoff and Fourcade all ended up in prison. Victor perhaps thought that as he'd never practiced illegalism he would get away with it, and so desperately sought to show that a gulf separated the 'intellectual' from the 'illegalist'—indeed, it was for this very reason that he and the illegalists had parted company. Naturally, Victor was angry at being judged for what others had done, but unfortunately his bitterness at the whole affair—the execution of Raymond, his oldest friend, the suicide of Édouard, the deaths of André and René, and the separation from Rirette, his lover—coloured his judgement, so that his later interpretation of events was twisted into a harsh condemnation of his former comrades.

Thus, with only a few exceptions, the entire anarchist movement came out against illegalism. Lionel, however, tried to go back to basics, and questioned the primacy imparted by many anarchists to the collectivity at the expense of the individual:

"The anarchist is in a state of legitimate defence against society. Hardly is he born than the latter crushes him under a weight of laws, which are not of his doing, having been made before him, without him, against him. Capital imposes on him two attitudes: to be a slave or to be a rebel; and when, after reflection, he chooses rebellion, preferring to die proudly, facing the enemy, instead of dying slowly of tuberculosis, deprivation and poverty, do you dare to repudiate him?"

"Besides, the revolution that you preach isn't it the collective rebellion, the collective crime? And this crime that you've justified in so many admirable theories, why do you reject it when it is individual?"

"If the workers have, logically, the right to take back, even by force, the wealth that is stolen from them, and to defend, even by crime, the life that some want to tear away from them, then the isolated individual must have the same rights".

This was what separated the individualist anarchists from the rest: they denied the primacy of the collectivity. It was this question that was at the heart of much of the copious theorizing and moralizing. For instance, the moral commandment 'Thou shalt not kill' is upheld theoretically by both anarchism and capitalism; the latter, society, is nominally against killing, yet has laws with the death penalty for murder, allows its agents to kill in certain circumstances, and socially organizes death through the enforced conditions of existence of the working class—and all this is done in the name of the collectivity, society as a whole. At the same time, anarchists believe that it is wrong to kill except in specific situations (the assassination of dictators, agents of state repression, for example) or in the general conditions of revolution, in which revolutionaries will probably be forced to kill other proletarians who still defend the interests of the ruling class. In other words, there is no absolute morality of thou shalt not kill, whether for anarchists, capitalists or most human beings; killing is legitimate so long as it is based on the primacy of the collectivity—either killing on behalf of the masses, or in defence of society. This is why Stirner's argument, that behind the facade, society is basically organized violence, and that there should be no objection to individuals fighting back, has some appeal. If politics is the continuation of warfare by other means (to invert Clausewitz' dictum) then the Bonnot Gang simply went back to the basics of class warfare, albeit in a brutal, take-no-prisoners manner.

If the illegalists-to-be threw in their lot with the anarchist-individualists (and most of them did so in their teens) it was because, in the words of Victor Serge, this milieu in particular "demanded everything of us and offered everything to us".

The anarchist-individualist revolt was immediate, it was not a question of awaiting the improbability of the New Jerusalem—for this new generation of anarchists the revolution was to be lived here and now: deferred gratification was a religious, bourgeois concept. And so, from their various locations—Lyon, Brussels, Charleroi, Alais—the illegalists were drawn inexorably to Paris, that priming ground for revolution, the city that had lived through the revolutions of 1789 and 1848, the Commune of 1871, the anarchist 'terror' of the 1890s, and which was then to witness the intensity of the illegalist revolt.

Yet, if the illegalists found many of their thoughts and feelings reflected and articulated in this milieu, it was the particular oppressiveness of French society that provided a most fertile soil for these ideas to take root. The illegalists were proletarians who had nothing to sell but their labour power, and nothing to discard but their dignity; if they disdained waged work, it was because of its compulsive nature. If they turned to illegality it was due to the fact that 'honest toil' only benefited the employers and often entailed a complete loss of dignity, while any complaints resulted in the sack; to avoid starvation through lack of work it was necessary to beg or steal, and to avoid conscription into the army many of them had to go on the run.

Bonnot's life-history (ten years longer than most of the others), was a classic story of an ordinary working class lad who, after the normal youthful escapades, wanted to settle down into a decent job, get married and have a family. He was frustrated not just by 'bad luck' but by his inability to wield any power over his own conditions of existence. His early flirtation with anarchism, which might once have been dismissed simply as youthful exhuberance, now became a fully fledged *liaison dangereux*, but although his turn to crime may well have been influenced by his newfound anarchist contacts, he must have felt that he had very little to lose; he'd worked for years, done his military service, tried to support a family, and what had he got at the end of it? Nothing. Ideas and theories on the one hand, social experience on the other, it was a dialectical process that produced illegalism, and each individual's particular set of circumstances that produced illegalists.

Their attitudes were more or less formed before they congregated in Paris, although the concentration of comrades in Romainville doubtless reinforced their ideas, and the arguments between the 'activists' and the 'intellectuals' showed that the former were hardly keen pupils eager to learn from their ideological mentors. If Bonnot and Garnier's scribbled notes contained phrases lifted from the pages of *l'anarchie*, this was more a case that they saw their own feelings reflected in print. Yet besides their obvious motivation, they might have lacked opportunity had it not been for Garnier's driving energy and the chance arrival of Bonnot from Lyon. It's worth reflecting that if Bonnot had not been forced to throw in his lot with the Paris comrades, they might have all remained 'nobodies' rather than members of the infamous Bonnot Gang, a gang which, despite its spectacular actions, always had something of an amateur air about it.

Despite the backtracking of the 'theoreticians', the affair had its effect on the movement: the 'outrages' of the Bonnot Gang were blamed in their entirety on the individualist current by the wider anarchist movement. In August 1913 the Fédération Communiste-Anarchistes held a congress in the Union building on rue Cambronne. René Hemme (Mauricius), editor of *l'anarchie*, and other individualists who tried to put their point of view were cut short by an interruption from Martin of *Le Libertaire*: "Between you and us there can be no possible understanding"; Jean Grave threatened to leave if they did not, so the individualists walked out, declaring the congress authoritarian and anti-anarchist. For their part, the conference condemned all forms of individualism as bourgeois and incompatible with anarcho-communism. While they were in session, *Le Matin* was daily publishing instalments of Rirette's memoirs, which had begun: "I wish to repair the harm that others have done. May these memoirs stop those who, from bad example or improvident design, have strayed onto the slippery slope and are destined to become the all-too-easily-smashed playthings of illegalist illusions; for behind illegalism there are not even any ideas. Here's what one finds there: spurious science, lust, the absurd and the grotesque".

The anarchist-individualists were disgusted by this sell-out, but the damage was done; the activities of the illegalists were also held responsible for the apparent wave of reaction sweeping over France: "arrests and searches have become so frequent that they are hardly commented on; the police have prohibited several anarchist papers from being sold at railway stalls and shops". This, of course, ignored the general repression of the revolutionary and working class movements that had intensified since the *impasse* of the 1906 general strike, and the fact that, with a European war looking more and more on the cards, the French State needed forcibly to repress all those who might pose a threat to their mobilization plans. The appointment of Guichard as head of the Sûreté Nationale was indicative of the new mood of repression prior to the First World War, just as the 'new realism' of the Confédération Générale du Travail (CGT) was a response to their inability to counter it. However, the London-based journal *Freedom* indignantly located the cause of all this in "a number of individualists", who, "in the name of the 'right to live their lives' have committed a series of attacks on property accompanied by shooting and killing which has aroused widespread indignation among the people. The perpetrators claimed that their acts were the logical outcome of their anarchist ideas. The anarchist-communists considered, however, that these 'comrades' had as little right to their plunder as has a capitalist to the produce of the workers. But the harm was done. Simple-minded young comrades were often led away by the illegalists' apparent anarchist logic; outsiders simply felt disgusted with anarchist ideas and definitely stopped their ears to any propaganda". Kropotkin was probably the writer of this piece, taking his cue from the resolutions passed at the FCA congress the previous month; it was intended to hold an International Anarchist Congress in London the following August, in 1914. Mauricius was still intent on going, but individualists decided, collectively, not to attend and denied Mauricius any right to 'represent' them. In fact the congress was never held as, on the first of that month, the German armed forces mobilized, and so began the greatest slaughter that had yet been organized in world history.

All over Europe, workers went to war in a spirit of enthusiasm; any anger, boredom or frustration that they may have felt for society was resolved in this legitimized release of tension which channelled hostility onto an easily recognizable group. In France the war was presented as a classless national struggle which united bourgeois and proletarian alike, and this was reflected politically in the *Union Sacrée* of the parties of right, left and centre. The socialists, who had won a majority of seats in the Chamber of Deputies, abandoned the idea of working class internationalism (as did their fraternal counterparts abroad) and made common-cause with the bourgeoisie.[1] Throughout Europe the ideology of class war was abandoned for the practice of imperialist war. Many socialists complained that, faced with the pro-war hysteria of the masses, they had no other choice, and besides, it was only a 'defensive' war. Even the anarchists were not immune to the war fever and the argument that a victory for German imperialism would set back the revolutionary process: Kropotkin, Grave, Hervé, Paul Reclus and Charles Malato, who had not hesitated to condemn the Bonnot Gang for killing fellow proletarians and robbing banks, aligned themselves behind the Allies—Russia, France and Great Britain—who, in turn, did not hesitate to squander sixty thousand lives in a single day if it aided their fight for imperialist dominance. Despite the years of resistance to militarism, most syndicalist and anarchist militants of military age went to the colours without

---

1   The popular and antimilitarist leader of the French Socialist Party, Jean Jaurès, was assassinated in a Paris cafe on 31 July 1914, neutering the socialist leadership. The assassin was acquitted by a patriotic jury in 1919, but later fled France for Ibiza. Republican militia, rumoured to be members of the Federación Anarquista Ibérica (FAI) shot him in July 1936.

resistance; the State did not even need to round up all those 'subversives' on the *Carnet B*—a list of those thought to pose a threat to the effective mobilization of working class support for the war. Lorulot, Armand, Sébastien Faure, most individualists and anarcho-communists stood their ground, as did a handful of mainly foreign revolutionaries, such as Lenin, Rosa Luxemburg and Karl Liebknecht. But the bulk of the European revolutionary movement capitulated wholesale in the face of the reality of war.

The Bonnot Gang had already faced this type of hysteria, as well as the latest weapons of war—machine-guns and melinite—at the sieges of Choisy and Nogent. In the light of the appalling barbarism of the Great War, the 'outrages' of the illegalists seem very minor; it could be argued that society was enraged by their actions not because they had killed individuals or stolen property, but because they were not authorized to do so. If, rather than dying behind mattresses or beneath the guillotine, they had died in the trenches, they would have been lauded as heroes, no matter how many fellow workers they'd killed. It is perhaps unlikely that the illegalists would have gone willingly to war given their contempt and cynicism for the 'stupid masses'; if they had gone underground to escape conscription in peacetime, they were hardly likely to join up now as slaves in uniform killing other workers on orders from their officers. The illegalist revolt was fought without illusions as a negation of the State and society, and an affirmation of the self, realized through a duel to the death with the agents of the former. Unfortunately, 'living their lives' meant, in a topsy-turvy world, doing so at the expense of others, but they were no more trapped within the logic of capital than the rest of the population. After all, even the 'creative' side of the revolution, those working in unions, cooperatives, soup kitchens, collectives, in campaigns and for newspapers, etc, were forced to some extent to compromise with the ruling order of things, the economic variant of compromise being syndicalism, the political one, socialism.

If the illegalists felt that they could only assert themselves through violence, they still needed to make use of the latest technology such as automatic firearms and fast cars to give them, albeit briefly, an edge over the forces of the State; they even provided themselves with potassium cyanide to give them power over their manner of death. They remained defiant to the end. In court they refused to admit to their crimes, preferring to spin out the game until the last possible moment—we admit nothing, we dare you to prove it! The 'tragedy' of the gang lay in the fact that while people identified, to some extent, with their revolt, the ultimate outcome was known in advance—that they would kill and be killed. Yet despite the attempts of the bourgeois, socialist and anarchist press to deprecate illegalism, the Bonnot Gang became popular working class heroes, and probably the most well-known anarchists ever in France.

Some historians have seen in illegalism a reaction to the 'downturn' in class struggle after the defeats of 1908 and 1910, just as the anarchist 'terrorism' of the 1890s can be considered a prelude to an 'upturn'. This would dovetail neatly with the scheme that anarchists rushed into the *syndicats* and *bourses du travail* in 1894, but finally became disenchanted with the CGT's reformism after 1910 and drifted away into more 'marginal' activities. But there was never any simple advance from anarcho-communism to anarcho-syndicalism, or turn from 'illegal' methods to open ones; various currents and tactics of anarchism existed side by side throughout the period. Anarchists were always closely associated with working class struggle, and played an important role in the creation of class organizations in the 1870s and '80s—they did not suddenly enter these organizations as a response to the 'Wicked Laws' of 1894. The class struggle itself of course took various forms, and criminal activity could be a part of it, sometimes class-conscious, sometimes not. The illegalists wedded together the 'natural criminality' resulting from one's socio-economic position as a member of the exploited class, with the theoretical affirmation of illegality valorized by anarchists. In this they differed both from 'straight' criminals who simply wanted to make money, and from anarchist intellectuals who only made propaganda.

As a theory, illegalism was well-grounded in basic anarchist ideas: the legitimacy of re-appropriation, the primacy of the socio-economic sphere over the narrowly political, direct action rather than representation, the emphasis on freedom of the individual and the immediacy of revolution. Nevertheless, even Marius Jacob, the famous anarchist burglar, considered illegalism to be "fundamentally an affair of the temperament rather than of doctrine. That is why it cannot have any educative effect on the working masses as a whole". The illegalists did not really consider the educational aspect of their acts, being more concerned with their individual revolt against society; temperamentally, they were quite different from each other, although they all agreed on one thing—this society held no future for them.

One young man, Émile Bachelet, who had lived only a few yards from the *Causeries Populaires* in Montmartre, and who had been, "irresistably drawn by the ambience of the milieu", recalled: "Over several years, I lived this 'intense life', and there I met a few of those whose names became, sadly, famous—Raymond-La-Science, Octave Garnier, 'Simentoff' above all. I knew them well enough to be able to say that the *Bandits Tragiques* were neither more wicked, nor more cynical, nor more rebellious than any of us. But perhaps they had more courage in deciding to live what we were content only to contemplate".

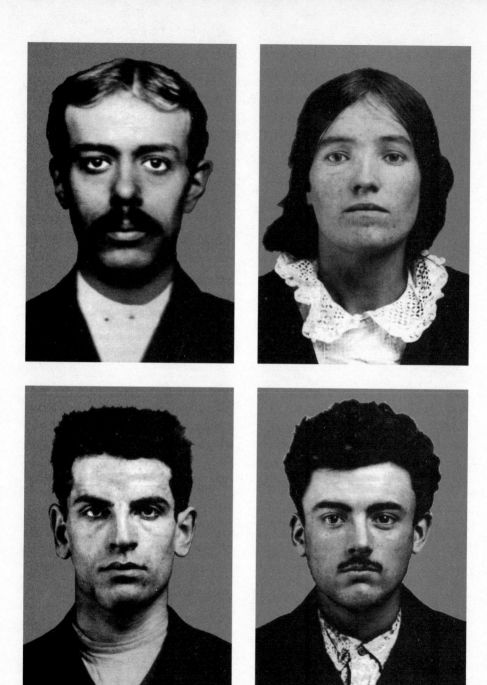

Crozat de Fleury (top left), a middle class fence for the rue Ordener bonds, sentenced to five years. Barbe Le Clech (top right), charged with receiving jewellery from Metge, her lover. Poyer (bottom left) and Bénard (bottom right), who robbed the gun shop in boulevard Hausmann and supplied the gang with Winchester rifles.

Epilogue

Soudy, Callemin and Monier were not the last victims in this story:

Judith Thollon, her husband and Henri Petitdemange had already been put on trial in Lyon in 1912 after Bonnot's death and convicted of receiving stolen goods. But whereas the two men got one year each, Judith was sentenced to no less than four, in revenge for the fact that not only had she been Bonnot's lover, but she had refused to disown him in the course of the trial. Judith died in prison.

Marie Besse, shop assistant and Élie Monier's young lover, was allowed to visit him one last time prior to his execution. But she never recovered from the shock of his execution and passed away just two months later.

Barbe Le Clech, girlfriend of Metge, was acquitted at trial of receiving stolen goods. She was released only to die of tuberculosis before the end of the year.

There were also more positive outcomes:

Of the other women on trial, Marie Vuillemin went back to Belgium, only dying in 1963, while Anna Dondon, who had avoided prosecution, lived to the ripe old age of ninety-five, dying in 1979.

Of those who were transported to French Guiana, no less than three of the four managed to escape:

Alphonse Rodriguez, acquitted at the mass trial of the illegalists, was immediately sent to the Lille Assises where he was convicted of counterfeiting and sentenced to eight years hard labour. Ironically, given that his statement helped convict Dieudonné, he then joined him and De Boe and Metge in the penal colony in French Guiana. In 1920 he escaped via Venezuela and made his way to the USA from where he contributed articles to Armand's *L'En Dehors*. Returning to Europe in 1932 he spent the Second World War in neutral Switzerland. Rodriguez had his memoirs published as *Confessions et révelations d'un anarchiste authentique*. He died in Paris in 1969.

Jean De Boe had almost served his sentence when he decided to escape, via Surinam, from where he headed back to Belgium in 1922. He resumed his work as a typographer and took part in strikes in 1925 and 1930. In 1937 he went to aid the Republicans in Spain, and adopted the two daughters of a fallen comrade. As a confirmed anarchist he was sought by the Gestapo during the German occupation in World War Two but went into hiding. He died in 1947.

Eugène Dieudonné, transported aboard the prison ship *La Martinière* with De Boe, was waved off from the quayside by his wife Louise. He made three attempts to escape, the second only got him as far as the coast of Guiana (in itself an achievement) but the third took him to Brazil and freedom. A vociferous press campaign on his behalf, above all by the journalist Albert Londres, resulted in him being given a presidential pardon. Returning to France in 1927, he found Louise still waiting for him. After writing of his experience of prison in *La Vie des Forçats*, published in 1930, he opened a small cabinet-maker's shop on the rue du Faubourg St Antoine and lived a quiet life. He died in August 1944, just as Paris was liberated from the Nazis.

Marius Metge served eighteen years of his life sentence, being released in 1931. Still a good cook, he decided to stay in Cayenne, where he worked in a restaurant. He died of a fever in 1933.

Others stayed in France:

Antoine Gauzy, convicted at trial of harbouring Bonnot, also received much strong support from some sections of the press who thought that the evidence supported his innocence. He was released in July 1913 not long after the conclusion of the trial, only to be shot three times by a former detective of the Sûreté still enraged by the murder of Jouin and shooting of Inspector Colmar. He recovered from his wounds, and, anarchist to the end, refused to press charges. He died in Paris in 1963.

Louis Rimbault had avoided the trial and imprisonment by feigning madness. One of the indicators of this supposed madness was his insistance that Bonnot was "a great man whose name will pass into legend!" He was released from hospital and continued his quest for personal liberation founding the vegan, naturist colony *Terre Liberée* in Luynes, close to Tours in 1923. A confirmed individualist all his life, he eventually found the term 'anarchist' too restrictive and declared he was no longer one. He died in 1949.

Rirette Maîtrejean sold a story about her experiences with the illegalists to the Parisian daily newspaper *Le Matin* who published them in August 1913. This did not endear her to her former comrades. She married Victor Kibalchich in Melun prison in August 1915, being allowed one hour together. They did not meet again until his release in 1917 when he was exiled from French territory and went to Barcelona. Being unable financially to support her two daughters, Rirette returned to Paris. They divorced after Victor left for Russia, but they maintained a lively correspondence, Rirette deprecating his acceptance of Bolshevism. She remained an anarchist, working as a *correcteuse* for *Libération* until her retirement. She died aged eighty in 1968.

Victor Kibalchich, served his full five-year term, yet continued to contribute articles to Émile Armand's anti-war magazines (using a new pseudonym, Victor Serge). On his release in early 1917 he was expelled from France and went to Barcelona where he witnessed the failure of the insurrection led by the anarcho-syndicalist CNT. Forced back to Paris he was arrested and interned as an undesirable alien in October 1917 just as the Bolshevik revolution took place. Despite offering to enlist in the Allied Army as a way of getting to Russia, he was not released until January 1919. Finally making it to Petrograd (formerly, and now once again, St Petersburg) soon after, he threw in his lot with the Bolsheviks, and became better known to the world as Victor Serge. Taking the side of Trotsky against Stalin he was lucky not to have been shot. Instead, he was exiled to Orenburg in central Asia, and then deported in 1936, after a determined press campaign in the West for his release. Among the many works confiscated by the NKVD secret police was his memoir of the French anarchist illegalists entitled *Les Hommes Perdues* (sadly still untraceable in the Moscow archives). Victor still maintained relations with anarchists in Western Europe, and, according to his son Vlady, even met up again with Eugène Dieudonné in Paris as well as Émile Armand. He managed to flee France in advance of the Nazi invasion in 1940, and so was one of the very few celebrated revolutionaries to have escaped the twin horrors of Stalinism and Fascism. A prolific writer, his novels are deserving of a wider audience. He died in Mexico in 1947.

Lastly, Lieutenant Fontan, hero of the siege of Choisy, and promoted to the rank of Captain, was one of over six million French casualties of 'The Great War', the outbreak of which the syndicalists, socialists and anarchists proved unable to prevent. He died in the mud and blood of the trenches like so many others, on the Somme, December 1914.

And the weapon that sparked that war? The 9mm Browning semi-automatic, the revolutionary's weapon of choice, wielded by Gavrilo Princip as he gunned down Archduke Franz Ferdinand in the streets of Sarajevo on 28 June 1914.

FN Model 1910.

Appendix 1

A letter from Lorulot to Armand about Kibalchich's conduct at the trial *[undated]*

My attitude to the trial of the bandits:

[. . .] M. Kibalchich said [at the trial]: "I am astonished that M. Lorulot has not been prosecuted as I have been. I am accused of having been the editor of *l'anarchie* and having known the 'Bandits'. Now, Lorulot has been, equally, at *l'anarchie* and he knew them like me. Why this difference in treatment?"

M. Kibalchich was in the dock with the accused. I was in the box as a witness in order to help the defence. Between him and me, therefore, argument was not possible. That's why I did not reply. Which doesn't mean I had nothing to say! Here is what I could have replied:

M. Kibalchich declares that he has always been an adversary of illegalism. *Untrue.* One may read in his article in *l'anarchie*, shortly after the rue Ordener outrage, *"Les bandits sont grands, les bandits sont beaux".*

For my part, I defy anyone who believes it to find ten lines written by me advocating illegalism. On the contrary, I wrote in *l'anarchie* (August 1911) in order to establish the *bankruptcy of illegalism.* And at that time M. Kibalchich (who edited *l'anarchie*) welcomed an article by Levieux in response to mine, which treated me as an honesty-freak, comparing me to Jean Grave and mocking my ideas, which he ridiculed.

Hence the truth is the opposite of Kibalchich's assertions. Of the two of us, he was the only one to have some sympathy for illegalism, *as the aforementioned facts prove.*

I had been editor of *l'anarchie*, it's true. But I had left the paper in June 1911, well before the affair of the rue Ordener. The first *coup* of the *Bande Tragique* took place in December 1911. I had therefore been away from *l'anarchie* for six months and had totally ceased all relations with those who would later come up before the courts (moreover, it is known that they were never my friends, and were, on the contrary, the principal cause of my departure from *l'anarchie*).

Therefore I see no grounds in all this to justify the thesis of M. Kibalchich.

Why should I have been prosecuted? Because I had known people who subsequently became criminals, and with whom I had never had any link? That is not tenable. They didn't prosecute M. Kibalchich because he had known the 'bandits' or because he had edited *l'anarchie*. They prosecuted him and found him guilty because he had received firearms, those from the burglary of an armoury, firearms from same source as those which were found on the bandits. These arms, therefore, established a link between Kibalchich and his co-defendants which the prosecution could make use of, whereas, against me, the law couldn't uncover a single material fact and wasn't even able to invoke, as one can see from above, the feeble 'subversive opinion' charge.

That is what Kibalchich didn't say, when he posed as an honest journalist, and when he broke solidarity, during the trial; of those in court with him.

That is what I didn't wish to reply! That's why I had nothing to say, preferring to remain proper and dignified to the end.

It would have been enough for me to have cried:

"But Kibalchich don't make fun of us! You find it amusing that I haven't been prosecuted and you're making insinuations that the law welcomes with pleasure, as it will bring into disrepute a militant and propagandist, perhaps the only one who has warned thoughtless youngsters to the dangers of illegalism! The only one who never advocated it! The only one who can't be reproached with having populated the penal colonies and the prisons! I was in the way, certainly, of the work of provocation which was under way in the anarchist milieu. What better way to get rid of me than to excite vile slanders, 'of which something always sticks'—so many men are stupid and evil . . ."

"So, M. Kibalchich, I wasn't prosecuted because there wasn't the slightest little thing to invoke against me. They never found any stolen revolvers at my place, and that's why I'm not sitting next to you!"

I didn't want to say that—and yet it was the only reply to make to a man of bad faith who attacked me. That is the dilemma which I found myself in. If I had talked like that, I would have supplied the law with weapons to use against him, helping his conviction. Never would I do such a thing.

André Lorulot

A letter from Victor Kibalchich about his conduct at the trial

Barcelona, 28 March 1917
My Dear Armand,

[. . .] I didn't repudiate anyone at the trial. I even had the thanks of R C[allemin] and all of the others. But it was they, playing the leading roles (alas!), who piteously repudiated themselves. RC denied being an anarchist, etc, etc. . . . I said, and I would willingly repeat it, that I was disgusted to see our ideas, so rich and beautiful, ending up in such a foul waste of youthful energy, in mud and blood. And that I was deeply aggrieved to suffer for such a cause. I haven't begged for sympathy from anyone. At any time. See the published accounts. I defended myself without compromising, too aggressively even. I concluded by asking to be judged, not for what others might have done but for my own acts and my own ideas. Raymond reproached me, it's true, with disapproving too strongly of the horror and nastiness which were in question. A thoughtless reproach, and exceedingly tactless since, feigning innocence and repudiating his so-called ideological errors of yesteryear, he should not have effected such a censure. However, no matter! Our ideas, for me, came before people who debased them; and even in front of a jury I think I have the right to make use of mine (so long as I don't wrong anyone).

I'm astonished to have to tell you things which you know very well. [. . .]

Victor

Appendix 2

A *chanson* by Raymond-La-Science, 1912

Designed to be sung in working class cafe style, these lyrics draw on the infamous bomb attack in 1892 when Émile Henry placed a bomb (inside a pot or 'marmite') at the offices of a mining company who were locked in a vicious struggle with the strikers of Carmaux. On discovery of the bomb an over-zealous police officer transported it to the local police station on the rue des Bons-Enfants where it exploded, killing four police officers. Émile Henry, son of a Communard, was later caught and executed. In keeping with his nickname, 'La Science', Raymond's conclusion is that the best friend of the proletariat is chemistry.

La Java des Bons-Enfants

Dans la rue des Bons-Enfants,
On vend tout au plus offrant.
Y avait un commissariat,
Et maintenant il n'est plus là.

Une explosion fantastique
N'en a pas laissé une brique.
On crût qu'c'était Fantômas,
Mais c'était la lutte des classes.

Un poulet zélé vint vite
Y porter une marmite
Qu'était à renversement,
Et la retourne imprudemment.

Le brigadier, l'commissaire,
Mêlés au poulet vulgaire

Partent en fragments épars,
Qu'on ramasse sur un buvard.

Contrairement à c'qu'on croyait,
Y'en avait qui en avaient.
L'étonnement est profond:
On peut les voir jusqu'au plafond.

Voilà bien ce qu'il fallait
Pour fair' la guerre aux palais.
Sach' que ta meilleure amie,
Proletair', c'est la chimie.

Les socialos n'ont rien fait
Pour abréger les forfaits
D'l'infamie capitaliste,
Mais heureusement vient l'anarchiste.

Il n'a pas de préjugés.
Les curés seront mangés.
Plus d'patries, plus d'colonies.
Et tout pouvoir, il le nie.

Encore quelques beaux efforts,
Et disons qu'on se fait fort
De régler radicalement
L'problème social en suspens.

Dans la rue des Bons-Enfants,
Viande à vendre au plus offrant.
L'avenir radieux prend place,
Et le vieux monde est à la casse!

A poem by Raymond-La-Science, 1912

While the lyrics above express Raymond's anger with injustice and give voice to his desire for vengeance, this poem, without a title, gives expression to the torment of a soul that was unable to live in a world of of its own choosing. It starts gently enough but becomes darker.

Il est des désirs qui frôlent le coeur
De leur caresse légère et fugace,
Comme la suave harmonie d'un choeur
Caresse l'air sans y laisser de traces.

Il est des désirs qui bercent longtemps
Le pauvre coeur de leur douces chimères,
Qui restent jeunes à travers le temps
Et qui éffacent les larmes amères.

Il est des désirs aux sombres desseins
Qui rôdent longtemps autour l'âme
Et qui peu à peu glissent dans son sein
Le feu de leurs attouchements infâmes.

Il est des désirs vagues et troublants
Qui font briller les yeux de feux étranges,
Comme en ces nuits d'été ou des rais blancs
Courent sur la mer en légères franges.

Il est des désirs qui, pleins de malheur,
Sanglotent sourdement dans le silence,
Qui brûlent les yeux et rongent le coeur,
Et qui, un jour, sombrent dans la démence.

Il est des désirs qui sont capricieux,
Bien rarement le réel les contente.
Il est des désirs qui sont trop precieux
Qui vivent et qui meurent dans l'attente.

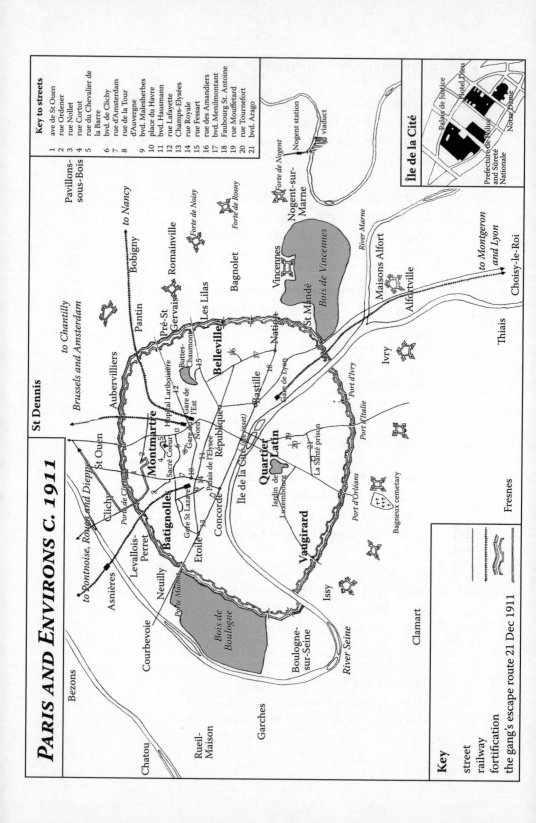

PARIS AND ENVIRONS C. 1911

St Dennis

Pavillons-sous-Bois

to Nancy

to Chantilly

Brussels and Amsterdam

Bobigny

Aubervilliers

Pantin

Pré-St Gervais

Romainville

Les Lilas

Forte de Noisy

Forte de Rosny

Forte de Nogent

Nogent station

viaduct

Nogent-sur-Marne

River Marne

Bagnolet

Bois de Vincennes

Vincennes

St Mandé

Maisons Alfort

Alfortville

Choisy-le-Roi

to Montgeron and Lyon

Thiais

Fresnes

Clamart

Garches

Rueil-Maison

Chatou

Bezons

Asnières

to Pontmoise, Rouen and Dieppe

Clichy

St Ouen

Porte de Clichy

Courbevoie

Levallois-Perret

Neuilly

Etoile

Porte Maillot

Bois de Boulogne

Boulogne-sur-Seine

Issy

River Seine

Port d'Orléans

Bagneux cemetary

La Santé prison

Jardin de Luxembourg

Vaugirard

Quartier Latin

Concorde

Palais de l'Elysée

Gare St Lazare

Batignolles

Montmartre

Sacré Coeur

Gare de l'Est

Gare du Nord

Hôpital Lariboisière

Buttes-Chaumont

Belleville

Nation

Bastille

Gare de Lyon

République

Île de la Cité (see inset)

Port d'Italie

Port d'Ivry

Ivry

Île de la Cité

Palais de Justice

Hôtel Dieu

Prefecture de Police and Sûreté Nationale

Notre Dame

Key

street

railway

fortification

the gang's escape route 21 Dec 1911

Sources

Archive collections consulted

1. *Archives de la Préfecture de Police,* rue Basse des Carmes, Paris 75005
    (Now on a new site at 25-27 rue Baudin, 93310 Le Pré-Saint-Gervais)
La Serie B (documents postérieurs à 1870):
Ba/134, Ba/135, Ba/136, Ba/137 (rapport quotidien du Préfet),
Ba/303, Ba/308, Ba/309 (rapports sur les anarchistes),
Ba/394 (menées des socialistes et anarchistes a Lyon),
Ba/752 (rapport mensuel du Préfet),
Ba/765, Ba/766, Ba/767, Ba/768, Ba/769 (rapports quotidiens),
Ba/894 (attentats anarchistes),
Ba/928 (Joseph Albert dit 'Libertad'), includes photos of Bonnot Gang
Ba/1360 (Chemins de fer du Nord),
Ba/1363 (Grève des Chemins de Fer),
Ba/1403 (Grève des terrasiers),
Ba/1498 (Rapports et informations concernent les menées anarchistes
    1899–1906),
Ba/1499 (Rapports et informations concernant les menées anarchistes
    1907–14),
Ba/1500, Ba/1501(anarchistes étrangers),
Ba/1502 (chiffres secrets de correspondence entre les anarchistes),
Ba/1503, Ba/1504 (surveillance des anarchistes),
Ba/1506 (rapports sur les groupes anarchistes),
Ba/1507, A/1508, A/1510 (Anarchistes en Angleterre, Allemagne,
    Belgique),
Ba/1643 (Bonnot, Garnier et Carouy), *l'anarchie,*
Ba/1693 (Police étrangères, Belgique).
*A prime source for l'anarchie, and the Bonnot Gang. The intelligence
    reports are essential reading. Surprisingly helpful staff.*

2. *Archives Nationales de France,* 60 rue des Francs-Bourgeois, 75003 Paris. (Now on a new site for documents post-1789 at 59 rue Guynemer, 93380 Pierrefitte-sur-Seine)

La Serie F7 (Police générale):

F7 12504-12518 agissements anarchistes 1880–1913,

F7 12554-12559 rapports quotidiens de la Préfecture de Police 1904–13,

F7 12522-12525 congrès divers, 1878–1914,

F7 12528-12534 Premier Mai, 1898–1911,

F7 12581-12601 Police des étrangers 1886–1906,

F7 12560-12565 Notes de police 1901–9.

F7 13053 Rapport sur les menées anarchistes.

Essential research material for La Belle Époque.

3. *The National Archives* (formerly the Public Records Office), Bessant Drive, Kew, TW9 4DU.

HO/45 Home Office records, concerning international action against anarchism, arms to Russian revolutionaries etc.

HO/144 Home Office records, anarchism 1904–1907, aliens and disturbances etc.

FO/371 Foreign Office records, includes activities of Russian nihilists in Paris, Lettish revolutionaries in London, and Indian anarchists in Paris, anarchist conference in Amsterdam etc. (1906–1912).

4. *International Institute for Social History,* Cruquiusweg 31, 1019 AT, Amsterdam (formerly at Kabelweg, 51)

AN series 55, 64, 69, 126, 246, 270, 320,

F fol A, *L'anarchie Paris* 1905–14

F fol.G, *La Guerre Sociale* 1912–13

F fol H, *L'Humanité* 1913

F 8*I, *L'Idée Libre* 1912

F fol I, *L'Intransigeant* 1912–13

F fol L, *Le Libertaire* 1913

F 8*T, *Les Temps Nouveaux* 1912–13

F 8*V, *Vie Ouvrière* 1912

F 8*H, *Hors du Troupeau* 1911–12, *Le Révolté* 1908–13

Superb collection, wonderful staff. Now on a new site.

Library collections accessed

1. *Bibliotheque Nationale de France*, 75706 Paris Cedex 13. Previously somewhat difficult for non-academics to access, and with a complicated retrieval system, now relocated to modern premises by the River Seine not far from Ivry. Excellent and accessible with super helpful staff, plus the fantastic online resouce Gallica (gallica.bnf.fr).
2. *Bibliotheque Public d'Information*, Centre Beaubourg, rue St Martin 75004, Paris. Very accessible and open to all.
3. *Library of the London School of Economics and Political Science*, 10 Portugal Street, London WC2A 2HD. The library has a very good anarchist collection.
4. *The British Library*, 96 Euston Road, London, NW1 2DB. Previously in the famous round Reading Room, the library has moved to the excellent new facilities on Euston Road.

Museums

Cité de l'Automobile (Collection Schlumpf), 15 rue de l'Épee, Mulhouse 68100, France. Fantastic collection, said to be the biggest in the world, which includes several De Dion Boutons and two beautiful Delaunay-Bellevilles from the period.

Wanted poster offering 100,000 francs reward for the arrests of Bonnot, Garnier and Carouy. The poster also depicts the "tragic toll", weapons and vehicles used and the haul of loot from the two bank robberies.

Bibliography

Contemporary newspapers

L'anarchie (1905–14, Paris)
La Croix (1911–13, Paris)
L'Echo de Paris (1911–13, Paris)
L'Eclair (1911–13, Paris)
L' Excelsior (1911, Paris)
Le Figaro (1911–13, Paris)
Le Gaulois (1911–13, Paris)
La Gazette des Tribuneaux (1913, Paris)
La Guerre Sociale (1912–13, Paris)
Hors du Troupeau (1911–12, Orleans)
L'Humanité (1913, Paris)
L'Idée Libre (1912, Paris)
L'Illustration (1912–13, Paris)
L'Intransigeant (1912–13, Paris)
Le Journal (1913, Paris)
Le Journal Officiel (1912, Paris)
Le Libertaire (1912, Paris)
Le Matin (1912–13, Paris)
Le Mercure de France (1913, Paris)
La Patrie (1912–13, Paris)
Le Petit Journal (1911–13, Paris)
Le Petit Parisien (1911–13, Paris)
La Presse (1911, Paris)
Le Révolté (1908–13, Brussels)
Les Temps Nouveaux (1912–13, Paris)
Vie Ouvrière (1912, Paris)

Books and Pamphlets

Adam, George, 'La Bande à Bonnot' in Guilleminault, Gilbert (ed.) *Le Roman Vrai de la 3e République* (1957).

Adam, George, *La Bande à Bonnot* (1963).

Armand, Émile, *Ce que sont les anarchistes individualistes* (Paris, 1923).

Armand, Émile, *L'anarchisme comme vie et activité individuelle*, (Romainville, 1911).

Armand, Émile, *L'illegaliste anarchiste, est-il notre camarade?* (1927).

Ashton-Wolfe, H, *The Underworld* (1926)

Becker, Émile, *La Bande à Bonnot* (1968).

Berlandstein, Lenard, *The Working People of Paris, 1871–1914* (1984).

Bernède, Arthur, *Bonnot, Garnier et Cie* (1933).

Carr, Reg, *Anarchism in France: The Case of Octave Mirbeau* (1977).

Carter, April, *The Political Theory of Anarchism* (1971).

Conrad, Joseph, *The Secret Agent* (1907).

Damiani, Gigi, *Cristo e Bonnot* (1927).

Darien, Georges, *Biribi* (1897).

Darien, Georges, *Le Voleur* (1898).

Dieudonné, Eugène, *La Vie des Forçats* (1930).

Dumas-Vorzet, F., *La Bande à Bonnot* (1930).

Dupeux, Georges, *French Society 1789–1970* (1976).

Duplay, Maurice, 'La Bande à Bonnot', in *Historia* (1961).

Duval, Clément, *Memorie autobiografiche* (1917).

Ego, *Illégalisme et* Légalisme (éditions de l'anarchie, 1912).

Fleming, Marie, *The Anarchist Way to Socialism* (1979).

France, Anatole, *Les dieux ont soif* (1912; Engligh trans., *The Gods Will Have Blood*, 1979).

Georgano, G.N., *A Source Book of Veteran Cars* (1974).

Girard, André, *Anarchistes et Bandits* (1914).

Gordeaux, Paul, *La Bande à Bonnot* (1970).

Grierson, Francis Durham, *The Compleat Crook in France* (1934).

Guérin, Daniel, *Ni Dieu Ni Maître* (4 vols. 1970).

Horowitz, Irving Louis (ed.), *The Anarchists* (1964).

Lanoff, Robert, *De la rue Ordener aux Aubrais* (editions de l'anarchie, 1912).

Le Roi, Alexandre, *La Bande à Bonnot* (1968).

Levieux, *L'Outil de Meurtre* (éditions de l'anarchie, 1910).

Levieux, *Hommes Libres* (1912).

Libertad, Albert, *Le Culte de la Charogne* (1909).

Libertad, Albert, *La Joie de Vivre* (1909).

Libertad, Albert, *Le Travail Anti-social et les Mouvements Utiles* (1909).

Lori, Luigi, *La Banda Tragica* (date unknown)

Lorulot, André, *Chez les Loups* (1922).

Lorulot, André, *L'individualisme, Doctrine de Révolte* (1910).

Lorulot, André, *La Vie Nomade* (1912).

Lorulot, André, *Les Vrais Bandits* (1912).

Lorulot, André, and Alfred Naquet, *Le Socialisme Marxiste, l'Individualisme Anarchique* (1911).

Magraw, Roger, *A History of the French Working Class, Vol. 2: Workers and the Bourgeois Republic, 1871–1914* (1986).

Magraw, Roger, *France: The Bourgeois Century 1815–1914* (1983).

Maîtrejean, Rirette, *Souvenirs d'anarchie* (1913)

Maitron, Jean, 'De Kibalchich à Victor Serge: Le Rétif', in *Le Mouvement Social* (1964).

Maitron, Jean, *Le Mouvement Anarchiste en France* (2 vols. 1956).

Maitron, Jean, *Ravachol et les Anarchistes* (1964).

Manévy, Raymond, and Philippe Diolé, *Sous les Plis du Drapeau Noir* (1949).

Mauricius, *L'Apologie du Crime* (1912).

Mauricius and Le Rétif, *Contre le Faim* (1911).

Mell, Ezra Brett (aka Albert Meltzer), *The Truth about the Bonnot Gang* (1968).

Menzies, Malcolm, *En Exil Chez les Hommes* (1985).

Méric, Victor, *Les Bandits Tragiques* (1926).

Michon, Émile, *Un Peu de l'Âme des Bandits* (1913).

Nataf, André, *La Vie Quotidienne des anarchistes en France 1880–1910* (1986)

Normand, Jean, *La Bande Tragique* (1953).

Paraf-Javal, Mathias-Georges, *L'Absurdité de la Propriété* (1906).

Paraf-Javal, Mathias-Georges, *Evolution d'un Groupe sous une Influence Mauvaise* (1908).

Périchard, G-L, *La Bande à Bonnot* (unknown date).

Quail, John, *The Slow-Burning Fuse* (1978).

Rabani, Émile, *L'anarchie Scientifique* (1907).

Rédan, *Biribi* (editions de l'anarchie, 1910).

Rédan, *Les Criminels devant la Justice* (1913).

Rosmer, Alfred, *Le Cas Bonnot* (1912).

Roudine, Victor, *Max Stirner* (1910).

Ryner, Han, *Petit Manuel Individualiste* (1903).

Sanborn, Alvan, *Paris and the Social Revolution* (1905).

Serge, Victor, 'Meditation sur l'anarchie' in *Revue Esprit* (1937).

Serge, Victor, *La Pensée anarchiste in Le Crapouillot* (1938).

Serge, Victor, *Memoirs of a Revolutionary* (1951; English trans. Peter Sedgewick, 1967).

Serge, Victor, *Men in Prison* (1931; English trans. Greeman R, 1972).

Sergent, Alain, *Un Anarchiste de la Belle Époque: Alexandre Marius Jacob* (1970).

Sergent, Alain, *Les Anarchistes. Scènes et Portraits* (1951).

Stirner, Max, *L'Unique et Sa Propriété* (1899; English trans. *The Ego and Its Own*, Steven Byington, 1982).

Tancredi, Libero, 'L'enigma di Bonnot', in *La Rivolta* (1913).

Thomas, Bernard, *La Bande à Bonnot* (1968).

Thomas, Bernard, *Jacob* (1970).

Valera, Paolo (ed.), *Memorie di Giulio Bonnot* (2012).

Woodcock, George, *Anarchism* (1971).

Woodcock, George (ed.), *An Anarchist Reader* (1986).

Xo d'Axa, *Le Grand Trimard* (1895).

Zeldin, Theodore, *History of French Passions* (5 vols., 1973–77; English trans. 1979–81).

Zola, Émile, *Paris* (1898; English trans. Ernest Alfred Vizetelly).

Books appearing since publication of first edition in 1987 (in date order):

Pagès, Yves (ed.), *Victor Serge—Le Rétif. Articles parus dans l'anarchie 1909–1912* (1989).

Caruchet, William, *Ils ont tué Bonnot. Les révelations des archives policières* (1990).

Marshall, Bill, *Victor Serge: The Uses of Dissent* (1992).

Bertin, Claude, *Les Grands Procès—La Bande à Bonnot* (1995).

Jacob, Marius, *Écrits* (2 vols. 1995).

Delacourt Frédéric, *L'Affaire Bande à Bonnot* (2000).

Nemeth, Luc, *Victor Serge et les anarchistes* (paper given 1991, available online 2000).

Weissman, Susan, *Victor Serge* (2001).

Cacucci, Pino, *In Ogni Caso Nessun Rimorso* (1994; English edition, *Without a Glimmer of Remorse*, trans. Paul Sharkey, 2006).

Lambert, Christophe, *La Bande a Bonnot contre les Brigades du Tigre* (2006).

Beaudet, Celine, *Les Milieux Libres. Vivre en anarchiste à la Belle époque* (2006).

Legendre, Tony, *Expériences de vie communautaire anarchiste en France: Le milieu libre de Vaux (Aisne) de 1902 a 1907, La Colonie naturiste et* végétalienne de Bascon (Aisne) de 1911–1951 (2006).

Thomazo, Renaud, *Mort aux bourgeois! Sur les traces de la Bande à Bonnot* (2007).

Abidor, Mitchell, *The Great Anger: Ultra-revolutionary Writing in France from the Atheist Priest to the Bonnot Gang* (2008).

Ladarre, Benoît, *La Bande à Bonnot—Memoires Imaginaires de Garnier* (2008).

Lavignette, Frédéric (ed.), *La Bande à Bonnot—à Travers la Presse de L'Époque* (2008).

Salmon, André, *La Terreur Noire* (2008, new edition of the 1959 publication).

Steiner, Anne, *Les en-dehors Anarchistes Individualistes et illegalistes à la "Belle Époque"* (2008).

Hoobler, Dorothy and Thomas, 'The Motor Bandits' in *The Crimes of Paris* (2009).

Pécherot, Patrick, *L'homme à la Carabine* (2011).

Leclercq, Pierre-Robert, *Bonnot et la Fin d'une Époque* (2012).

Valera, Paolo (ed.), *Memorie di Giulio Bonnot* (2012).

Thomas, Bernard, *Jacob Alexandre Marius* (English trans. Paul Sharkey, 2015).

Serge, Victor, *Anarchists Never Surrender! Essays, Polemics and Correspondence on Anarchism 1908–1938* (trans. Mitchell Abidor, 2015).

Greeman, Richard, Les Frères de Bruxelles (unpublished manuscript).

Index

Page numbers in *italic* refer to illustrations. 'Passim' (literally 'scattered') indicates intermittent discussion of a topic over a cluster of pages.

Jouin in, 98; Libertad and, 17;
repression of Paris Commune,
1; as strikebreakers, 28, 29,
47; use of against illegalists,
172–74, *172. See also* military
service and resistance
arson, 3, 5, 6, 26, 113, 158
assassination, 2–3, 6, 26, 84;
attempt on Leopold II, 37n4;
Alexander II, 2, 31; Franz
Ferdinand, 218; Jaurès, 210n1;
moral aspects, 207
Association internationale anti-
militariste. See International
Antimilitarist Association
(AIA)
automobile industry, 72, 83–84
automobile theft. *See* car theft

Bachelet, Émile, 213
Bakunin, Mikhail, 19, 36
Le Balai Social, 159n4
bank messenger robberies, 82,
86–94 passim, 107–8, 110, 188
bank robberies, 133–38 passim, *140*
Baraille, Bartholémy, 144
Barcelona, 44–45, 217
Barrès, Maurice: *Le Culte de Moi*,
8–9
Barthelmess, Ida, 103
Bedhomme (taxi driver), 130, 131
Belardi, Jeanne, 55–62 passim,
82–85 passim, 96, 100, 113,
120, 150
Belgian Congo, 37n4
Belgian Socialist Party. *See*
Socialist Party (Belgium)
Belgium, 31–42, 100–101, 103,
138, 141; DeBoe return to,

216; Joseph Renard in, 109;
Monier in, 108, 109; Rodriguez
expulsion from, 121. *See also*
Boitsfort, Belgium; Charleroi,
Belgium; Ghent
Bellegarrigue, Anselm, 19
Belonie, David, xiii, 73, 75, *80*, 81,
87, 117; Rodriguez relations,
xvii; rue Ordener robbery
aftermath, 94, 100, 103, 108,
120–26 passim; trial, 187, 194
Bénard, Kleber, 188, 194, *214*
Berck-sur-Mer, 65, 143, 144
Berger, Léon, 82
Bertillon, Alphonse, 128, 188, 196
Besse, Marie, 120, 157, 201, 215
bicycles and bicycling, 58, 145,
146, 170; police, 137, 139
Bill brothers, 103, 108, 168
Blanc, Louis, 32
Bloody Sunday, 2005, 19
boat-trains, 92
Boitsfort, Belgium, 34, 196
Bolsheviks, 26–27, 217
bombs and bombing, 2, 3, 27, 36,
223; Russia, 31
Bonnot, Jules, ix, xv, xvii, 3,
67–79 passim, *74*; absolution
of acquaintances, 163, *177*;
belongings, 156, 164–65; *Le*
Bourgeois, 75, 204; capsule
bio, xiii; car theft, 57, 83–85;
Choisy-Le-Roi shoot-out and
death, vii, 160–67 passim;
Dieudonné view of, 198; in
fiction and film, vii–viii; Gauzy
claim, xvii, 189; hijacking,
Chantilly robbery, and aftermath, 133–38 passim, 144,

About the Author

RICHARD PARRY STUDIED medieval and modern history at University College London and took a master's degree in European social history at the London School of Economics, as this was the only course in the UK that offered anarchism as a core subject. He subsequently became a respected criminal defence lawyer, specializing in defending protesters and those on drugs charges. He continues to live and practice law in London.

ABOUT PM PRESS

PM Press was founded at the end of 2007 by a small collection of folks with decades of publishing, media, and organizing experience. PM Press co-conspirators have published and distributed hundreds of books, pamphlets, CDs, and DVDs. Members of PM have founded enduring book fairs, spearheaded victorious tenant organizing campaigns, and worked closely with bookstores, academic conferences, and even rock bands to deliver political and challenging ideas to all walks of life. We're old enough to know what we're doing and young enough to know what's at stake.

We seek to create radical and stimulating fiction and non-fiction books, pamphlets, T-shirts, visual and audio materials to entertain, educate, and inspire you. We aim to distribute these through every available channel with every available technology—whether that means you are seeing anarchist classics at our bookfair stalls; reading our latest vegan cookbook at the café; downloading geeky fiction e-books; or digging new music and timely videos from our website.

PM Press is always on the lookout for talented and skilled volunteers, artists, activists, and writers to work with. If you have a great idea for a project or can contribute in some way, please get in touch.

PM Press
PO Box 23912
Oakland, CA 94623
www.pmpress.org

FRIENDS OF PM PRESS

These are indisputably momentous times—the financial system is melting down globally and the Empire is stumbling. Now more than ever there is a vital need for radical ideas.

In the years since its founding—and on a mere shoestring—PM Press has risen to the formidable challenge of publishing and distributing knowledge and entertainment for the struggles ahead. With hundreds of releases to date, we have published an impressive and stimulating array of literature, art, music, politics, and culture. Using every available medium, we've succeeded in connecting those hungry for ideas and information to those putting them into practice.

Friends of PM allows you to directly help impact, amplify, and revitalize the discourse and actions of radical writers, filmmakers, and artists. It provides us with a stable foundation from which we can build upon our early successes and provides a much-needed subsidy for the materials that can't necessarily pay their own way. You can help make that happen—and receive every new title automatically delivered to your door once a month—by joining as a Friend of PM Press. And, we'll throw in a free T-shirt when you sign up.

Here are your options (all include a 50% discount on all webstore purchases):
- **$30 a month** Get all books and pamphlets
- **$40 a month** Get all PM Press releases (including CDs and DVDs)
- **$100 a month** Everything plus PM merchandise and free downloads

For those who can't afford $30 or more a month, we have **Sustainer Rates** at $15, $10 and $5. Sustainers get a free PM Press T-shirt and a 50% discount on all purchases from our website.

Your Visa or Mastercard will be billed once a month, until you tell us to stop. Or until our efforts succeed in bringing the revolution around. Or the financial meltdown of Capital makes plastic redundant. Whichever comes first.

Anarchists Never Surrender
Essays, Polemics, and Correspondence on Anarchism, 1908–1938

Victor Serge
Editor: Mitchell Abidor
Foreword: Richard Greeman

$20.00
ISBN: 978-1-62963-031-1
8.5 by 5.5 • 256 pages

Anarchists Never Surrender provides a complete picture of Victor Serge's relationship to anarchism. The volume contains writings going back to his teenage years in Brussels, where he became influenced by the doctrine of individualist anarchism. At the heart of the anthology are key articles written soon after his arrival in Paris in 1909, when he became editor of the newspaper *l'anarchie*. In these articles Serge develops and debates his own radical thoughts, arguing the futility of mass action and embracing "illegalism." Serge's involvement with the notorious French group of anarchist armed robbers, the Bonnot Gang, landed him in prison for the first time in 1912. *Anarchists Never Surrender* includes both his prison correspondence with his anarchist comrade Émile Armand and articles written immediately after his release.

The book also includes several articles and letters written by Serge after he had left anarchism behind and joined the Russian Bolsheviks in 1919. Here Serge analyzed anarchism and the ways in which he hoped anarchism would leaven the harshness and dictatorial tendencies of Bolshevism. Included here are writings on anarchist theory and history, Bakunin, the Spanish revolution, and the Kronstadt uprising.

Anarchists Never Surrender anthologizes Victor Serge's previously unavailable texts on anarchism and fleshes out the portrait of this brilliant writer and thinker, a man I.F. Stone called one of the "moral figures of our time."

> "One of the most compelling of twentieth-century ethical and literary heroes."
> —Susan Sontag

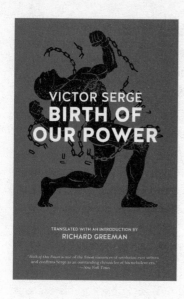

VICTOR SERGE
BIRTH OF
OUR POWER

TRANSLATED WITH AN INTRODUCTION BY
RICHARD GREEMAN

"Birth of Our Power is one of the finest memoirs of revolution ever written, and confirms Serge as an outstanding chronicler of his turbulent era."
—New York Times

Birth of Our Power

Victor Serge

Introduction and Translation:
Richard Greeman

$18.95
ISBN: 978-1-62963-030-4
8.5 by 5.5 • 256 pages

Birth of Our Power is an epic novel set in Spain, France, and Russia during the heady revolutionary years 1917–1919. Serge's tale begins in the spring of 1917, the third year of mass slaughter in the blood-and-rain-soaked trenches of World War I. When the flames of revolution suddenly erupt in Russia and Spain, Europe is "burning at both ends." Although the Spanish uprising eventually fizzles, in Russia the workers, peasants, and common soldiers are able to take power and hold it.

Serge's "tale of two cities" is constructed from the opposition between Barcelona, the city "we" could not take, and Petrograd, the starving, beleaguered capital of the Russian Revolution besieged by counter-revolutionary Whites. Between the romanticism of radicalized workers awakening to their own power in a sun-drenched Spanish metropolis to the grim reality of workers clinging to power in Russia's dark, frozen revolutionary outpost. From "victory in defeat" to "defeat in victory."

The novel was composed a decade after the revolution in Leningrad, where Serge was living in semicaptivity because of his declared opposition to Stalin's dictatorship over the revolution.

> "Nothing in it has dated. . . . It is less an autobiography than a sustained, incandescent lyric (half-pantheist, half-surrealist) of rebellion and battle."
> —*Times Literary Supplement*

Men in Prison

Victor Serge

Introduction and Translation:
Richard Greeman

$18.95
ISBN: 978-1-60486-736-7
8.5 by 5.5 • 232 Pages

"Everything in this book is fictional and everything is true," wrote Victor Serge in the epigraph to Men in Prison. "I have attempted, through literary creation, to bring out the general meaning and human content of a personal experience."

The author of *Men in Prison* served five years in French penitentiaries (1912–1917) for the crime of "criminal association"—in fact for his courageous refusal to testify against his old comrades, the infamous "Tragic Bandits" of French anarchism. "While I was still in prison," Serge later recalled, "fighting off tuberculosis, insanity, depression, the spiritual poverty of the men, the brutality of the regulations, I already saw one kind of justification of that infernal voyage in the possibility of describing it. Among the thousands who suffer and are crushed in prison—and how few men really know that prison!—I was perhaps the only one who could try one day to tell all... There is no novelist's hero in this novel, unless that terrible machine, prison, is its real hero. It is not about 'me,' about a few men, but about men, all men crushed in that dark corner of society."

Ironically, Serge returned to writing upon his release from a GPU prison in Soviet Russia, where he was arrested as an anti-Stalinist subversive in 1928. He completed *Men in Prison* (and two other novels) in "semi-captivity" before he was rearrested and deported to the Gulag in 1933. Serge's classic prison novel has been compared to Dostoyevsky's *House of the Dead*, Koestler's *Spanish Testament*, Genet's *Miracle of the Rose*, and Solzhenitsyn's *One Day in the Life of Ivan Denisovitch* both for its authenticity and its artistic achievement.

This edition features a substantial new introduction by translator Richard Greeman, situating the work in Serge's life and times.

"No purer book about the hell of prison has ever been written."
—Martin Seymour-Smith, *Scotsman*

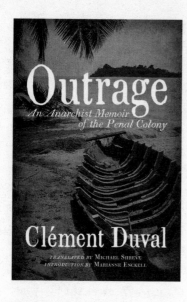

Outrage
An Anarchist Memoir of the Penal Colony

Clément Duval
Translator: Michael Shreve
Introduction: Marianne Enckell

$20.00
ISBN: 978-1-60486-500-4
9 by 6 • 224 Pages

"Theft exists only through the exploitation of man by man . . . when Society refuses you the right to exist, you must take it . . . the policeman arrested me in the name of the Law, I struck him in the name of Liberty."

In 1887, Clément Duval joined the tens of thousands of convicts sent to the "dry guillotine" of the French penal colonies. Few survived and fewer were able to tell the stories of their life in that hell. Duval spent fourteen years doing hard labor—espousing the values of anarchism and demonstrating the ideals by being a living example the entire time—before making his daring escape and arriving in New York City, welcomed by the Italian and French anarchists there.

This is much more than an historical document about the anarchist movement and the penal colony. It is a remarkable story of survival by one man's self-determination, energy, courage, loyalty, and hope. It was thanks to being true and faithful to his ideals that Duval survived life in this hell. Unlike the well-known prisoner Papillon, who arrived and dramatically escaped soon after Duval, he encouraged his fellow prisoners to practice mutual aid, through their deeds and not just their words. It is a call to action for mindful, conscious people to fight for their rights to the very end, to never give up or give in.

More than just a story of a life or a testament of ideals, here is a monument to the human spirit and a war cry for freedom and justice.

Anarchy, Geography, Modernity
Selected Writings of Elisée Reclus

Elisée Reclus

Editors: John P. Clark and
Camille Martin

$22.95
ISBN: 978-1-60486-429-8
9 by 6 • 304 Pages

Anarchy, Geography, Modernity is the first comprehensive introduction to the thought of Elisée Reclus, the great anarchist geographer and political theorist. It shows him to be an extraordinary figure for his age. Not only an anarchist but also a radical feminist, anti-racist, ecologist, animal rights advocate, cultural radical, nudist, and vegetarian. Not only a major social thinker but also a dedicated revolutionary.

The work analyzes Reclus' greatest achievement, a sweeping historical and theoretical synthesis recounting the story of the earth and humanity as an epochal struggle between freedom and domination. It presents his groundbreaking critique of all forms of domination: not only capitalism, the state, and authoritarian religion, but also patriarchy, racism, technological domination, and the domination of nature. His crucial insights on the interrelation between personal and small-group transformation, broader cultural change, and large-scale social organization are explored. Reclus' ideas are presented both through detailed exposition and analysis, and in extensive translations of key texts, most appearing in English for the first time.

> "Maintaining an appropriately scholarly style, marked by deep background knowledge, nuanced argument, and careful qualifications, Clark and Martin nevertheless reveal a passionate love for their subject and adopt a stance of political engagement that they hope does justice to Reclus' own commitments."
> —*Historical Geography*

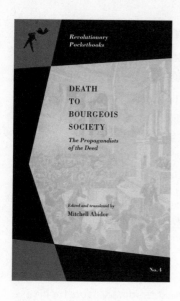

Death to Bourgeois Society
The Propagandists of the Deed
Editor and translator: Mitchell Abidor

$14.95
ISBN: 978-1-62963-112-7
8 by 5 • 128 pages

Perhaps no period has so marked, so deformed, or so defined the anarchist movement as the three years in France from 1892 to 1894, the years known as the Age of Attentats, the years dominated by the Propagandists of the Deed.

Death to Bourgeois Society tells the story of four young anarchists who were guillotined in France in the 1890s. Their courage was motivated by noble ideals whose realization they saw their bombs and assassinations as hastening. In a time of cynicism and political decay for many, they represented a purity lacking in society, and their actions when they were captured, their forthrightness, their defiance up to the guillotine only added to their luster.

The texts collected in *Death to Bourgeois Society* focus on the main avatars of this movement: the grave robber/murderer/terrorist Ravachol; Auguste Vaillant, who bombed the Chamber of Deputies; Emile Henry, who attacked both the bourgeois in their class function and their very existence; and the Italian immigrant Santo Caserio, who brought down the curtain on the age when he assassinated the French president Sadi Carnot.

The volume contains key first person narratives of the events, from Ravachol's forbidden speech and his account of his life, to Henry's questioning at his trial and his programmatic letter to the director of the prison in which he was held, to Vaillant's confrontation with the investigators immediately after tossing his bomb, and Caserio's description of the assassination and his defense at his trial.

"It is quite wrong and anachronistic to call the practitioners of 'propaganda by the deed' at the end of the nineteenth century 'lifestyle anarchists.' They were part and product of a social movement which was consciously anarchist and socialist."
—Peter Marshall, author of *Demanding the Impossible*

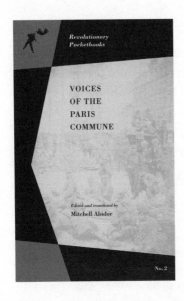

Voices of the Paris Commune

Editor: Mitchell Abidor

$14.95
ISBN: 978-1-62963-100-4
8 by 5 • 128 pages

The Paris Commune of 1871, the first instance of a working-class seizure of power, has been subject to countless interpretations; reviled by its enemies as a murderous bacchanalia of the unwashed while praised by supporters as an exemplar of proletarian anarchism in action. As both a successful model to be imitated and as a devastating failure to be avoided. All of the interpretations are tendentious. Historians view the working class's three-month rule through their own prism, distant in time and space. *Voices of the Paris Commune* takes a different tack. In this book only those who were present in the spring of 1871, who lived through and participated in the Commune, are heard.

The Paris Commune had a vibrant press, and it is represented here by its most important newspaper, *Le Cri du Peuple*, edited by Jules Vallès, member of the First International. Like any legitimate government, the Paris Commune held parliamentary sessions and issued daily printed reports of the heated, contentious deliberations that belie any accusation of dictatorship. Included in this collection is the transcript of the debate in the Commune, just days before its final defeat, on the establishing of a Committee of Public Safety and on the fate of the hostages held by the Commune, hostages who would ultimately be killed.

Finally, *Voices of the Paris Commune* contains a selection from the inquiry carried out twenty years after the event by the intellectual review La Revue Blanche, asking participants to judge the successes and failures of the Paris Commune. This section provides a fascinating range of opinions of this epochal event.

> "The Paris Commune of 1871 has been the subject of much ideological debate, often far removed from the experiences of the participants themselves. If you really want to dig deep into what happened during those fateful weeks, reading these eyewitness accounts is mandatory."
> —Gabriel Kuhn, editor of *All Power to the Councils! A Documentary History of the German Revolution of 1918–1919*

Pino Cacucci
Without a glimmer of remorse

Without a Glimmer of Remorse

Pino Cacucci
Illustrator: Flavio Costantini

$14.95
ISBN: 978-1-62963-1-868
7.5 by 5 • 368 pages

A fascinating dramatized fiction of the life and times of Jules Bonnot, his "gang," and associates, the individualist anarchists of the time, including the young Victor Serge. An affectionate, fast-paced, but historically accurate account of the life of the extraordinary Bonnot—worker, soldier, auto-mechanic, driver to Sir Arthur Conan Doyle—a man with a long-cherished dream of absolute freedom, and the first bank-robber to use a getaway car; an anarchist who felt it his duty to lash out at bourgeois society, staking his all. A tragically romantic hero, Jules Bonnot emerges from these pages as a wounded dreamer who was to deeply affect the lives of so many other unforgettable characters. Beautifully illustrated by Flavio Costantini.